# MANAGING
# INTERNATIONAL MANUFACTURING

# Advanced Series in Management

## Volume 13

*Series Editors:* **A. BENSOUSSAN** and **P. A. NAERT**

*University of Paris-Dauphine*
*and INRIA*
*Paris, France*

*INSEAD*
*Fontainebleau, France*

NORTH-HOLLAND
AMSTERDAM · NEW YORK · OXFORD · TOKYO

# MANAGING INTERNATIONAL MANUFACTURING

*Edited by*

Kasra FERDOWS
*European Institute of Business Administration (INSEAD)*
*Fontainebleau, France*

1989

NORTH-HOLLAND
AMSTERDAM · NEW YORK · OXFORD · TOKYO

ISBN: 0 444 87351 1


*Publishers:*

ELSEVIER SCIENCE PUBLISHERS B.V.
P.O. Box 1991
1000 BZ Amsterdam
The Netherlands

*Sole distributors for the U.S.A. and Canada:*

ELSEVIER SCIENCE PUBLISHING COMPANY, INC.
655 Avenue of the Americas
New York, N.Y. 10010
U.S.A.

PRINTED IN THE NETHERLANDS

# PREFACE

Manufactured goods are crossing national boundaries more than ever before. International trade in manufactures is now worth more than two-thirds of total world trade. In 1986, this meant that more than 1.5 trillion dollars worth of manufactured goods crossed national boundaries. Trade in manufactures has consistently outperformed international trade in general and is expected to continue to do so in the foreseeable future. National markets are clearly becoming more exposed to manufacturers worldwide.

What are the implications of this trend for the management of manufacturing function in the firm? One may logically deduct that a) the strategic importance of superior manufacturing for capturing global markets will increase further, and b) the very structure of the manufacturing operations in many firms will become more internationalised. These deductions are supported by even cursory observations.

However, in spite of its substantial reality and accelerated growth, internationalisation of manufacturing has not received much attention from the researchers in the production and operations management area. Most of the body of the knowledge on international manufacturing has been from the perspective of the economists, political scientists, industry analysts, or others. Their works are useful, but there is a need to assess the relevance of their findings for management of the manufacturing function in the firm. More important, production management scholars themselves need to step up their generation of new knowledge about this phenomenon. The idea behind this book has been to move towards meeting these needs.

The book is addressed to researchers and senior managers in manufacturing management. Its purpose is to present the current state of knowledge and pending questions in the internationalisation of manufacturing from the perspective of production management. Its contents to a large extent are based on a Research Symposium held at INSEAD on 7 to 9 September 1987 entitled "Issues in International Manufacturing". Earlier versions of eleven of the thirteen papers in this book were among the thirty two papers of the Symposium. However, the book is not a proceedings of the Symposium.

There are three parts in the book. Part One contains five papers which examine the internationalisation of the manufacturing base in the firm. These papers address various issues in the management of an international network of factories. The focus in Part Two is on the cross country comparisons of manufacturing management practices. Among the many papers available on this subject, I have selected four--two dealing with new areas of comparison and two with large-sample based studies. Part Three looks into the role of manufacturing in the global competition. Again four papers are presented here, each very different from the others both in substance and in research methodology. I have selected these papers to provide illustrations of the type of research that is done in assessing the creation of global competitive advantage through manufacturing.

I am greatly indebted to the distinguished participants of the Symposium. My thanks go particularly to the Symposium Committee: Proessors William Berry, Arnoud De Meyer, Robert Hayes, Terry Hill, Jeffrey Miller, Jinichiro Nakane, Roger Schmenner, Wickham Skinner, Roland Van Dierdonck, Chris Voss, and Steven Wheelwright.

The Symposium was sponsored by INSEAD with the cooperation of the Operations Management Association and the European Institute for Advanced Studies in Management. As Chairman of the Symposium, I would like to express my gratitude to these organisations and to Ford of Europe for providing financial assistance. Many thanks also to Gisèle Zuliani for her efficiency, care and cheerfulness while helping me with the final editorial work of this book.

Roya Movahedi organised and coordinated the Symposium and also provided editorial assistance. Her support throughout the entire project has been invaluable. I offer her my deep appreciation.


Kasra Ferdows

Fontainebleau
November 1988

# Contents

PART TWO

PART THREE

# INTERNATIONAL MANUFACTURING:  THE ISSUES IN PERSPECTIVE

Manufacturing is becoming more internationalised in two ways: first, more manufactured goods are crossing national boundaries every year; second, a larger number of companies are investing in foreign manufacturing facilities.

The statistics show that both these trends are accelerating. The first trend--increasing trade in manufacturing goods--is clearly visible from the statistics published by GATT (The General Agreement on Tariffs and Trade) and other sources.  GATT data show that between 1950 and 1986, the volume of manufactures trade rose by fifteen fold.  They also show that trade in manufactures has consistently outperformed international trade in general--now accounting for two-thirds of total world trade. [1]

Consider also the fact that growth in world trade has historically exceeded growth in world output.  That is, the share of world output which has been traded has increased through the years.  This was particularly true in the 1960's when world trade grew 2 1/2 percentage points a year more than world output.  In recent years, this difference has been narrowed to about 1 percent, but it is still quite significant. [1]

Taken together, these trade trends indicate that every year a larger share of world output of manufactured goods is exported to a country other than where produced.

The statistics for the second trend--larger investments in foreign manufacturing facilities--are more sketchy but still convincing.  In Japan, for example, according to the Ministry of International Trade and Industry (MITI), the share of inudstrial output that is produced abroad rose to 3.3 percent of domestic production in the fiscal year ended March 31, 1988, from 3 percent a year earlier.  This is still less than other leading industrial nations.  (The ratio for the United States is 17 percent of total production, and West Germany 19 percent). [2]  But the pace of Japan's overseas manufacturing investment has been accelerating by the rise in the value of the yen since 1985, and some predict that the share of the output of the Japanese firms produced abroad will approach the present American level within five years.

But the Americans are not standing still.  The weak dollar, contrary to many predictions, has not hindered the expansion of the already sizeable network of American operations abroad.  This network, built over 40 years, surpasses that of any other nation.  According to the US Commerce Department, in 1987 the American companies continued investing in foreign plants, particularly in Europe, at a record rate.  The net outflow of investment abroad (total amount spent on foreign operations less amount brought back for use in the United States) in 1987 was $22.6 billion--a record amount and nearly twice the $11.8 billion net outflow in 1986. [3]

West Germany, already with a large foreign manufacturing base, also continues to invest in production abroad. So are the British, French, Italians, and many other industrialised nations. In short, more firms are establishing more manufacturing bases in different countries.

So manufacturing is becoming more internationalized because more manufactured goods are entering international trade and because firms are establishing more manufacturing bases abroad. And the pace is accelerating. In spite of all this, little can be found in the literature on how to manage this process.

The bulk of the literature in the so called "international business" essentially focuses on marketing and financial issues. Other studies are done from the perspective of the economists, sociologists, historians, anthropologists, political scientists, or industry analysts--not the firms's director of production.

Why has the production management perspective not received the attention it deserves? The simple answer is because given the traditional way manufacturing has been managed in most companies, it has been difficult to see the need for it. By being at the back end of the strategy formulation process, manufacturing decisions have been made in fragments and as consequences of essentially marketing or financial considerations.

The reactive strategic role assigned to manufacturing seems to be under critical questioning in recent years. The literature in the last decade reflects a growing recognition that manufacturing can provide a significant and defensible competitive advantage on a global scale [4]; that instead of being at the back-end, it can be a strategic spearhead. In fact, the international competition in manfactured goods explained earlier has provided examples in every industry of companies that have succeeded in the market on the basis of manufacturing strength, and as such convinced more managers and researchers of the value of strategic manufacturing capabilities.

The growing recognition of the strategic role for manufacturing on the one hand, and more intense internationalisation of manufacturing on the other hand, have made the gap in the international manufacturing literature now more visible. Specific events like 1992 in Europe, trade deficit in the United States, and trade surplus and high value of the yen in Japan have heightened the interest in the international dimension of manufacturing. In the next few years, as more managers and scholars see this gap, it is likely to be filled. But a great deal of work remains. This book presents some of the recent research in this area.

## ORGANISATION OF THE BOOK

This book is organised into three parts:

    Part One:    Internationalisation of Manufacturing Base

    Part Two:    International Comparisons of Manufacturing Management

    Part Three: Manufacturing and Global Competition

The objective in Part One is to present the research on both the process of internationalisation of a firm's manufacturing and logistics base, and on the operational management of an international network of factories and suppliers. Internationalisation of manufacturing and logistics pose a set of unique complications: currency fluctuations, tariffs, variations in industrial relations rules and practices, local value-added requirements, languages and cultural differences are but some of the factors which contribute to the complexity. Moreover, the advances in telecommunications, the drive towards just-in-time delivery and smaller order quantities, and stricter quality standards for vendor items have direct implications for the management of an international network of factories, since these are more recent phenomena, they pose unique challenges and opportunities.

The research in this area is still at its infancy. Large sections of this field are still uncharted. The five papers presented in this Part aim to make contributions in various corners of this unchartered field.

The first paper (written by myself) aims to examine the strategic role of various manufacturing sites of an international company. I propose that the organisation of the factory network, the nature of the linkages in this network, and the management systems for individual factories are contingent upon the factory's strategic role. The second paper, that of Michael McGrath and Roberto Bequillard, is based on an in-depth study of the electronics industry and they suggest a model for gauging the degree of internationalization of the manufacturing base of the company and provide a guideline for internationalization.

Third, Michael Oliff et al apply a model to assess choice of international manufacturing sites. Fourth, Marshall Fisher et al present an optimisation model to determine the flow of components and finished goods in an international network of suppliers, factories and markets.

Fifth and last paper in this Part is by Therese Flaherty in which the evolution of internationalisation of the manufacturing base is analyzed and a model for effective flow of information and products between factories is proposed.

Part Two, international comparisons of manufacturing management, is relatively a more researched topic. Comparisons of manufacturing practices in different countries--particularly the North American, European, and East Asian countries--have received considerable attention lately. Each of the four papers presented in this part focus on a particular aspect of this type of comparative analysis. Kim Clark and Takahiro Fujimoto's paper focuses on the comparison of the product developent activities in the automotive industry in Japan, United States and Europe. Relatively little research has been done in this area to date, and their in-depth empirical research is significant contribution towards understanding the important linkage between development and production.

Jeffrey Miller et al's paper is based on a survey of large manufacturing companies in the United States, Europe, and Japan. Unlike many other studies which are essentially clinical in nature, this study is unique in the sense that it is based on a large sample, multi-year analysis of the evolution of manufacturing strategies in the three regions. In this paper, the focus is on assessing the gaps in the manufacturing capabilities and whether or not these gaps are narrowing.

Donald Gerwin and Jean-Claude Tarondeau's paper focuses on the development of another important capability in manufacturing, namely flexibility. Their comparison is between United States and France, paying particular attention to the implementation of similar flexible manufacturing systems in the two countries and drawing general lessons.

The final paper in this Part, by Aleda Roth et al, is also based on the same data base as Miller's et al, but the focus here is on the analysis of the manufacturing strategy formulation process in the three regions.

The papers in Part Three are intended to provide illustrations of the role of manufacturing in global competition. Marvin Lieberman's paper, by examining selected macro economic data and performance of a number of important firms in two industries, provides an explanation for the observed superior performance of some of the Japanese manufacturers, and suggests implications for the future.

Edward Davis' paper analyzes the trend in Japan towards "financial engineering" and considers the implications of this trend on the strategic role of manufacturing in large Japanese companies--whose success in global competition in most part has been due to manufacturing strength.

The third paper by Joel Goldhar examines the implications of the new manufacturing technologies on the way international manufacturing companies are likely to compete in global markets. And finally, Jack Baranson's paper, while comparing the rate of adoption of these new technologies in the economies of the Eastern block countries with the Western block (a subject deserving much more attention than it has received so far), analyzes the prospects of the manufacturers in the Eastern block in global competition.

As can be seen from these short descriptions, the papers in this book do not cover the full spectrum of issues in international manufacturing. However, they do address many of the important ones and make important contributions towards their better understanding. Many other issues still remain, and more work is needed to provide more clarity on all the issues in international manufacturing--including those addressed in this book. The intention in this volume is not to consolidate the knowledge on international manufacturing. It is too early to do that. Rather, it is to explore the various fronts of this unchartered field.

**NOTES**

[1]   Source:   GATT, as reported in The Economist, September 26, 1987, pp 78.

[2]   Source:   MITI, as reported in The International Herald Tribune, June 2, 1988 (Business Section).

[3]   Source:   US Commerce Department, as reported in The International Herald Tribune, May 21-22, 1988, pp 13.

[4]   For example, see Hayes R.H., Wheelwright and Clark, Dynamic Manufacturing, Free Press, New York, 1988.

PART ONE


INTERNATIONALISATION OF MANUFACTURING BASE

MANAGING INTERNATIONAL MANUFACTURING
K. Ferdows (Editor)
© Elsevier Science Publishers B.V. (North-Holland), 1989

# MAPPING INTERNATIONAL FACTORY NETWORKS

Kasra FERDOWS

INSEAD

The volume of world trade in manufactured goods has increased 15 times in the last three decades, and this long-term trend is not slowing down.[1] More products manufactured in one country are finding their ways into other countries. These products are not just finished goods; they are also components, intracompany transfers, and processed materials.

No company can stay indifferent to this trend. The competitive threats posed by foreign manufacturers should of course be constantly monitored, but, looking at this trend more positively, all companies should examine more vigorously the cost/benefits of establishing or expanding their own manufacturing base internationally. Variations in tariffs, fluctuations in currencies, proximity to markets, and access to foreign technology are but some of the reasons why existence of an international manufacturing base would provide a company with more room to maneuver. Without an international network of factories, a firm has simply less strategic options, and given the trend in the global competition, the consequence of this limitation in options is becoming more dire.

The decision to establish, expand, or change an international network of factories is complex. A large number of factors should be taken into account, many of which are intractible, unmeasurable, or unpredictable. Consequently, the decision-making process is usually long and costly. Rightly so, because such decisions bind the firm for a long time and there are many pitfalls on the way. So experience is particularly important here, and given the accelerated pace of internationalisation of manufacturing called for at present, a prudent company would be looking around hard to learn more about how to go about making these decisions.

But where should one look? Who are the ones that provide the lessons for internationalisation of manufacturing? The answer is simply those that have been at it for a long time, and they do not include many Japanese firms. They are mostly American and European multinationals. This is one area in manufacturing management where the Japanese have not matched the strength of Americans and Europeans.

The American multinational companies have been setting up foreign manufacturing facilities rather aggressively in the last four decades. Thanks mostly to them, the total foreign manufacturing base of the United States is larger than that of any other nation.[2] German, British, and other European companies also already have a large manufacturing base outside their countries. The Japanese multinationals have started this more recently but are on an accelerated course.[3]

How have some of the experienced multinational companies developed their international factory networks? How have they divided work among different plants? What strategic roles have they assigned to each? In short, how have they managed the process of internationalising their manufacturing operations, and what general lessons can be derived from their experience?

These were the questions which prompted this investigation. The answers are not found easily. My research to date has yielded a model which, essentially through reduction of complexity, helps the search for the answers. Specifically, what I report in this paper is a model for a) identifying the strategic role of each plant in the firm's international network of factories, and b) suggesting a pattern for evolution of these strategic roles through time.

The research leading to this paper consisted of analysis of international factory network of eight large multinational companies in the electronic industry. Five were American, one Dutch, one Italian, and one Japanese.[4] For most of them, I focussed on their European factories. I have also drawn on the data collected from multinational manufacturers in other industries--both through publically available documents and personal observations--to show that the model I propose in this paper applies more generally.

The model has two important limitations which I should point out at the outset. First, it covers only factories which are essentially owned and/or operated by the firm itself; joint ventures, contract manufacturing, technological partnerships, long-term supply contracts, non-integrated affliates and other forms of engaging in manufacturing activity in a foreign country have not been included. This is not because these other forms are less important than own manufacturing; rather, it only reflects my choice in keeping the scope of this research manageable.

Second, only the long-term decisions are addressed. Day-to-day operational decisions are not covered here. Management of operations of an international factory network is complicated and needs further work. Nevertheless, the model I propose in this paper provides an insight into how the network of international factories should be organised and has a few direct implications on the communication links among factories and between factories and headquarters.

## PATTERNS OF INTERNATIONALISATION OF THE MANUFACTURING BASE

If a typical manufacturing company in the industrially advanced region of the world were to follow the "product life cycle" model proposed by Vernon [5], and modified by Wells [6], and Stobaugh [7], one would expect to see a shift in the manufacturing base of its more mature products from developed to developing countries. Applied to an American company, a simplistic version of this model (as proposed in the early 1970's) would predict five phases in the shift of the manufacturing base as a new product moves towards maturity: in Phase I, when the new product is just introduced, all manufacturing is done in the United States; in Phase II, production is started in Europe; in Phase III, production in Europe is expanded to export also to the developing countries; in Phase IV, production is started in the developing countries and Europe also exports to the United States; and finally in Phase V, the developing countries start exporting to the United States.

Even if we adjust for the changes in the industrial power and economic growth of different countries since the early 1970's, still the model has little explanatory power for the evolution of the manufacturing base at the firm level. In fact Vernon himself states:

> Neither the theory of international trade nor the theory of international capital movements has much to offer in explanation of managerial decisions to invest in production facilities abroad. [8] (Emphasis added)

The main problem, as I see it, is that these theories assume only a subset of possible motivations for a company to locate a manufacturing facility in a new country. Access to cheap production input factors and proximity to market form the foundation of these theories. Both are valid and important motivating forces. But since companies have more than just these reasons for putting a factory abroad, these theories lose their explanatory power.

They also lose their normative power because the key for answering how a company should expand its manufacturing base internationally is simply in the why. In other words, the reasons for establishing a factory abroad determine the way the company should plan, design, construct, and commission that factory. What is the strategic role of the factory--that is the starting question.

Later in this paper I suggest a simple framework to differentiate among a set of generic strategic roles for factories in the firm's international manufacturing network. The premise of this framework is that a factory's strategic role is defined to a large exent by two variables: a) the primary reason for establishment of the factory and b) the extent of "technical activities" planned for that site. In the next section, I describe five categories of primary reasons for establishing a factory in a new country. By "technical activities" I mean a selected set of

activities which go beyond the mere production of the product--
activities such as procurement, process engineering, product
engineering, product development, warehousing and distribution, finance,
after-sale service, and the like. More on this is also explained later.

## MANUFACTURING IN A DIFFERENT COUNTRY

There are always a combination of different reasons why a firm puts a
factory abroad. I suggest most of the reasons can be grouped into five
categories:

> >Access to low cost production input factors
> >Proximity to market
> >Use of local technological resources
> >Control and amortisation of technological assets
> >Pre-emption of competition

Here is a brief description of these categories.

### Access to low cost production input factors

Economists have long argued that the primary reason for locating
manufacturing abroad is exploitation of low cost production factors.
Among the four factors of labour, materials, energy, and capital, the
foremost has been, of course, labour. Proximity to cheaper raw materials
and energy, too, have provided compelling reasons in certain industries.
However, the fourth factor, capital, has seldom been a _primary_ reason
for locating manufacturing facilities abroad. Availability of cheaper
capital (in the form of grants or low interest loans) seem to be a
factor in choosing among alternative manufacturing sites, but not the
driving force behind internationalising the manufacturing base of the
firm.

### Proximity to market

Existence of a manufacturing base often allows a better customer serv-
ice--particularly in product customisation and delivery--and enhances
customer confidence in the company. Some of the reasons put forward by
Vernon's product life cycle model [5]--stipulating movement of manufacturing base from developed to developing countries as the product
matures and size of the market reaches certain thresholds--are such
market-driven reasons.

Davidson [9] in a study of US based multinationals, suggested that the
primary reason for locating manufacturing abroad has been essentially to
serve a new market or to reduce financial and trade restriction risks.
When a national market is served from a manufacturing base in the
country, production costs and sales revenues are denominated in the same
currency, reducing uncertainty related to currency and price fluctuations; furthermore, by being inside, the rise of trade barriers would in

fact enhance the position of the company. Many observers suggest that the current rush of the Japanese automobile and electronic companies setting up manufacturing facilities in North America and Europe is mainly due to these reasons.

## Use of local technological resources

A manufacturing base can be an effective way to tap into local technological resources. If keeping up-to-date with technology is critical to a company, then proximity to universities, research centers, and sophisticated suppliers, competitors, and customers assumes strategic importance. Having a manufacturing base not only increases the frequency of interactions with the environment, but may be the most efficient way to distill the available information and experience into useful knowledge for the company.

A primary reason for establishing manufacturing facilities in the Silicon Valley, in Japan, or in many industrially advanced European countries, among other places, fall in this category.

## Control and amortisation of technological assets

By using its own processes in foreign manufacturing, a company may earn better returns on its technology than would be possible through licensing. Moreover, by expanding internationally, a firm may benefit from scale economies. Flaherty [10] found these to be among the important reasons for internationalisation of the manufacturing base in the five companies she studied.

The same is true for many other European manufacturers, particularly those coming from smaller countries such as Holland, Denmark, Belgium, and Sweden. For many of the manufacturers in these countries, access to international markets, especially the United States market, is crucial. Without that they simply would not be able to afford the resources which are needed to establish and maintain a technological leadership. Desire to control the know-how can be a strong reason why they may establish their own factory as opposed to entering into partnerships, joint ventures or licensing agreements, even though the latter may be cheaper.

## Pre-emption of competition

In a developing country with an underdeveloped market, a company may establish a manufacturing base in order to pre-empt the competition. The goal is to expand as the market grows, and through government permits, accumulated local experience, and customer dependence and confidence, maintain a high barrier to entry for others. Many tobacco factories in the African and South American countries are illustrative cases; so are tire factories, breweries, artificial textile fibres, and automotive component plants.

In oligopolies, the necessity to establish a manufacturing base in some of these countries go beyond the potential returns to be earned in that

country: there is also a motivation to deny the competitors an incuba-
tion zone to grow and become strong. Car manufacturers are a case in
point. By going to the Federal Republic of China, Volkswagen and Peugeot
not only benefit from the potential growth in that market, but also they
may be pre-empting other competitors from growing strong there and
attacking other markets. One may argue that if Ford and General Motors
had kept or re-established their manufacturing facilities in Japan after
World War II--as they did in Europe--the shape of the car industry in
the world today would have been very different.

Some of these reasons are of course more frequently encountered than
others. In my research, I found the first three to be more prevalent
than the last two. For simplicity, in the framework that I suggest in
the next section, I consider only the first three categories. If needed,
the framework can be extended to include all five.

## IDENTIFYING STRATEGIC ROLE OF THE FACTORY

Identifying the role of a particular factory in the competitive strategy
of the company is indeed a complex task. Every case seems to be special,
meaning that a unique set of factors are dictating the role which is
assigned or played by the factory. Is there a way to reduce this complexity? Is there a way for categorising the strategic roles of various
factories in a firm's international manufacturing network?

My research suggests that looking at the primary reason for establishing
the manufacturing site together with examination of the extent of technical activities currently planned for that site provide significant
clues for understanding the strategic role which is assigned to the
factory (or if such assignment is not done consciously, the role actually being played by the factory). Figure 1 shows a framework which
incorporates this, and suggests six generic strategic roles:  Off-Shore,
Source, Server, Contributor, Outpost, Lead.

FIGURE 1: GENERIC ROLES OF INTERNATIONAL FACTORIES

| EXTENT OF TECHNICAL ACTIVITIES AT THE SITE | High ↑ Low | Source | Lead | Contributor |
| | | Off-Shore | Outpost | Server |
| | | Access to Low Cost Production Input Factors | Use of Local Technological Resources | Proximity to Market |

Primary Strategic Reason For the Site

## Off-Shore Factories

These are factories which are there essentially to utilise local cheap production input factors and supply components or final products to the home plant.

The basic characteristic of these plants is that managerial invest- ment in the plant is kept to the minimum essential to run the production. Usually no real engineering work--product or process related--goes on at the site; procurement decisions are reduced to managing day-to-day order follow up; accounting and finance primary purpose is to provide data for the management at home country; pattern of shipments out of the plant is kept simple and essen- tially out of the control of the plant management.

Many factories in the Far East established by American and European so- called "high-tech" companies fall in this category. During the 1970's almost all producers of integrated circuits shipped their wafers to the Far East to be assembled into a microchip. Other examples can be found in the Mexican Free Zones (Maquiladoras) where in the last decade the number of factories set up by mostly American companies to take advantage of low Mexican wages have increased several fold. The output of these factories are essen- tially all exported to the US.

## Source Factories

The primary reason for establishing these factories, too, is access to cheap production input factors. But they are given a more sub- stantial strategic role than the Off-Shore factories. They become a focal point for a company's efforts for specific components, products, or production processes. More managers and technical support staff are housed at the site, and the factory is given a greater autonomy in procurement, production planning, process changes, and distribution.

Apple Computer's factory in Singapore is such a factory. For a long time it supplied assembled printed circuits to other Apple fac- tories in the United States and Ireland. The factory specialised in this, and some of the advanced engineering work for this production process (burn-in, for example) was done at this site. Similarly, the Hewlett-Packard memory board plant in Puerto Rico and the Philips plant in Singapore (producing a variety of small electrical appliances such as irons and hair dryers) are Source plants in the sense that they carry responsibility for development and production of specific products or components--even if these products or components may be relatively minor ones--for worldwide distribu- tion.

## Server Factories

These factories are to serve specific national or regional markets.
Like the Off-Shore category, the investment in managerial talents
at these sites is kept to a level deemed essential to run the
production efficiently. There is, however, more autonomy at the
site for managing the flow of material and information between the
factory and its suppliers and customers.

Best examples are the soft drinks bottling plants and tobacco
factories spread over many developing countries. Many factories set
up by the Japanese in Europe and the United States are essentially
Servers--at least in the early phases before transfer of some
engineering work. Many of the companies trying to get into the
Chinese market are doing so with Server factories.

## Contributor Factories

These plants serve a specific national or regional market, but
their assigned role goes beyond just supplying products. Like
Source factories, they become focal points for certain company-wide
activities. They compete even with the company's home factories to
be the test bed for the newest process technology, newest computer
system, and for the introduction of new products. In short, they
are given explicit roles to develop and contribute know-how for the
company--going beyond the normal financial contributions expected
from the Server Factories.

Nestle's plant in Singapore (serving the south east Asian markets),
Apple Computer's plant in County Cork, Ireland (serving the
European markets), Baekart's (world's largest producer of steel
wires for tires) plant in Japan, Volvo in Belgium, Waertsila's
(Finnish producer of large diesel engines) factory in Singapore are
all examples of Contributor factories. All have a role which goes
beyond just serving their designated markets.

## Outpost Factories

Their main role is to collect information. They are located in
areas where technologically advanced suppliers, competitors, customers, or research laboratories are situated. The premise for
their establishment is that a factory would provide an efficient
mechanism to collect useful information. In my research, I have
not come across Outpost factories. Therefore this category is
perhaps only a theoretical possibility.

The companies which want to be present in technologically advanced
areas seldom set up a whole new factory. Instead they seem to
prefer acquiring an existing one, or going into a joint venture.
For example, Philips' acquisition of Signetics in the Silicon
Valley, Ciba-Geigy's acquisition of a biotechnology firm in the

same area, Ford's purchase of 25% of Mazda in Japan, have been
mostly driven by the desire to establish an outpost for collecting
data.

## Lead Factories

These factories serve as partners of headquarters in building
strategic capabilities in the manufacturing function. They tap into
local technological resources not only to collect data for headquarters, but also to use these resources themselves. Companies
would depend on Lead factories for development of specific manufacturing capabilities. Often they would be the sole or major producer
of certain products or components for the companies's global
markets.

Hewlett-Packard plants in France, Germany and United Kingdom are
good examples. They are situated in areas with a good supply of
engineers and in close proximity of other high-tech factories. Each
plant has responsibilities for many technical activities beyond
production; often at the same site one finds centers for development of certain products for world-wide applications. The same is
true for some of the European plants of IBM. These plants are
often the "Prime sites" for worldwide supply of new products and
processes.

Factories of Corning Glass in France, United Kingdom and Germany
can also be considered as Lead factories. The four plants in France
specialize in specific products (such as lenses and television
screens), and by being in close proximity to Corning's European
research center, have pioneered many new products and processes for
Corning world-wide. The two plants in the United Kingdom have
specialised in various other products including table-ware. The
German plant is where most of the work in fiber optics is going on.
Almost all these plants have significant roles in developing
manufacturing competence for Corning Europe.

## INTERNATIONAL FACTORY NETWORK IN A NEW PERSPECTIVE

Even though the boundaries of the above categories are not sharply defined, the model allows a company's factories to be viewed in a new perspective. This perspective is useful in three ways: first and most important, in tracking the patterns of changes in the strategic role of each factory through time; second, in the choice of the appropriate communication system for the factory network; and third, in the organisation design for a firm's international network of factories. These are explained below.

### Changes in Strategic Role of Factory

New factories generally start with clear strategic roles. Factories located abroad usually start as Servers or Off-Shores. (Outpost is another possibility, but as mentioned before, I have not come across any Outpost plants). A company many choose to keep the factories in these roles for a variety of reasons. Many global companies have highly centralised organisational structures and choose to keep all technology development near domestic operations. However, it should be noted that those Off-Shore and Server plants which do not gradually change to Source and Contributor plants, provide little benefit to the rest of the company in terms of locally generated technological knowledge. Moreover, there is a danger of stagnation and falling behind in technological progress in such factories. Not having the necessary human resources and organisational latitude, the factory is likely to be slow in improving its operations in transfering know-how and technology from the company's central staff. The net result is a deterioration of performance.

One way to avoid these risks is to build technical capabilities within plants. Process improvement, product customisation, making more decisions for procurement and distribution, and ultimately product development are examples of technical tasks which can be relocated at the manufacturing site. Expanding a factory's responsibilities for these tasks implies a change in the strategic role assigned to the factory in the international network. This can be depicted more clearly in Figure 2.

Figure 2 is a more detailed version of Figure 1. The movements shown are the natural ones in an evolutionary sense; they increase the chance of survival of the factory. The scale of "Technical Activities at the Site" in Figure 2 is meant as an illustration, and should be adjusted for relevant tasks in the specific company or industry being analyzed by this model.

FIGURE 2:  CHANGES IN STRATEGIC ROLES OF INTERNATIONAL FACTORIES

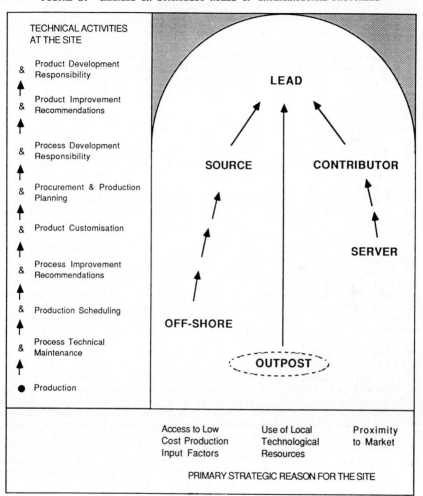

The arguments for the specific moves suggested in Figure 2 are three-fold:

> First, as mentioned above, Server and Off-Shore plants, by being essentially occupied with mere production and lacking slack resources, may fall behind technological progress. Lack of excitement in the plant is likely to drive the talented managers and engineers away; hence performance is likely to deteriorate and the site would become increasingly more dependent on central staff for long-term survival.
>
> Second, reducing the time to market for introduction of new products encourages moving the Off-Shore and Server factories towards Source and Contributors and eventually some of them to Lead plants. Reducing time to market requires increasing efficiency and speed of problem-solving in the design of both the product and the process. Shortening the communications link between design and production and allowing them to be done more in parallel (instead of sequentially) are effective methods for achieving these. Hence, putting more of the firm's technical resources physically close to the factories is helpful in this process. For the Server factories, the shortening of the cycle applies also to customisation of products to fit the local market needs, and sometimes to compliance with local government pressure for increasing local contents. As product technology matures, markets begin to segment and local substitution occurs. For sophisticated products, customers start demanding local changes to the product. As volumes increase, governments and local industry structure put pressure on factories to have more local contents. Thus, with time, there is more pressure to increase the extent of technical activities at the site.
>
> A third reason, and the principal one to move towards Lead factories, is to tap into local technological resources. Existence of a manufacturing site seems to be an important means for attracting local talent to join the company. Such talent would then be under-utilised if the factory is not given the broad strategic scope of a Lead plant. To keep successful managers sufficiently motivated, and to use the factory as an effective learning vehicle for the organisation, the company must let such factories grow in complexity and scope. Additional functions must be added once production becomes routine. These factories should be given the chance of competing for the company's new products and processes. They should have the resources to carry projects forward and transfer knowledge to the rest of the company.

All this implies that moving towards Source, Contributor, and Lead factories is desirable. As the model in Figure 2 suggests, there are specific paths for the development of these type of factories. Moreover, certainly not all factories in a multinational company can or should be turned into Lead plants. Some plants might be kept as Contributor or Source plants and remain effective. Of those, only the plants which are situated in technologically advanced environments--e.g. in certain parts of Germany, France, Japan, United States--are in a good position to move into the Lead position.

In the sample of eight multinational companies studied in this research [4], in almost all cases the international factories had been started in Off-shore or Server roles, and after a while, some of them had moved to Source, Contributor, or Lead plants. The Apple plant in Singpore started as an Off-Shore but moved to become a Source; the H-P plants in Germany, UK, and France, started as Servers, but since then developed into Contributor and Lead plants. Through the years, these plants have built up organisations which have become competence centers for development of specific systems, products, and processes for the company's worldwide operations.

To recap, Lead plants, and to a lesser extent Contributor, and Source factories, must have management teams and technical skills capable of learning from their environments and of using the knowledge effectively and innovatively in creating new products and processes. They must as well be continually striving for efficiency and flexibility within their plants to respond quickly to the changing customer needs. This requires a charter sufficiently broad at the outset to attract the quality of employees needed to spur innovation and to manage complexity. Site location is important, hence a plant with such a mandate must be strategically located, even though the site may look expensive for the early phases during which the factory has a simpler strategic role.

Why should a company go through all the trouble of spreading its technical resources in manufacturing sites around the world? The answer simply is because the abilities to learn from one's employees worldwide, to tap centers of excellence in various countries, and to be more responsive to changes in different parts of the global market are becoming more important.

These arguments have been put forth by many, most recently by Bartlett and Ghoshal [11] who state them eloquently and convincingly. If we were to apply Bartlett and Ghoshal's findings here, the successful multinational corporations are those which maximise learning from their international factory network by investing in local resources--i.e., in the context of Figure 2, moving from Off-Shore and Server positions up. Bartlett and Ghoshal would also advocate not staying in the Outpost position, because an Outpost factory is neither effective for the purpose of timely information collection, nor is it efficient in the use of resources. In fact, the Outpost factory fits what they call a "black hole".

## Communication Within Factory Network

Many speak of installing sophisticated telecommunications and management information systems within the international factory network. These include computer-aided design links, materials management links, engineering systems links, worldwide project teams, and uniform cost management reporting systems, amongst many others. Aside from the expense and irreplaceable management time which successful implementation of these systems demand, a persistent risk is that if not properly chosen, the information system may in fact be harmful! Too much data transfer reduces the ability of the management to sort out the useful information. Mere measurement of certain variables may send the wrong signals to some factories in the chain. In short, choosing a appropriate communication system for an international factory network is clearly not an easy task. Albeit only modestly, the model in Figure 2 helps determine the needed information links to and from each factory in the network.

The premise is a simple one: the communication links beween a factory and headquarters and the other factories in the network depend on the strategic role of the factory. This looks obvious, but it often gets buried in complexity of each factory being considered to be a special case. The usual result is that either the factories are left to develop their own systems or, paradoxically, senior management forces a common system for all. These might be good solutions in certain cases, but certainly not in all.

If all foreign factories of a firm are essentially Off-Shores, or all are Servers, aiming for a common system of communications would not be a problem. But if some are Off-Shores and some are Contributors and Source factories, then a common communication system would be a mistake. Again, the reasons are obvious. Information exchange with Off-Shore and Server factories is relatively limited in scope and flows mostly in one direction. The Contributor and Source plants, on the other hand , require a broader band for communication, more intensive and frequent exchanges, and need connections not only with the central staff but also with other plants. In the same vein, if the plant network contains Lead factories, then the entire communication system in the network--including the links with the Off-Shore and Server factories--becomes more complicated.

To be more specific, networks containing Source, Contributor, and Lead factories need complex yet efficient communication systems not only for transmitting the routine data--production plans, output, costs, engineering change notices, product documents, and the like--but also for frequent exchange of views and ideas on product and process designs. Personal contacts and informal channels become as important as the formal channels. De Meyer's [12] comments on formal and informal communication flows between international R & D facilities summarizes well the communication needs within such factory networks:

> The need for excellent communication between sites is critical for the effective transfer of technology. Much of the information that must flow to headquarters and between different sites can be routinized and one can rely on impersonal media, such as electronic mail, reports and global database networks. But for many stages of the innovation cycle, the personal face-to-face communication remains of primordial importance. Personal contacts play a preponderant role in the diffusion of knowledge between sites and in the

exploitation of research results. Lateral informational flows must be stimulated. Tools available include:

. A policy to stimulate travel and constant telephone contacts between managers and technological experts (both DEC and Ford have private planes for shuttling employees daily between their European sites).

. Regular formal meetings with extensive informal "appendices".

. Company culture stressing open informational exchange.

. Organization of international working groups or project teams leading to intense interaction between employess from different sites.

. An active policy of job rotation between sites.

. Language training.

The extent and the level of sophistication of the communication links in an international network of factories has thus less to do with the number in the network or the grographical spread of the factories and more with variety of strategic roles assigned to the factories. A bottling or a tobacco company with factories spread in fifty countries probably needs a simpler communication system than a car company that designs and manufactures in five.

All the nine companies in the sample [4], being very large multinational companies had factories in almost all the categories of Figure 2 (except fully owned Outposts). The communication systems in their factory networks were thus quite complex. Even so, one could discern the strong influence of the factory's strategic role in the design of the communication system. In Philips, for example, the lighting division had a distinctly different communication system from the electronics division.

In the lighting division, Philips operates Server factories for markets outside of those supplied by Lead plants in Holland. All lighting R&D is performed in Philips' Holland labs and first transferred to the Lead factories nearby for process development and validation. Mature products and processes are then transferred to its Server factories worldwide. In contrast, the consumer electronics division has mostly Contributor and Lead factories spread over the world. Most of product and process development tasks are housed in these factories. The intensity and nature of communications among the factories in these two divisions, as one expects, are vastly different. In the lighting division, the flow of the data to and from its mostly Server factories is rather routine, vertical (i.e. hierarchical) and rather regular. In the electronics division the communication between the factories consists more of sharing knowledge and experience. More tools for stimulating

lateral information flow--such as more face-to-face meetings, job rota-
tions, international work groups or project teams--are employed in the
electronics division.

Another example of extensive use of these tools is in Hewlett-Packard.
The international factory network of H-P consists of mostly Source,
Contributor and Lead factories, and a wide range of tools--from
electronic mail, to regular meetings and "retreats", and job rotations--
are employed to create and keep multiple lines of communication between
factories. Travel expenses seem to be a significant amount of each
factory's budget. Had H-P had mostly Off-Shore or Server factories, one
could question the need for all this. But with Lead, Contributor and
Source factories, such investment in communications becomes a necessity.

**Organisation of Factory Network**

Organisationally, the choice of reporting system in an international
network of factories has been confounded by many factors. The usual
solution is a matrix organisation where geography, product, or technology have shaped the decision. In addition to these three axes of
differentiation, the strategic role of the factory is certainly another
important axis which in some cases should perhaps prevail over the other
three. Identifying the current and planned strategic roles for each
factory should lead to a better choice for the worldwide manufacturing
organisation.

The premise here is that there are benefits in putting the factories
with similar strategic roles in the same organisational units--even if
they are scattered in different corners of the world. Because a
Contributor, Server, and an Off-Shore factories belong to the same
business unit and happen to be, say, in Europe or the Far East, they
should not be necessarily put under the same organisation.

The ways in which these factories need to communicate with each other,
with the rest of the international network, and with central manufacturing and development staff are vastly different. While the Server
factories and perhaps Off-Shores can be organised on a geographical
basis, Source, Contributors, and Lead plants need more direct and frequent access to units outside their region. Performance measure, too,
would be different for these factories depending on their strategic
roles. Whereas cost efficiency is important in an Off-Shore plant, or
profit margin in a Server one, the measure for Outpost, Source,
Contributor, and Lead plants is more complicated. Placing a mix of
these factories in the same organisational unit increases the level of
confusion, and cost allocations among factories and organisational units
become a more taxing affair.

## CONCLUSION

The international expansion of a corporation's manufacturing base is becoming a necessity for survival. With diverse and sometimes conflicting forces driving this expansion, the absence of a clear strategic map for the role of each factory within the firm's international manufacturing network can have dire consequences. Establishment of a plant is a binding and generally irreversible decision, locking the firm into long-term constraints, and there is no guarantee that a series of such decisions made incrementally would yield an optimal network. Moreover, once the factory is established, its development should be guided strategically, even though the operational considerations may seem overwhelming.

The model I suggest here (Figure 2) helps clarify the strategic role of each factory within the international network. Using it for analysis of factory networks provides a fresh perspective and yields a few insights. I suggest three as follows:

First, development of Lead plants in the network is a strategy that stimulates innovation and provides effective access to globally developed technology. No one nation has a monopoly on manufacturing strength now, and a multinational manufacturer without such plants would be at a strategic disadvantage. The building of these types of plants requires a large commitment and takes a long time. Seldom is it practical to establish a Lead factory from scratch. The usual way is to start with a Server, Source, or even Off-Shore factory, and build up technical resources and capabilities at the site. Turning an Outpost into a Lead factory seems to be less practical probably because without a clear staple production or market, it is difficult to justify investment of technical resources in Outpost factories.

Second, in analysing the international network of factories of a company, existence of Lead, Source, and Contributor plants indicates sophisticated international production experience, and potential for achieving lasting competitive advantage through worldwide manufacturing. Conversely, gaps in a company's network of international factories can raise new questions. Sheer numbers of international factories may give the wrong impression. Many Off-Shore plants or Server plants, but no Source, Contributor, or Lead plants are not signs of a mature network which can make long-term contributions to the competitive position of the firm.

Third, in the choice of the organisational structure for the international factory network, an important criterion is the current and future strategic role of each factory as defined from the perspective of this model. Often for international factories, geographical, product or technological criteria seem to shape the worldwide organisation. The strategic roles defined here can be a

new and powerful source of differentiation in the choice of grouping of the international factories in a company. Similarly, the
choice of communication systems among factories, and between them
and the central staff, can be helped by differentiation among the
strategic roles of the factories.


## ACKNOWLEDGEMENTS

I thank David Sackrider for his help throughout this research, particularly during the field work. I also thank Scott Marquardt, Arnoud
De Meyer, and Sumantra Ghoshal for their valuable comments on the earlier drafts of this chapter.


## NOTES

[1]  Source: GATT, as reported in The Economist, September 26, 1987,
pp. 78.

[2]  Source: US Commerce Department, as reported in The International
Herald Tribune, May 21-22, 1988, pp. 13.

[3]  Source: The Economist, August 20, 1988, pp. 62.

[4]  The companies studied were:

        Apple Computers
        Digital Equipment Corporation
        Hewlett Packard
        IBM
        LSI Logic
        Olivetti
        Philips
        Sony (France)

Data were collected through company documents, field visits, and
interviews with directors of these companies. Interviews were held
during Winter and Spring 1988.

[5]  Raymond Vernon, "International Investment and International Trade
in the Product Cycle," Quarterly Journal of Economics, Vol. 80 May
1966, pp. 190-207.

[6]  Louis T. Wells, "International Trade: The Product Life Cycle
Approach," in The Product Life Cycle and International Trade, Louis
Wells (Editor), Harvard University Press, 1972, pp. 3-33.

[7]  Robert E. Stobaugh, "The Product Life Cycle, US Exports, and
International Investment". Unpublished doctoral dissertation,
Harvard Business School, 1968.

[8] William H. Gruber, Dileep Mehta end Raymond Vernon, "The R&D Factor in International Trade and International Investment of United States Industries," in The Product Life Cycle and International Trade, Louis Wells (Editor), Harvard University Press, 1972, pp. 126.

[9] William H. Davidson, Experience Effects in International Investment and Technology Transfer, UMI Research Press, Ann Arbor, MI, 1980.

[10] Therese Flaherty, "Coordinating International Manufacturing and Technology," in Michael E. Porter (Editor), Competition in Global Industries, Harvard Business School Press, Boston, 1987.

[11] Christopher A. Bartlett and Sumantra Ghoshal, "Managing Across Borders," Sloan Management Review, Summer and Fall 1987.

[12] Arnoud De Meyer, "Internationalisation of Research and Development," INSEAD, Fontainebleau, 1988.

MANAGING INTERNATIONAL MANUFACTURING
K. Ferdows (Editor)
© Elsevier Science Publishers B.V. (North-Holland), 1989

### INTERNATIONAL MANUFACTURING STRATEGIES AND INFRASTRUCTURAL CONSIDERATIONS IN THE ELECTRONICS INDUSTRY


Michael E. MCGRATH and Roberto B. BEQUILLARD

Pittiglio, Rabin, Todd & McGrath


The growing importance of the international manufacturing function in the electronic industry is due to fundamental changes in new technology, automation, production volumes, and increased experience in international operations. The benefits of international manufacturing forced the management to re-think their operational strategies and pay closer atten- tion to developing an effective and appropriate infrastructure for international operations.

The aim of this paper is to help the management in this process. The paper starts with a presentation of a framework for classification of typical international manufacturing strategy, and is followed by a dis- cussion of the infrastructural requirements needed to support each type of strategy.


## 1. TYPICAL INTERNATIONAL MANUFACTURING STRATEGIES


Simply put, international manufacturing strategy is the manufacturing strategy of a multinational business. It is the overall plan for how the company will manufacture products on a worldwide basis to satisfy customer demand worldwide.

The benefits of a properly executed international manufacturing strategy can be very substantial. A well developed strategy can have a direct im- pact on the financial performance and ultimately be reflected in increased profitability. In the electronic industry, there are examples of com- panies attributing 5% to 15% reduction in cost of goods sold, 10% to 20% increase in sales, 50% to 150% improvement in asset utilization, and 30% to 100% increase in inventory turnover to their internationalisation of manufacturing.

To understand how companies view international manufacturing and what fac- tors affect these decisions, we conducted a study in which the inter- national manufacturing strategies of 56 electronic companies were reviewed. The result of the study reveals that there are five basic forms of international manufacturing strategy in the industry:

**Home country manufacturing** is mainly a centralized manufacturing strategy which consists of having almost all of the manufacturing operations conducted in the company's country of origin. These companies have a high degree of global sourcing performed through third parties and usually have a sales representation or a joint venture/licensing agreement for distribution to foreign markets.

**Regional manufacturing** is the strategy to deploy manufacturing operations into major markets. This strategy views the world as various regions having common characteristics (i.e., similar markets, distribution requirements, government policies, etc.) and deploys manufacturing activities in those regions, either at the product level (manufacturing the same product in each region) or at the component or sub-assembly level (manufacturing the same component and sub-assemblies in each region).

**Coordinated global manufacturing** is the classic strategy for taking advantage of low labor cost areas (or other low cost local resources) for manufacturing. Typically this strategy leads to having separate manufacturing facilities for components and sub-assemblies which are transferred for final assembly.

**Combined regional & coordinated global manufacturing** is a strategy which involves some component and sub-assembly manufacturing in low cost regions with final assembly in regions where the markets are located.

**Tax avoidance** is not a primary strategy. It is usually considered only after an international manufacturing strategy has been conceptually approved. It is, however, a very influential factor in deciding where to locate manufacturing of specific products within the overall international manufacturing strategy framework. For some companies, this strategy can translate into significant savings depending on the particular products and location.

|  | No. of Companies | Percent |
|---|---|---|
| Home Country Manufacturing | 20 | 36 |
| Regional Manufacturing | 17 | 30 |
| Coordinated Global Mfg. | 5 | 9 |
| Combined Strategy | 14 | 25 |
|  | 56 | 100 |

All the companies reviewed were classified according to their particular international manufacturing strategy.

Of the 56 companies, 9 companies (16%) followed tax avoidance as a secondary strategy. One interesting difference observed was the amount of worldwide movement of assemblies and sub-assemblies from plant to plant. A parameter called the product movement ratio (PMR) was developed to measure the total value of non-finished product transferred among major regions of the world. The PMR is computed as the ratio of the value of

material transfers to total sales and is normalized to eliminate accounting differences.

## POSITIONING OF COMPANIES ACCORDING TO
## PMR VS. FOREIGN SALES

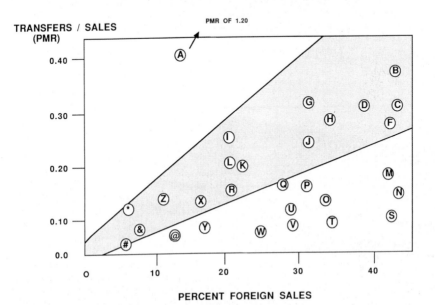

FIGURE 1

As can be clearly seen in Figure 1, there are significant differences in
the international product transfer strategies of different companies. One
company, for example, has a PMR of 0.08 indicating that only very little
product is transferred among regions. At the other extreme, is a company
with a PMR greater than 1, indicating that its dollar value of product
transfer is greater than its dollar value of total sales (normalized) or
that, on the average, every product is transferred more than once from
region to region. It is expected that companies will fall in the shaded
area, unless the level of regionality is high, in which case, companies
will fall below the shaded area (this is typical of companies manufacturing internationally to leverage foreign sales). If companies are
manufacturing internaticnally to supply their domestic market, they will
fall above the shaded area (this is typical of companies manufacturing internationally exclusively to take advantage of low cost opportunities).
Companies B, C, F, N and M are all similar-sized computer manufacturers,
yet the manufacturing approaches are significantly different. This is
seen in a wide variation of PMRs from .08 to .38.

## 2.  DIMENSIONS OF INTERNATIONAL MANUFACTURING STRATEGY

In general, international manufacturing strategy can be viewed as distinct sets of decisions which can be grouped into three different dimensions:

1. **The role international manufacturing plays within the overall strategy of the business.**

2. **Deployment decisions**

3. **Infrastructural requirements**

Although a great deal could be written about each of these areas, for the purpose of this discussion we will mention only briefly the key issues addressed in the first two dimensions and will concentrate on the third.

International manufacturing (the first dimension) is clearly a major factor in business strategy whether or not it is treated as such. Its ability to significantly contribute to the strategic objectives of the business makes it an ideal candidate for competitive analysis of opportunities, and therefore it should be an integral part of the business planning process. In reality, many companies plan their international manufacturing strategies at the operating level strictly by comparing their existing operations to available alternatives. Typically, they use only a single criterion (usually cost) and fail to see the other areas of opportunities that international manufacturing offers. The use of international manufacturing to leverage foreign sales, for example, is an opportunity frequently overlooked.

Deployment decisions (the second dimension) are closely linked to strategic planning. Although a decision may have been made based on its strategic merits, it may not be feasible due to tactical constraints. These types of decisions involve planning the number, size and location of plants, assigning products and sub-assemblies to individual plants and planning the level of vertical integration.

Once the strategy has been developed, management attention begins to focus on the organizational and infrastructural mechanisms required to coordinate and manage international manufacturing activities. Although infrastructural considerations should play a major role in the determination of the overall strategy, it is usually an area that is overlooked and not given the importance that it deserves. The shared belief is that organizational changes can be made along the way, risking only a delay in the implementation schedule. This fails to recognize the impediments that a poorly designed infrastructure can impose in the realization of the overall strategy. Another typical misconception is viewing international manufacturing operations in isolation and not as part of an overall international operations framework.

### 3. INTERNATIONAL MANUFACTURING INFRASTRUCTURE

The materials and manufacturing overhead functions can be the most critical operating functions in an electronics company's activities. Apart from the actual cost of material purchases, they constitute the highest cost elements in most large electronic companies and represent the highest value added in the manufacturing process. Their relative importance has also been increasing in relation to the total cost of making the product.

Given this cost structure, it is essential for a large company to be effective at managing its international operations, optimizing its performance in these overhead areas. This requires managing successfully each of the following three areas: materials planning/procurement, manufacturing, and distribution/logistics.

## INTERNATIONAL OPERATIONS ACTIVITIES

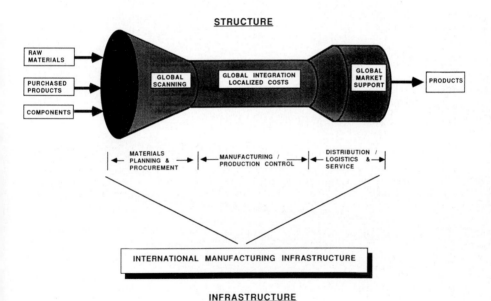

FIGURE 2

Because these three areas have strong linkages within themselves and among each other, they must be managed with an overall business perspective and in an integrative mode. Figure 2 shows how these organizations integrate to form the structure of international operations. It incorporates the total value added process of international activities starting with raw materials, components and purchased products which are funneled into the manufacturing process to produce a range of products which are subsequently distributed broadly to the world markets. The key organizational abilities that the corporation must master in each of the areas is also shown. The materials planning and procurement organization must have a keen ability for scanning the world for the highest quality and lowest cost resources. The manufacturing organization should have strong integrative mechanisms across functions and the ability to control the local environment. The distribution/logistics organization should have an ability to provide global market support for the finished products and must have the necessary flexibility and understanding of the distribution channel's operating policies and customer needs in order to provide adequate post sales support.

Given the positioning of the manufacturing activity in the international operations structure, it serves as the strategic link between global resources and global markets. It is also the focal point for the evaluation of trade off between product cost and customer service. Should a company locate manufacturing closer to its customers even though the product manufacturing cost will be higher?

To answer this type of question, the effects of decisions in all three areas of the structure must be carefully analyzed. Any major international operations planning program will have an impact in all three areas, and its implications must be carefully evaluated.

The overall framework for managing and integrating activities in these areas is the international manufacturing infrastructure. It is this infrastructure which establishes the guidelines in which manufacturing executes.

An international manufacturing infrastructure can be viewed as including five elements:

1. "Localization" of manufacturing strategy

2. International supply/demand management

3. Global and local sourcing techniques

4. Product/process technologies and new product introduction strategies

5. General organization and integration mechanisms

All these elements must interrelate with each other to make the structure work. The relative importance of each element within the structure, however, varies according to the overall strategy of the business and the particular mission of the international manufacturing plants. Companies having multiple plants in various countries and competing across a range of products selling in different markets must perform effectively in each of the five areas. Figure 3 shows the major elements of an international manufacturing infrastructure and the decisions that impact its overall form.

The sections which follow discuss each of these elements and identify the major issues which need to be addressed.

**INTERNATIONAL MANUFACTURING INFRASTRUCTURE**

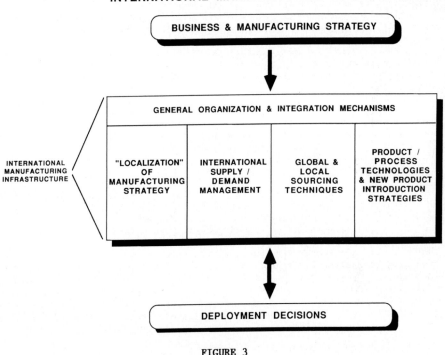

FIGURE 3

## 3.1 Localisation

As international manufacturing strategies are developed, specific missions need to be established for each of the manufacturing plants. These missions should be in line with the overall strategy of the business and must not lead to conflicting objectives among the manufacturing units. For example, a plant in one country is heavily dependent on a plant in another country for a critical component. The mission of the downstream plant was defined to be responsive to its customers and have short production runs in order to reduce delivery times while the mission of the upstream plant was defined to be a low cost producer and manufacture in large quantities to achieve economies of scale. The missions obviously conflict and need to be reconciled or the overall international manufacturing strategy will not succeed. However, specific strategies must also be developed for each plant in each country to consider the importance of the local environment in competitive positioning. For example, proximity to market, varying resource costs, capacity availability and the strength of the individual manufacturing units require variation in local plant strategies.

The guideline for determining the degree of localization of the manufacturing strategy is part of the infrastructure. It must provide guidance in resolving three basic issues:

**(a)  What is needed to maintain consistency within the overall international manufacturing strategy?** The development of overall business policies on international manufacturing and the definition of the interrelationships required among the manufacturing units are two activities necessary to achieve strategic consistency. Examples of this include:

> **Policies for managing the total supply chain** and meeting corporate inventory objectives

> **Interplant scheduling mechanisms** (e.g., which plants should feed others and in what volumes, frequencies, etc.)

> **Polices for guiding make/buy decisions** - For example, in some companies, manufacturing plants are required to buy components from other plants within the company. In other companies, they buy from the outside market if they believe that it is better.

> **Sourcing policies** - Should manufacturing plants buy through the corporate office or independently?

**(b) Which aspects of manufacturing need to be standardized across international plants?** Standardization may or may not be desirable in all areas. Evaluating the trade-offs between standardization of activities throughout all plants vs. the level of localization of individual activities is critical to the development of the international manufacturing strategy. These decisions should be reviewed, particularly as they relate to:

> **Manufacturing processes** - Certain investments in automation may only be viable with economies of scale realized from a multiplant implementation. If the processes are not standardized, this opportunity may not exist.

> **Manufacturing systems** - Should manufacturing plants be required to use common systems, training and procedures?

> **Inventory policies** - Should these policies be the same for all plants, training and procedures?

> **Vertical integration** - Should the vertical span be consistent across plants or should the manufacturing units be structured differently according to the local environment?

> **Quality** - Should product quality be consistent or are plant focuses different enough to allow quality requirements to vary?

**Image** – Should the company maintain a standard image in every country in which it operates or should it be permitted to differ according to the local environment?

**(c) What elements of manufacturing are clearly local prerogatives?** Some manufacturing functions must be managed with a local management perspective. Companies must identify these and manage them accordingly. They can include:

**Human resource polices** – Salaries, vacation, fringe benefits and other issues are frequently locally determined factors.

**Local sourcing** – Activities involved with the local procurement of raw materials, components and other products

**Vertical integration** – To the extent to which the manufacturing unit becomes a key influential player in the domestic economy of a foreign country, its policies will become subject to the political imperatives of the local environment and must be managed accordingly.

The level of "localization" in international manufacturing strategy is a key determinant of the degree of centralization of managerial control and of the mechanisms required to achieve strategic consistency.

## 3.2 International Supply/Demand Management

In an international manufacturing environment order scheduling and fulfillment, interplant scheduling and the management of the global pipeline are major success factors. This is the role of international supply/demand management and the issues that the infrastructure must support include the following:

**(a) How are customer orders with international multiplant requirements scheduled?** In the computer industry, for example, customer orders are placed for entire systems consisting of various modules (i.e., keyboards, disk drives, networks, etc.). These modules may be manufactured at plants in different countries and ultimately will require consolidation into a single order for delivery to the customer. There are three different approaches that companies commonly use to deal with this requirement: separate final assembly and test facility for order consolidation, a separate warehouse facility for merging modules into a single order or "site merging" modules delivered directly to the customer from the different manufacturing plants. The first has been the traditional alternative, however, several companies have found that entire facilities can be eliminated by putting the infrastructure in place for warehouse or site merging.

**(b) How is interplant demand scheduled?** A large computer company may have more than one million part numbers used to manufacture its product lines and may sell more than 10,000 catalog items. Obviously, interplant re-

quirements can not be scheduled at these levels. This requires a carefully designed and managed interplant scheduling system. Several approaches commonly used are:

>    **Top level scheduling** – Centrally scheduling the top 2-3% of the
>    items and letting the individual plants schedule the rest can  be
>    a successful approach.

>    **Treating plants as vendors** – Component plants are viewed as  ven-
>    dors and treated on an "arms length" basis.

>    **Interplant MRP** – This requires the company to have a  centralized
>    or  integrated  MRP  system  to  schedule all interplant require-
>    ments.

**(c)  How  is  the  global pipeline managed?** The global pipeline should be
managed so as to balance the overall corporate customer service,  capacity
utilization  and  inventory  objectives. Inventory policies, manufacturing
cycle times, the international transportation network,  in-transit  times
and customer lead time are all examples of areas requiring coordination on
an international level.

International  manufacturing companies must address these three key issues
and establish the appropriate  infrastructure  for  international  supply/
demand management.

### 3.3  Global & Local Sourcing Techniques

Sourcing  refers  to the process of determining how and where manufactured
goods and raw materials will be procured.  Its impact on profitability can
vary greatly depending on the products but the upside potential of a well-
designed and implemented sourcing strategy is so high that it is an essential part of the organizational infrastructure of electronic companies.

Over the last few years two major trends have developed:  global  sourcing
and  local  sourcing.  While on the surface these trends appear to be contradictory, what is necessary is for companies to reconcile when to  apply
each.  This  reconciliation  is  done  through  the  global sourcing infrastructure. Companies  need  to  resolve  three  basic  issues  in  this
process:

**(b)  How should the inconsistencies between global and local  sourcing  be
evaluated?  What are the trade-offs?** Just-In-Time (JIT) sourcing has become very popular in the electronics industry.  In many ways JIT &  global
sourcing  are  contradictory.  On  the  one  hand, a Just-In-Time program
implemented at a domestic level can have very impressive results including
significant  cost reductions, better product quality and increased responsiveness to customers.  The significance of JIT/Sourcing can  be  seen  by
the actions of several countries to promote and develop the vendor base to
provide this capability.  This is more frequently becoming a major  factor
for plant location.

On the other hand, due to the availability of low-priced commodity type components in the world market, sourcing some components globally instead of domestically is critical for electronic manufacturing. Without it, most companies could not compete in the global market.

How are these divergent goals reconciled? In the first case, companies that have achieved JIT benefits have had to change many of their organizational strategies to meet the needs of the new environment. They have changed their overall business philosophy from choosing the lowest cost suppliers to developing close relationships with a selected group of local suppliers in order to reduce total cost, even if it means paying more for the component itself. In the second case, companies have had to continue buying components in the traditional way and have developed internal mechanisms that allow them to scan the world and be flexible in their procurement patterns.

The only way these divergent goals can be reconciled is by establishing the appropriate guidelines. This requires understanding and evaluating the potential benefits of a JIT program implemented on a domestic level and classifying components into categories in order to provide guidelines on which ones should be locally sourced and which ones should be sourced globally. This solution, as simple as it may sound, has been very difficult for companies to implement. Many companies do not have the infrastructural capabilities to guide global and local sourcing decisions on an ongoing basis.

**(b) What is the best approach to international procurement?** Deciding how international procurement will be performed is critical for electronics companies. A survey of procurement practices of 18 major companies reveals the following data:

| Purchasing Mode | Percentage of Procurement Using This Approach |
|---|---|
| Overseas Buying Office | 12% |
| Buying Trips | 28% |
| Buying through Sellers' Local Sales Offices | 40% |
| Buying through a Company-Owned Manufacturing Plant Offshore | 16% |
| Other | 4% |

Companies must decide which approach is most appropriate to their overall strategy and organize accordingly. This requires a high degree of organizational flexibility.

**(c) What organizational mechanisms are used for international procurement?** Proper vendor management is important to achieve the benefits of global sourcing. There are three ways of doing this:

**Centralized Procurement** – All major components are purchased by a corporate purchasing group. Each plant submits its sourcing requirements to the purchasing department where they are aggregated

into a master purchasing plan. This gives the company higher ne-
gotiating leverage but reduces manufacturing flexibility.

**Lead plant responsibility** - Some companies assign to different
plants the responsibility for selecting vendors and buying
specific components. The plant buying the largest quantity of a
particular component is usually the one assigned the task of ne-
gotiating agreements for the whole company.

**Commodity teams** - These are independent teams that have responsibility for vendor selection and procurement of products in different commodity areas within the company. They include representation from various manufacturing plants and other corporate
functions and make decisions based on majority vote. A large
company that uses this process has found small teams to be more
effective than large teams and has revised its approach leaving
smaller plants out of the process.

## 3.4  Product/Process Technology and New Product Introduction Strategies

According to the product/process innovation life cycle concept [1], in the
early stages of the life cycle of a product, product innovation is much
more prevalent than process innovation, with the reverse being true as the
product matures. This framework is particularly applicable to the
electronics industry, where the trade-offs between product and process innovation are becoming less clear as the life cycle of the products are
shortened and where the technology content of both product and process is
high.

The international manufacturing infrastructure must provide the mechanisms
to effectively deal with these issues where multiple similar plants are
involved. It should be designed to address the following organizational
concerns:

**(a) How are products "internationalized"?  How standardized should they be
across countries?  How varied?** There are many electronics products which
must be modified to meet the requirements of different natural markets.
Examples include: all products requiring software adaptation for the local
languages, computer keyboards which require different characters for the
different languages, and, in general, most electronic products which require a change to the power source for the different voltages found in the
various countries around the world.

This raises an interesting question that has a direct impact on manufacturing decisions:  Should a product be designed for world use and include
all the features needed in every country, even though not all features are
needed in all markets, and the cost of manufacturing the product is
higher?  A simple example is a standard product built for the U.S. and
European markets with a dual voltage power source built in and a switch to
change it to the desired voltage.  These types of decisions can have major
implications for manufacturing.

Other types of product "internationalization" are less clear. These relate to the different preferences or customs of individual countries. One multinational manufacturer of control systems faced this kind of problem in developing a new product. The US designed and specified a keyboard/CRT input panel. European product managers believed strongly that a larger control panel with individual analog switches was required in the European market. These local preferences changed the product so significantly that a common product could not be manufactured and worldwide manufacturing economies not achieved.

**(b) How standardized should the manufacturing processes be internationally?** The level of technology that is appropriate in one country may not be appropriate in another. For example, some manufacturing operations performed in third-world countries, where labor is cheaper and technology scarce, may utilize a different manufacturing process than its counterpart in more developed countries, where automation may be most appropriate.

**(c) How should the product/process introduction activities be managed?** One large computer manufacturer uses an approach called the "production management center" concept. This consists of committees formed by representatives of R&D, marketing and manufacturing that are responsible for developing manufacturing processes in a particular product area, designing the process once and then using it wherever the process is used. A schematic of the different functional areas that are represented in a production management center is shown in Figure 4. The "production management center" is a good mechanism to integrate product and process innovation techniques with the needs of global management. Also, by designing for manufacturability and testability from the start, the number of product or process changes is reduced, allowing the company to move down the experience curve more quickly and achieve maximum profitability on short-lived products.

Another approach used for implementing manufacturing process changes is to develop training modules. This consists of internal teams of experts trained on particular processes and assigned the task of visiting all international manufacturing plants, conducting on-site training and helping them implement the new techniques.

The particular role that manufacturing plants play in the product/process introduction scheme is dictated by the trade-offs between the importance of their local environment and the strength of the particular manufacturing unit. International manufacturing plants will either be the **leaders** in a certain product or market, **contributors** to the strategies of the leaders or **implementors** of the strategy developed by the leaders.[2]

**(d) How should new products be introduced?** Basic issues to consider include:

      **Proper timing** - When should the product be intro-duced?

      **Location** - Should it be introduced at one plant first or all plants simultaneously?

**Phasing** – What is the product introduction strategy? Should it be introduced in one country first and others later after learning from the initial experience?

## PRODUCTION MANAGEMENT CENTER CONCEPT

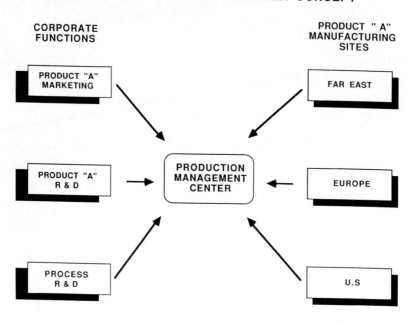

FIGURE 4

## 3.5  General Organisation and Integration Mechanisms

The way in which companies organize and manage their international manufacturing activities vary according to the overall strategy of the business. "Structure follows strategy",[3] a discussion on the type of organization structure that is most appropriate to the particular international manufacturing strategy, is outside of the scope of this paper, but it should be emphasized that regardless of the strategy and structure of the company, there must be mechanisms in place to integrate all the previously discussed infrastructural elements with the overall organization and business strategy.

Large international electronics companies use a variety of integration mechanisms. Some of these were discussed previously. In our study of this area, the following integration mechanisms were seen:

> Centralized high-level manufacturing staff functions can be effective in providing worldwide coordination where plants are decentralized. Centralized manufacturing on a worldwide basis is rare in companies greater than $1 billion.
>
> Selected plants can take lead responsibility for certain functions which need to be coordinated.
>
> Company-wide plans, policies or guidelines can serve to provide the coordination needed.
>
> Steering Committees or task force teams, if properly integrated, can serve as the link between decentralization and centralized coordination.
>
> Information systems designed to integrate the needed functions can be applied to supplement other means of coordination.

These mechanisms will be different from company to company depending on its manufacturing strategy, operational configurations, key strengths and control needs, but their main function is the same. They serve to tie together all the other elements of the infrastructure.


## 4. RELATING STRATEGY AND INFRASTRUCTURE

Depending on the particular international manufacturing strategy of the company, the impact of the five infrastructural elements on performance will vary. For example, a home country manufacturing strategy, by its very nature, will require less infrastructural sophistication overall than a combined regional/ coordinated global strategy, but it may require a high degree of focus and performance on a single element of the infrastructure, since the overall success of the strategy may lie in the ability to effectively exploit that particular capability.

Figure 5 shows the strategic impact of the five infrastructural elements previously defined and how they vary across and within strategies. Companies transitioning from one strategy to another or solidifying their position in a particular strategy must recognize the importance to build an infrastructure that maximizes performance in those elements most critical to success.

Most significantly, Figure 5 shows that more complex strategies require a more sophisticated infrastructure to be successful. This means that the investment in international manufacturing infrastructure is significant, and the risk of failure is higher for companies following these strategies. While this may seem obvious, it is frequently ignored, and

there have been cases where companies following the same strategy had differing degrees of success because one ignored the infrastructure requirements.

# INFRASTRUCTURE IMPACT ON STRATEGIC PERFORMANCE

| | | INTERNATIONAL MANUFACTURING STRATEGY | | | |
|---|---|---|---|---|---|
| | | HOME COUNTRY | REGIONAL | COORDINATED GLOBAL | COMBINED REGIONAL AND COORDINATED GLOBAL |
| INFRASTRUCTURAL ELEMENTS | LOCALIZATION OF MANUFACTURING STRATEGY | LOW | HIGH | HIGH | HIGH |
| | INTERNATIONAL SUPPLY / DEMAND MANAGEMENT | MED | MED | HIGH | VERY HIGH |
| | GLOBAL AND LOCAL SOURCING MECHANISMS | HIGH | HIGH | VERY HIGH | VERY HIGH |
| | PRODUCT / PROCESS TECHNOLOGY AND NEW PRODUCT INTRODUCTION TECHNIQUES | LOW | MED | HIGH | VERY HIGH |
| | GENERAL ORGANIZATION SUPPORT MECHANISMS | MED | MED | HIGH | VERY HIGH |

FIGURE 5

## CONCLUSION

A well developed international manufacturing strategy is a key element of
the overall business strategy of electronics companies. Although international manufacturing strategy decisions should be the result of a long-
term strategy plan, it is apparent that many companies are either frequently shifting their strategies or making decisions in reaction to
short-term factors. Companies that do have a long-term strategy, however,
have gained a significant competitive advantage and have been able to accommodate short term changes.

Some of the reasons why international manufacturing has been such an important issue in an electronics company's planning process have been discussed here. It is expected that the trends driving companies to international manufacturing will continue and that the need to successfully
accommodate their strategies to the changing environment will accelerate.

Companies should try not to make the mistakes other companies have made. Most unsuccessful international manufacturing efforts have resulted from the following deficiencies:

The long-term strategy for international manufacturing is not clearly defined.

The strategy is based on inappropriate information (typically this comes from using "standard" accounting data).

The company cannot make the decisions required to implement the strategy.

The strategy is based on improper assumptions (or inexperience).

The strategy is inconsistent with other elements of a company's business strategy.

The strategy is not successfully implemented because of a poor international manufacturing infrastructure.

As the paper describes, five elements are needed for an effective international manufacturing infrastructure. Their relative importance changes according to the particular strategy of the company, but they all form an integral part of the strategic management process of an international manufacturing company.

Many companies are successful at planning international manufacturing requirements but fewer are successful at implementing it effectively because of the infrastructural support that the organization needs. Putting in place the international manufacturing infrastructure in a large company is a major task. Individual elements can require multiple millions of dollars and take several calendar years. The financial returns and strategic benefits, however, are so significant that companies cannot afford not to do it right.

One large company, for example, found that it's manufacturing cycle time on an international level was 18 months from the initiation of component manufacturing to final system assembly. By making major improvements to the key elements of its international manufacturing infrastructure, it was able to reduce the cycle time, over a three-year period, to less than six months. The resulting benefits in market responsiveness, new product introduction, manufacturing cost and inventory reduction were dramatic.

Our hope is that what was presented here will provide guidance to companies planning their international manufacturing strategies and will serve to advance the academic thinking in the field. Companies that understand how the elements of the infrastructure relate to their international manufacturing strategy will manage to meet the needs of the constantly changing environment and will remain competitive in the future. Those that do not will not be able to compete in this global industry.

**FOOTNOTES**

[1] Ghoshal S., and Bartlett C., "Tap Your Subsidiaries for Global Reach" Harvard Business Review, November-December 1986.


[2] Abernathy, W.J., and Utterback, "A Dynamic Model of Product and Process Innovation," Omega, December 1975, pp. 639-657.


[3] Chandler, A., The Visible Hand: The Managerial Revolution in American Business, Harvard University Press, Cambridge, Mass., 1977.

GLOBAL MANUFACTURING RATIONALIZATION: THE DESIGN
AND MANAGEMENT OF INTERNATIONAL FACTORY NETWORKS

Michael D. OLIFF and Jeffrey S. ARPAN
University of South Carolina


Frank L. DuBois
American University

## 1. INTRODUCTION

The last twenty years have seen an explosion in the magnitude of international business competition and operations due to reductions in trade
barriers, advances in technology, global standardization of products and
a heightened awareness of improvements in living standards resulting
from international trade. As a result, managers must now take a proac-
tive stance with respect to competition in the international environment
[1]. This evolving scenario has created both hardships and opportunities for firms seeking to maintain competitive advantages over
global competitors. On one hand, firms failing to respond to challenges
posed by global competition have suffered substantial losses in market
share and have often undergone painful restructuring or divestiture of
operations to recapture competitiveness. On the other hand, firms that
were quick to recognize the evolving nature of global competition and
took steps to mitigate its adverse effects have prospered [2].

Firms that have benefited from the new economic order have done so in
large part through the recognition of recent changes in global competition, the enhanced role that the manufacturing function now plays in
global competitiveness, and the diminishing returns in seeking domestic
solutions to this challenge. In large part, much of the success of
these firms can be traced to a renewed focus upon the manufacturing
function to exploit opportunities available in the international environment.

The economic integration or rationalization of production operations
across national boundaries has evolved rapidly in this atmosphere.
Multinational Enterprises (MNEs), by virtue of their simultaneous
presence in many different locations are in many cases able to shift
productive resources to those environments with the most desirable combination of factor inputs required for the manufacture of their
products. This factor has been a key element in the protection of competitive advantage from global adversaries. Some of these MNEs have
established what can best be called global manufacturing networks with
stages of the production process dispersed internationally to those
locations that offer the most advantageous operating conditions and
least expensive inputs for particular stages of the process.

A key question then confronting the management of the MNE is the configuration and coordination of global manufacturing networks to best
meet the challenge of global competition. Configuration refers to the
strategic dispersal of manufacturing activities. Thus, one MNE might
choose to establish a single fully integrated and autonomous plant to
serve a particular host country and external markets while another
chooses to construct multiple plants designed to accommodate single
stages of the production process and, hence, capitalize on the comparative advantages available at each particular location. In the latter
case, outputs are shipped to other plants or unaffiliated business units
for further processing into a final product.

The second issue, coordination, relates to the development of linkages
between dispersed manufacturing activities in an effort to minimize the
costs associated with the ongoing management of dispersed but interdependent production activities. This activity is extremely critical
for the MNE characterized by a multiplicity of dispersed production
stages, and entails the coordination of forecasts, production plans,
shipping schedules, vendor lists, and other operations necessary to the
achievement of corporate objectives. Coordination requires a balance
between the initial production costs resulting from dispersal on one
side and subsequent logistics and coordination related costs on the
other.

Unfortunately, little work has been done with respect to the development
of conceptual frameworks within which these issues can be examined.
Tools are needed that allow the management of the MNE to systematically
analyze the problems that must be confronted in the configuration and
coordination of international manufacturing networks; i.e., the country-
specific and international environmental constraints that restrict the
firm's behavior. In an effort to redress this omission, a modification
and extension to a conceptual framework originally presented in the mid
1960s by Richard Farmer and Barry Richman [3] is proposed. Known as
the Farmer-Richman comparative management matrix it has been used historically to address: 1) Why one country's industry may be more
efficient or effective than another country's, 2) Why management of the
firm and its activities may need to be altered if performed in another
country, and 3) Why specific business practices differ among countries.
However, little application of the framework has been made to the
development of international manufacturing network strategies in the
MNE. For the purposes of this paper, we propose several modifications
to the matrix and show how it can be used by a firm in the evaluation
of different international manufacturing rationalization strategies.
Case studies of three firms serve to illustrate the linkages between the
environmental constraints and global manufacturing strategies.

## 2. RESEARCH ON INTERNATIONAL MANUFACTURING STRATEGIES

Little work in the area of international manufacturing strategies and
the management of international factory networks is available before the
mid 1970s. Prior to this time, manufacturing was treated as a poor
stepchild to the marketing and finance functions in many organizations.
Since then many authors have stressed the importance of the manufacturing function in the pursuit of strategic objectives. Skinner, Banks and
Wheelwright, Hayes and Abernathy and others were among the first to take

a stand for the integration of the manufacturing function into the strategic plans of the firm [4]. However, their primary focus has been on the domestic firm seeking to recapture or enhance competitive advantage through a revitalization of its manufacturing function, thus, global rationalization strategies are treated only tangentially.

Much of the flavor of this early work is captured by Haas (1987) as she describes eight firm-specific manufacturing decisions where a "strategic breakpoint" induces a disproportionate sales volume increase. Again, however, global issues are given little attention.

Porter's (1986) "value chain" concept is useful in conceptualizing a manufacturing network composed of upstream and downstream activities. The major issues confronting the globally competitive firm can be regarded as the configuration of the upstream activities (i.e. where productive capacity is located) and the coordination of these activities (i.e. how these elements of the chain are linked together and how process technology is disseminated among the various elements in the network).

Multiplant manufacturing strategies are discussed by Schmenner (1983) within the context of the plant location decision. Five basic versions of multiplant strategies are discussed with each reflecting company attitudes toward configuration objectives. The type of strategy most pertinent to the rationalization framework is referred to as a Process Plant strategy or a configuration that separates the constituent stages of the production process on a plant by plant basis. Stages are dispersed by function to those locations where the greatest production efficiencies can be achieved. Again, however, the focus is on the firm having operations in only one country. No attention is given to the firm desiring to integrate globally dispersed operations.

By virtue of its simultaneous presence in different countries, the firm with globally dispersed activities is in a propitious position vis-a-vis purely domestic competitors with respect to its ability to exploit the volatility inherent in international markets. Kogut (1985b), explores the implications this advantage has for the operational flexibility of the MNE. Involved are both the arbitrage of market imperfections and the creation of leverage over host country stakeholders. To this end, the creation of a centralized planning and control function along with integrative systems to link subsidiary operations is proposed.

The information system requirements in a globally integrated firm are discussed by Ghopal (1986). But he gives little attention to the dynamics of international operations. That is, the effects of country-specific macro-economic variables (e.g., exchange rate fluctuations and inflation rates in the host country) and the effect of host country attitudes towards the centralized (external) control of what may well be a dominant economic force in the host country (e.g., transborder data flow restrictions) are given no mention.

Difficulties in the implementation of global manufacturing rationalization strategies are addressed qualitatively by Doz (1978) in diagnosing the need for rationalization and for the management of the rationalization process. Doz presents an analysis of the barriers to multi-country rationalization and offers some suggestions for managers approaching a rationalization project. Other authors such as Starr and Bitran et al. take a different approach to the analysis of rationalization.

Starr (1984), develops a global network model focusing on the exploita- tion of those factors that provide the MNE with a competitive advantage in international markets. The objective is to provide a framework for the MNE – through the use of the transhipment model – to determine the optimal allocation of global productive capacity. The transhipment model (also called the transportation algorithm) requires the determina- tion of the costs and volume constraints involved in the movement of resources from a set of origins to a set of destinations within the MNE's global infrastructure. The model is then solved for the optimal combination of variables to minimize an explicit cost function. However, initial capacity allocations are considered fixed and hence, decisions regarding allocation of productive capacity are not addressed.

Bitran et al. (1985) consider the adaptation of a single plant Materials Requirements Planning (MRP) system to a multi-plant environment by in- tegrating the transportation algorithm into the solution framework. The firm then treats its network of manufacturing facilities as an in- tegrated whole rather than as a collection of related but autonomous units managed with independent production systems. However, Bitran et al. give only scant treatment to the international barriers to multi- plant integration in their analysis.

At present, the research on global manufacturing strategies appears to lack a systematic framework within which the choices available to the MNE can be examined objectively. The number of relevant variables and constraints that must be considered in a firm's location decision is onerous enough in a purely domestic setting but multiply rapidly when the international dimension is introduced. Not only must the firm con- sider the same variables appropriate in a domestic location analysis but international variables distinct to each particular location possibility must also be recognized. The following sections present a detailed framework for the systematic analysis of these issues.

## 3.  THE COMPARATIVE MANAGEMENT MATRIX

Farmer-Richman present a classification scheme whereby the critical ele- ments of the general management process are contrasted with country- specific environmental variables in matrix format [5]. Figure One provides an overview of the linkages between the external constraints-- both country-specific and international--on the firm operating in a foreign environment, the critical elements of the management process, and management and managerial effectiveness. These three components combine to determine both firm efficiency and system (or total) ef- ficiency.

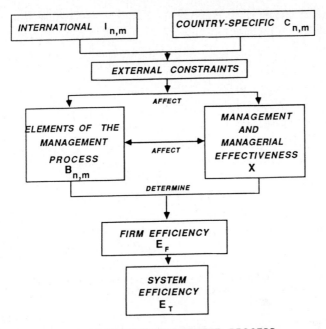

CONSTRAINT-MANAGEMENT  PROCESS
MANAGERIAL  EFFECTIVENESS/EFFICIENCY
RELATIONSHIPS

**Figure One**

Source: Comparative Management and Economic Progress
          R. Farmer and B. Richman (1965)

The critical elements of the management process include those items pertinent  to  the  firm–specific  managerial functions and critical policy
decisions in the firm.  These categories are presented in Table 1.

*M.D. Oliff, J.S. Arpan and F.L. Dubois*

## TABLE 1: CRITICAL ELEMENTS OF THE MANAGEMENT PROCESS

$B_1$    Planning and Innovation

$B_2$    Control

$B_3$    Organization

$B_4$    Staffing

$B_5$    Direction, Leadership, and Motivation

$B_6$    Marketing (Policies Pursued)

$B_7$    Production and Procurement

$B_8$    Research and Development

$B_9$    Finance

$B_{10}$ Public and External Relations

Source: Farmer & Richman (1965)

Within each of these categories, various subelements are identified. For example, the subelements of the production and procurement category are presented in the following table:

## TABLE 2: ELEMENT OF THE PRODUCTION AND PROCUREMENT PROCESS

$B_{7,1}$    The Make or Buy Decision

$B_{7,2}$    The Number, Types and Locations of the Major Suppliers to the Firm

$B_{7,3}$    The Timing of Procurement of the Major Supplies

$B_{7,4}$    Average inventory levels

$B_{7,5}$    Minimum, Maximum, and Average size of Production runs

$B_{7,6}$    The degree to which production operations are stabilized

$B_{7,7}$    Combination of factor inputs used in the major products produced

$B_{7,8}$    Basic Production Processes Used

$B_{7,9}$    Extent of Automation and Mechanization in Operations

Source: Farmer and Richman (1965)

With the Farmer-Richman classification scheme it is possible to examine the underlying causes of differences or modifications that must be made in the management processes of firms operating in different countries. As such, each of these elements can be examined in light of the country-specific variables impacting on firm operations. Farmer-Richman refer to these as the environmental variables or constraints within which the formulation of management policies and strategies take place. These are the factors or conditions that work to prevent the firm from operating in a certain way and are useful in explaining modifications to firm behavior that must be made in order to operate efficiently and effectively in a foreign environment.

The critical environmental constraints are disaggregated into four major categories: 1) Educational Constraints 2) Sociological Constraints 3) Political-Legal Constraints, and 4) Economic Constraints. A finer distinction is made within each of the environmental variables by further decomposition into subelements. Each of these categories and subelements are shown in the following table.

48             *M.D. Oliff, J.S. Arpan and F.L. Dubois*

## TABLE 3: CRITICAL ENVIRONMENTAL CONSTRAINTS

$C_1$:   Educational Variables       $C_2$:   Sociological Variables

$C_{1,1}$  Literacy Level            $C_{2,1}$  Attitude Toward Managers

$C_{1,2}$  Specialized Vocational Training & Education     $C_{2,2}$  View of Authority

$C_{1,3}$  Higher Education       $C_{2,3}$  Interorganizational Cooperation

$C_{1,4}$  Management Programs     $C_{2,4}$  Attitude towards Achievement & Work

$C_{1,5}$  Attitude Towards Education

$C_{1,6}$  Educational Match     $C_{2,5}$  Class Structure and Individual Mobility

$C_{2,6}$  Attitude Toward wealth and Material Gain

$C_{2,7}$  Attitude Toward Scientific Method

$C_{2,8}$  Attitude Toward Risk Taking

$C_{2,9}$  Attitude Toward Change

$C_3$:   Political-legal Variables   $C_4$   Economic Variables

$C_{3,1}$  Legal Rules of the Game     $C_{4,1}$  Economic Framework

$C_{3,2}$  Defense/Military Policy     $C_{4,2}$  Central Banking Systems and Monetary Policy

$C_{3,3}$  Foreign Policy     $C_{4,3}$  Fiscal Policy

$C_{3,4}$  Political Stability     $C_{4,4}$  Economic Stability

$C_{3,5}$  Political Organization     $C_{4,5}$  Organization of Capital Markets

$C_{3,6}$  Flexibility of Law     $C_{4,6}$  Factor Endowment

$C_{4,7}$  Market Size

$C_{4,8}$  Social Overhead Capital

$C_{4,9}$  Exchange Rate Stability

Source: Farmer and Richman (1965)

From this categorization it is possible to examine each of the critical elements of the management process with respect to each of the environmental variables salient to that element. Relationships can be written as equations with the element of the management process as the dependent variable and the relevant environmental constraints as the independent variables. For example, the time horizon of plans and planning (a subset of the Planning and Innovation process) may be written as a function of specialized vocational and technical training and general secondary education, higher education and special management development programs, all of which are a part of the educational constraint. Other variables in the environmental constraints impact on this issue but are omitted in the interest of brevity.

An important addition must be made to the environmental constraints in light of changes in the international financial order that have evolved since the original development of the Farmer-Richman model. As many international manufacturing decisions in the MNE may be contingent on exchange rate relationships and variability of exchange rates with respect to the home country of the MNE, this economic constraint is included in the set of environmental variables as variable $C_{4,9}$.

Given the critical elements of the management process and the environmental constraints hypothesized as relevant to each element, Farmer-Richman weave these components into the comparative management matrix. This matrix provides a general framework within which the workings of the firm can be analyzed on a country by country or region by region basis. The task of establishing interrelationships between the environmental constraints and the elements of the management process is performed in the original presentation of the model. However, interrelationships can be easily modified to fit each particular situation. If, for example, the educational level of the population is not a relevant variable impacting as hypothesized on one of the elements of the management process, it can easily be eliminated from consideration in the matrix. This classification scheme is by no means all inclusive but provides a useful starting point for a more complete analysis of the environmental variables and their influence.

International constraints are added to the model to reflect the additional complexities of operating in an international environment. These constraints are presented in Table 4. The international constraints refer to those variables relevant only to firms operating in a foreign environment which act to restrict or constrain behavior in a certain way.

## TABLE 4: INTERNATIONAL CONSTRAINTS

$I_1$: Sociological Constraints

$I_{1,1}$   National Ideology
$I_{1,2}$   View toward Foreigners
$I_{1,3}$   Nature and Extent of Nationalism

$I_2$: Political-Legal Constraints

$I_{2,1}$   Political Ideology
$I_{2,2}$   Relevant Legal Rules for Foreign Business
$I_{2,3}$   International Organization and Treaty Obligations
$I_{2,4}$   Power on Economic Group Blocking
$I_{2,5}$   Import-Export Restrictions
$I_{2,6}$   International Investment Restrictions
$I_{2,7}$   Profit Remission Restrictions
$I_{2,8}$   Exchange Control Restrictions

$I_3$: Economic Constraints

$I_{3,1}$   General Balance of Payments Position
$I_{3,2}$   International Trade Patterns
$I_{3,3}$   Membership and Obligations in International Financial Organizations

Source: Farmer & Richman (1965)

International constraints may be rules or laws regarding the behavior of foreign firms in a particular host country (e.g. minimum hiring quotas for host country nationals) or they may be rules or laws promulgated by the home country affecting the behavior of any firm - whether foreign or domestic - with international operations (e.g. U.S. tariff regulations 806.3/807.0 allowing the reentry to the U.S. under reduced tariffs goods that are sent offshore for intermediate processing [6]). International constraints also encompass sociological constraints and economic constraints that affect MNE behavior. Figure 2 presents the linkages between the international constraints and the environmental variables.

| | Educational 1 2 3 4 5 6 | Sociological 1 2 3 4 5 6 7 8 9 | Political-Legal 1 2 3 4 5 6 | Economic 1 2 3 4 5 6 7 8 9 |
|---|---|---|---|---|
| *Sociological Constraints:* | | | | |
| National Ideology | x x x   x | x x   x x x x x x | x   x x | x |
| View towards Foreigners | x x x   x x | x x   x x x x x x | x   x x | x |
| Amount of Nationalism | x   x | x x   x x x x x x | x   x x | x |
| *Legal-Political Constraints:* | | | | |
| Political Ideology | x   x   x | x   x x x x x x | x   x x x x | x |
| Rules for Foreign Firms | | x x x x x x x | x x x x x x x | x |
| International Obligations | | x   x | x x   x x | x |
| Economic Blocs | | x x | x x x   x | x |
| Import/Export Restrictions | | | x x x   x | x x x x x x x |
| Investment Restrictions | | x   x | x x x | x x x x x |
| Profit Remission Restr. | | x   x | x x x | x x x x x |
| Exchange Controls | | | x x x | x x x x x x |
| *Economic Constraints:* | | | | |
| Balance of Payments | | | x x x x x x | x x x x x x x x x |
| Intl. Trade Patterns | | | x x x | x x x x x x x x x |
| Intl. Financial Orgs. | | | x x x | x |

**Country-Specific and International Constraint Interrelationships**
**Figure Two**

Source: Farmer and Richman (1965).

While the Farmer-Richman matrix has served the international business community well in the twenty years since its development, applicability in the manufacturing community can be increased with the addition of a more detailed categorization of variables relevant to the international manufacturing strategies of the MNE. This extension is made to reflect the greater emphasis now placed on international manufacturing as a solution to the problems of global competition and to provide a conceptual framework for the analysis and management of international factory networks and logistics in the global environment.

## 4. REFINEMENTS TO THE MATRIX

In the following section a model of the factors influencing global manufacturing configuration and coordination strategies is proposed. This model is a refinement of the Comparative Management Matrix discussed in section 4.

In view of the greater emphasis now placed on the international manufacturing and rationalization objectives of the MNE, expanded production and procurement and research and development categories are proposed. Based on work by Flaherty (1986) and Hayes and Wheelwright (1984), the proposed categorization offers a more detailed presentation of the issues pertinent to the manufacturing strategies of the firm. In an international setting, the evaluation of each of these elements of strategy with respect to both country-specific environmental constraints and international constraints is critical to the success of the global manufacturing strategies of the MNE. These elements of the manufacturing decision process are presented in table 5.

TABLE 5:  CRITICAL ELEMENTS OF THE GLOBAL MANUFACTURING
STRATEGY DECISION PROCESS


Manufacturing Configuration Decisions:

+ strategic (long-term) Forecasts

+ logistics (including, the number, size, and location of plants)

+ process technology and equipment choice

+ assignment of materials, components, and products to be made by specific manufacturing facilities

+ vertical span of the manufacturing process


Manufacturing Coordination Decisions:

+ Policies for Manufacturing Support Activities

   - intermediate term forecasting
   - procurement
   - distribution and logistics
   - aggregate production planning
   - production planning and control
   - quality management
   - employee management and development
   - manufacturing engineering

+ Policies for Technology Support Activities

   - product design and improvement
   - process design and improvement
   - new product and process introduction

Manufacturing decisions are disaggregated into two basic categories: configuration decisions and coordination decisions. As discussed in Section 1, configuration decisions involve the large lump-sum, not easily reversible decisions of how international manufacturing activities should be configured to meet MNE objectives for profitability and performance. Coordination decisions refer to the decisions made on an on-going basis with respect to linkages between the different international manufacturing activities of the MNE such as planning and scheduling and product and process improvement.

In the proposed categorization, configuration activities are decomposed into decisions regarding strategic forecasts, logistical imperatives, process technology and equipment choice, facility assignment decisions, and vertical span of the manufacturing process. Coordination decisions are decomposed into two elements, policies for manufacturing support activities and policies for technology support activities. These two areas encompass and extend the original production and procurement and research and development categories in the original Farmer-Richman matrix.

Manufacturing support activities include the managerial functions associated with the day to day operation of the production process. These involve intermediate term sales forecasting, translation of forecasts into production plans and schedules, inventory management, quality management, directing purchasing activities, employee development and solving ongoing manufacturing engineering problems. Technology support activities encompass staff activities involved with the continual improvement of products and production processes. Responsibility for new product and process introductions are included in this area.

Figure 3 presents a matrix of these manufacturing strategy decisions and critical environmental constraints. A relationship between each of the strategy decisions and relevant environmental constraints is hypothesized. For example, process technology decisions are hypothesized as being a function of all six of the educational variable constraints. The assertion here is that the educational variables of the country have a very important influence on the type of process technology selected for use. Other elements in each of the environmental constraint categories are suggested as relevant to the selection of production process and are also presented.

| | Educational | | | | | | Sociological | | | | | | | | | Political-Legal | | | | | | Economic | | | | | | | | |
|---|---|---|---|---|---|---|---|---|---|---|---|---|---|---|---|---|---|---|---|---|---|---|---|---|---|---|---|---|---|---|
| | 1 | 2 | 3 | 4 | 5 | 6 | 1 | 2 | 3 | 4 | 5 | 6 | 7 | 8 | 9 | 1 | 2 | 3 | 4 | 5 | 6 | 1 | 2 | 3 | 4 | 5 | 6 | 7 | 8 | 9 |
| **Configuration Decisions:** | | | | | | | | | | | | | | | | | | | | | | | | | | | | | | |
| Strategic Forecasts | | | x | x | | | | | | | | | x | x | | x | x | x | | x | | x | x | x | x | | x | x | | x |
| Logistical Imperatives | x | x | | | x | x | | | x | | x | | | | | x | | x | | | | | | | x | x | x | | | |
| Process Technology | x | x | x | x | x | x | | | | | | x | x | x | | | | x | x | | | | | x | | x | x | | | |
| Facility Assignments | x | x | x | | x | | | | x | | | | | | | | | x | x | | | | | | | x | x | | | |
| Vertical Span of Process | x | x | x | | x | | x | x | | | | | | | | x | x | x | x | | | | | | x | x | x | x | | x |
| **Coordination Decisions:** | | | | | | | | | | | | | | | | | | | | | | | | | | | | | | |
| **Mfg. Support Functions:** | | | | | | | | | | | | | | | | | | | | | | | | | | | | | | |
| Mid-Term Forecasts | | | | | | | | | | | | x | x | | | x | x | | | | | | | | x | | x | | | |
| Purchasing & Procurement | | | | | | | | | x | | | x | x | | | x | x | x | | | x | | | | x | x | x | x | | x |
| Distribution and Logistics | | | | x | | | | | x | | x | | | | | x | | x | | | | | | | x | | x | | | |
| Aggregate Prod. Planning | | | | x | | | | | x | x | | | | | | | | | | x | | | | | x | | x | | x | |
| Prod. Planning & Control | | | | x | | | | | | x | x | | | | | | | | | x | | | | | x | | x | | | |
| Quality Mgt. & Improvement | | | x | x | | | | | | | | | | | | | | | | | | | | | | | | | | |
| Employee Development | | | x | x | x | x | x | x | | x | | x | x | | x | x | | x | x | | | | | | | | | | | |
| Mfg. Engineering | x | x | | | | | | | x | | x | | x | x | | x | | | | | | | | | | | | | | |
| **Tech. Support Functions:** | | | | | | | | | | | | | | | | | | | | | | | | | | | | | | |
| Product Improvement | | x | | | x | | | | x | | x | x | x | | | | | x | x | | | x | | | | | | | | |
| Process Improvement | | x | | | x | | | | x | | x | x | x | | | | | x | x | | | x | x | | | | | | | |
| New Product Intro | | x | | | x | | | | x | | x | x | x | | x | | | x | x | | | x | | x | | | | | | |
| New Process Intro | | x | | | x | | | | x | | x | x | x | | x | x | x | x | x | x | | x | x | | | | | | | |

**Environmental Constraints and Critical Elements of Manufacturing Strategy**
**Figure Three**

Application of the model within the framework developed in the previous section is now examined. The objective in any configuration/coordination decision is to achieve the best possible "fit" between host country endowments and constraints and firm-specific managerial assets when confronted with an array of possible options. The proposed framework offers a means by which management of the MNE can systematically evaluate the issues relevant to each choice in order that undesirable options can be quickly eliminated and attention focused on the most attractive alternatives.

Using the expanded comparative management matrix the MNE can evaluate each issue relevant to an investment project for a particular foreign environment. Management can rank each of the environmental variables impacting on the element of the management process with respect to the closeness of "fit" of each of the variables to the needs and characteristics of the firm. A simple 5 or 10 point rating scale will suffice for this purpose.

Given a portfolio of investment projects and possible investment locations, the firm must first determine which of the environmental variables are critical to the project. Experts knowledgeable about the conditions prevailing in each of the location possibilities would meet with project managers to rank the criticality of each of the relevant variables. Farmer-Richman suggest the use of the Delphi technique in order to assure objectivity in the ranking process.

Once a numerical ranking is assigned to each of the variables and consensus achieved among participants, the rankings for each location are totaled and comparisons between countries are made. The major benefit of the model is the ability of the firm to focus in on key decision areas that may need correction or modification. The firm can immediately eliminate projects based on the analysis or determine that alterations of internal operating techniques are necessary in order to reflect external constraints. Conversely, some of the external constraints may be subject to modification by the host country depending on the political clout of the firm and the importance of the project to the development objectives of the host country. This is particularly true with respect to the international constraints. In this event, the firm must assess the viability of this option and its long-term consequences on operations in that country.

## 5.  CASE STUDIES IN THREE INDUSTRIES

### 5.1 Introduction

In an attempt to gain a better understanding of the most critical environmental constraints affecting the global manufacturing operations of multinational enterprises, interviews were conducted with representatives of companies operating in three distinct industries, each of which is heavily impacted by global competition. Participating organization included Liz Claiborne Inc., representing the Apparel and Fashion industry, General Motors Corporation, of the Automotive and Transportation industry, and NCR Corporation, of the Computer and Office Equipment industry.

The case study subjects are characterized by varying levels of product complexity that have to a great extent shaped their global manufacturing strategies. These product-driven strategies provide an interesting basis from which to examine and compare the constraints relevant to the design and management of international manufacturing networks. The following sections present brief company profiles and a discussion of the impacts that environmental constraints have had on each firm's international manufacturing strategies.

## 5.2 Profiles of Case Study Participants

Operating in the highly competitive Apparel and Fashion industry, Liz Claiborne Inc. has established an enviable reputation offering stylish, high quality, and moderately priced apparel to the working woman. In existence only 11 years, the firm in 1986 had sales of $813 million, 42% above 1985 levels. A major component of Claiborne's competitive strategy permitting such rapid growth has been an emphasis on the development of offshore supply sources for both raw textile materials and manufactured garments. To this end, the firm relies almost exclusively on globally dispersed contract manufacturers to meet requirements.

In a similar fashion, the NCR Corporation has evolved into one of the least vertically integrated of all of the major firms competing in the computer and office equipment industry. NCR develops, manufactures, installs, and services business information processing systems for global markets. Sales in 1986 were $4.9 billion putting NCR in fifth place in revenue generation behind IBM, Digital Equipment, Unisys, and Hewlett-Packard in the data processing industry. This performance is impressive given the fact that in the early 1970s, NCR's competitive strategy was focused toward the manufacture and sale of (soon to be obsolete) mechanical cash registers. Faced with sizable losses during this period, the company shifted focus in 1972 to the expanding data processing industry and its basis in microelectronics technology. NCR now competes globally in product markets based on this technology. Approximately 50% of 1986 revenues were derived from overseas operations.

With the number 1 spot in the 1986 Fortune 500 and over $100 billion in sales revenue, General Motors Corporation is by far the largest of the interview participants. GM has a long and rich history of international involvement, devoting considerable effort to the design and coordination of overseas manufacturing operations to exploit the comparative advantages of the countries in which it has operations. In the execution of international manufacturing strategy, GM relies to a large extent on wholly-owned subsidiaries and joint venture partnerships. Approximately 12% of GM's manufacturing capacity is located outside of North America closely paralleling the distribution of sales revenue from overseas operations. Global capacity includes both dispersal of stages of the production process and construction of local-for-local assembly and manufacturing facilities. GM plants and accompanying support systems have significant impact on the host country and local economy in terms of employment and multiplier effects, hence, the firm is confronted with a multitude of environmental variables influencing its configuration and coordination decisions.

## 5.3 Constraints Impacting Company Operations

Company interviews were conducted with three major questions in mind. First, for each company, which are the most critical environmental constraints? Second, what have been the effects of their impact upon firm operations? And finally, what adjustments has the organization made to operations to reflect the influence of these constraints? Based on these company interviews, varying degrees of criticality of the environmental constraints was evident. Some constraints arose as being highly critical to the successful design and management of firm operations while others, although important, were not examined with any degree of rigor by the firms.

In particular, as would be expected with any firm involved globally, political-legal constraints on the part of both the home and host country had a significant impact on the overseas activities of each of the companies. Educational constraints in the host country tended to be most significant for NCR while sociological constraints were extremely important to Liz Claiborne. Country-specific economic constraints impacted most heavily on GM's global operations.

The political-legal constraints impacting on firm operations were, for the most part, the result of either host nation regulations concerning the nature and impact of foreign direct investment (e.g. localization requirements, import-export controls, foreign exchange restrictions, etc) or home country regulations concerning imports (e.g. tariffs and quotas). These constraints were the ones most commonly mentioned by the executives who participated in the study.

In the sections that follow, these critical environmental constraints and their impact in shaping each company's operations strategy are addressed in more detail. A concluding section summarizes these findings and provides suggestions for future research.

## 5.4 Liz Claiborne Inc.: Global Manufacturing Strategies

Liz Claiborne Inc. is heavily involved in the use of offshore suppliers and manufacturers to provide its raw materials and product needs. Manufacturing is performed worldwide by independent manufacturers working under contract, primarily in the Far East, but also in Latin America, the Caribbean, Europe, and Israel. In contrast to many of its competitors, Claiborne sources approximately 90% of its garment needs from contract manufacturers. For piece goods, the raw material inputs that go into the construction of the garment, the percentage is approximately the same. Relationships with over 450 different garment manufacturers and 70 - 75 different textile suppliers are maintained. Contractors take textiles that have been selected and purchased by Claiborne and work closely with company personnel to produce the required products. This gives Claiborne the flexibility and freedom to focus company efforts on the market research and product development required to ensure the success of a collection. Thus, the establishment and maintenance of long-term relationships with fabric suppliers and manufacturers is critical to the execution of company strategy. As stated by company co-chairman Arthur Ortenberg:

"... the manufacturing function is second in importance only to the design function with respect to competitive strategy. The company has a strong conviction that the future of the industry belongs to the organization with the strongest supply base, both from the standpoint of production facilities and from the standpoint of procurement of raw materials."

In the design of procurement and manufacturing strategies, Claiborne makes every effort to reduce logistics related costs by keeping production of the garment in the same country or region where the fabric is sourced. However, this is often not possible due to the existence of political-legal constraints on the part of both the U.S. and the country of origin.

Presently, the U.S. regulates the import of certain types of fabric and textiles under a quota system. All apparel imports are subject to regulation under the Multifiber Arrangement, the international accord governing textile and apparel trade, in which the U.S. has negotiated agreements with 34 different countries setting quotas on 600 individual items. It is often the case that an apparel importer may not be able to get products imported into the U.S. due to the quota for an item from a particular country being filled. In this event, a company has two options: 1) attempt to get the product reclassified into a different attempt to get the product reclassified into a different import category by changing the fabric content of the item or 2) move the manufacturing of the item to a location with unfilled quota. For Claiborne, with its strong quality emphasis, fabric substitution is usually an unacceptable option. The flexibility of quickly changing the location of manufacture allowed under contract manufacturing - a facility assignment decision - is critical to dealing with a variable, C (foreign policy), and the international constraint, $I_{2,5}$ (import-export restrictions), are relevant to the decision.

There are several key elements considered in the selection of the suppliers of piece goods and the selection of the manufacturers who convert piece goods sourced by Claiborne into the final product. As Claiborne competes on the basis of superior product quality vis-a-vis its competitors, selection of suppliers able to provide the requisite quality on a continuous basis is paramount. For this reason, sociological constraints are relevant to the determination of supply source, in particular, $C_{2,1}$ (attitude toward industrial managers and management), $C_{2,3}$ (inter-organizational cooperation), and $C_{2,4}$ (attitude toward achievement and work). These variables are examined carefully during the supplier selection process.

Second in importance to the supply source decision is delivery reliability. In addition to the four customary seasons, Claiborne has created two additional fashion offerings (pre-spring and pre-fall), thus, the need for timely delivery of the required products to retailers is accentuated. Inventory control is complicated by long lead times (as much as one year from product design to retailers' racks), a short selling season, and multiple suppliers for the many items that comprise that season's product offerings. In discussions with company executives, it was emphasized repeatedly that Claiborne sells a "collection" of related and complementary fashion items and not just individual garments. As a collection may be composed of garments provided by several different manufacturers, delivery reliability on the part of globally dispersed suppliers is mandatory.

Of tertiary importance to the supplier selection decision is price. With a highly differentiated product image and a sales force attuned to retailer's needs, Claiborne is to some degree immune from much of the price competition affecting the operations of other firms competing in this industry. Thus, Claiborne will not chase the low cost producer for a particular fabric or garment item to the exclusion of quality or delivery reliability but seeks rather to develop a long-term supplier/manufacturer relationship that is mutually beneficial to all concerned parties.

In a more qualitative sense, the firm places a high priority on the impact of their business on the development goals of the host country. In some instances manufacturing strategies have been modified to accommodate host country desires for a particular type of employment. In the Philippines, many firms reduced operations during the instability that characterized the transition from the Marcos to the Aquino government. Claiborne, however worked with the Aquino government to adapt operations to provide jobs for people in the countryside that had previously been considered unemployable. It was felt that a long-term relationship with the Philippines government could be enhanced with this strategy. Plentiful factor endowments ($C_{4,6}$) and favorable attitudes toward dealings with foreign firms ($I_{1,2}$) were enough to offset weakness in the educational variables. This philosophy and concern for the host country has made an important contribution to the continued success of the firm.

## 5.5 NCR Corporation: Global Manufacturing Strategies

With manufacturing facilities in Canada, Japan, Scotland, Germany Mexico, and Brazil, NCR is not new to international involvement. International operations began in 1900 and have expanded to the point that 51% of 1986 sales were derived from overseas operations. Non-U.S. manufacturing accounted for the production of just over 25% of manufactured items in 1986.

As discussed earlier, the nature of the product and manufacturing strategy shifted away from mechanical products to the manfuacture of electronic data and information processing devices in the early 1970s. With this shift also came a shift away from the high labor content of mechanical devices to the lower labor content but higher material content of electronic equipment. NCR moved from manufacturing in the pure sense of materials conversion to operations characterized by large levels of assembly and testing of purchased components. At present, labor comprises only 4% of the value-added portion of the product while materials comprise 70% and factory overhead the valance. This shift in the economics of product manufacture has forced a reorientation of locations strategy away from the search for low cost labor to complement the high labor content of earlier products to a search for locations having the technical and engineering infrastructure able to support the manufacture of technology-intensive products. The nature of these types of products dictates the need for a strong relationship between the engineering and manufacturing functions.

In the examination of NCR's global manufacturing strategy, it is apparent that the nature of the data processing industry implies a radically different configuration strategy than that of a firm such as Liz Claiborne Inc., or General Motors. Configuration decisions reflect two basic criteria: 1) whether the local market can support a manufacturing presence and 2) whether the location allows NCR to attract and keep qualified technical and engineering personnel. In the first case, the Farmer-Richman variables $C_{4,7}$ (market size) and $C_{4,4}$ (economic stability) are critical to the location decision. In the second case, quality of life and availability of educational opportunities are two strong location incentives, particularly for U.S. operations. Consequently, the Farmer-Richman educational variables, $C_{1,2}$ (specialized vocational and technical training), $C_{1,4}$ (management development programs), and $C_{1,5}$ (attitude toward education) play an important role in shaping location strategy.

In the case of operations in the developing economies of Brazil and Mexico, international political-legal and economic constraints on the part of these countries require some firms to establish a manufacturing presence simply in order to serve these markets. NCR Brazil is under a severe constraint due to government efforts to conserve foreign exchange. Management of the Brazilian operation must attempt to balance exports with imports to satisfy government restrictions. As a result, NCR finds that it can only order materials on a quarterly basis. This produces a corresponding increase in the amount of pipeline inventory, a compromise of customer service levels, and complications in production planning and control decisions. Thus, the Farmer-Richman international variables, $I_{2,2}$ (relevant legal rules for foreign businesses), $I_{2,5}$ (import-export restrictions), $I_{3,1}$ (general balance of payments position), and $I_{3,2}$ (international trade patterns) force significant modifications to NCR's production planning and control decisions. Also relevant are the political-legal constraints $C_{3,1}$ (relevant legal rules of the game), and $C_{3,6}$ (flexibility of law and legal changes) specific to all firms having operations in Brazil.

Purchasing policies for domestic operations are also affected by import-export restrictions on the part of the home country. U.S. foreign policy ($C_{3,3}$) and defense and military policies ($C_{3,2}$) may impact NCR's future procurement strategies. Presently the U.S. government is considering the imposition of sanctions against the Toshiba Corporation of Japan for their role in violating an international agreement preventing the sale of high technology equipment to the Soviet Union. As Toshiba is NCR's only qualified supplier for one-megabyte RAM (Random Access Memory) microchips, this could have a serious impact on NCR's ability to build products that use this component.

In sum, NCR's manufacturing strategy variables have been shaped by global forces over which the firm has little control. Configuration decisions are made taking into account the relevant economic and educational assets of the prospective host country. Coordination decisions are the direct result of the various international political-legal constraints impacting upon company operations. Given the present state of international trade patterns NCR's procurement policies reflect the realities of the global marketplace and the potential for import-export restrictions on the part of countries in which NCR has substantial sales revenues. In the future it is expected, to the extent it is possible, that NCR will source more of its component needs locally.

## 5.6  General Motors Corporation: Global Manufacturing Strategies

Due to the inherent scope and potential impact on an economy that an automotive manufacturing or assembly operation has, a firm such as General Motors is faced with a number of conflicting objectives emanating from the people and governments affected by its decisions. This requires a skilful response on the part of management in order to vitiate any negative reactions which may occur as a result of strategic decisions.

The first major constraint arises with respect to GM's dealings with labor and labor representatives; what Farmer-Richman would classify as the Sociological variable, $C_{2,3}$(inter-organizational cooperation). The effect that a reconfiguration decision has on domestic employment is obviously a non-trivial issue. This is true not only in U.S. plants but in the heavily unionized plants of Western Europe and Australia. Decisions made with the objective of lowering costs and improving efficiency may first have to be approved through a union hierarchy resulting in long delays and frustration on the part of company executives. In some instances, organized labor has blocked or caused considerable modification to plans to transfer productive capacity to more economic locations.

Local content regulations also impact capacity configuration decisions. These fall into the Farmer-Richman category, $C_{3,1}$(relevant legal rules of the game). This is an especially acute problem in LDC operations as these countries attempt to balance job creation objectives with a mandate to earn foreign exchange through greater exports. While the construction of a large manufacturing facility in an LDC creates both employment opportunities for the indigenous population and multiplier effects in satellite industries, it necessitates a concomitant increase in the amount of imports of components and raw materials. This, in turn, puts pressure on the host country's balance of payments position, its ability to earn foreign exchange and can adversely affect exchange rate relationships. This illustrates the linkages that exist between the environmental variables in the Farmer-Richman matrix.

In responding to a scenario such as that illustrated above, the host country may enact legislation designed to ensure that vehicles produced in that country have a certain minimum percentage local content. However, localization requirements in automotive manufacturing beyond the 30-35% range necessitate substantial capital investment in the manufacture of major components and can change the economics of location decision dramatically. For many automotive components there is a minimum efficient plant size or economic module that must be achieved for construction to be feasible. For output levels below this threshold, economic considerations and scale requirements may preclude capacity addition. Thus, local content requirements - both present and perceived future requirements - must be factored into the location decision.

Other important considerations influencing firm behavior are host country attitudes and regulations concerning the import of manufacturing technology. In figure 3 a strong relationship between the selection of process technology and the educational constraints in the host country was hypothesized. For a country such as India, logic would dictate a low level of sophistication with regard to manufacturing technology in an effort to take advantage of immobile factor endowments of the host country (e.g. plentiful and inexpensive labor). Again, however, there have been conflicts between the host country and General Motors.

In India, GM has had to reconcile the government's desire for the latest in manufacturing technology producing an automobile competitive in international markets with company objectives of producing a basic transport vehicle to be sold only in India and surrounding regions. GM feels that at this stage of India's economic development a less ambitious project than that which the government wishes is the most appropriate strategy. Likewise, in Egypt, negotiations to build an assembly and parts sourcing facility for the Middle East region have stalled because of intractable government positions with regard to export projections and local sourcing. Both of these cases are examples of international investment restrictions ($I_{2,6}$) and their effects on GM operations.

Educational contraints in the host country are considered but only tangentially. They are not a top priority in the evaluation of manufacturing sites but are considered controllable by the firm in all but the most extreme cases. GM contends that their training program is sufficient to negate any deficits in educational levels of the workers. On the domestic side, U.S. laws promoting the location of firms in Mexico adjacent to the U.S. border (the Border Industrialisation Program) has allowed GM to move sourcing of some of its high labor content components to this low wage environment. For this same reason engines destined for assembly into some U.S. made vehicles are sourced from GM's Brazilian operation. Domestic demand in Brazil is too low to support the minimum efficient plant size required for engine manufacture. However, given import prohibitions, lower wage rates, and adequate supporting infrastructure ($C_{4,8}$) in Brazil, local manufacture with export to the U.S. and other markets is feasible.

General Motors is confronted with the problem of balancing many different and sometimes mutually exclusive objectives. Process technology decisions are affected by host country investment restrictions, production planning by import-export constraints and local content requirements, and plant size by the supporting infrastructure of the host country and potential export markets. The evaluation of these issues and others is therefore crucial to the satisfaction of configuration and coordination objectives.

## 5.7 Conclusions and implications arising from the case studies

The global manufacturing strategies of the firms participating in the case studies were influenced to varying degrees by the environmental variables postulated by Farmer and Richman. For all of the firms, sociological and economic constraints had the greatest impact on configuration strategies (the location of productive resources) while political-legal constraints shaped tactical-level operational policies such as production planning and control, purchasing and procurement, and logistics.

The type of product manufactured and the complexity of the production process also influenced the degree of impact of the variables. For a high labor content product such as apparel, educational constraints were not considered as critical as the sociological and cultural constraints of the host country. For Liz Claiborne Inc., quality was as much a function of workers' attitudes as any other variable. It was NCR's experience that a complex product with low labor content required strongest consideration of the educational variables in the prospective host country. The complexity of the product required a high degree of automation in the production process and frequent engineering changes with a concurrent need for experienced technical personnel for manufacturing engineering and product design purposes. For General Motors, economies of scale in auto manufacture required the construction of relatively large facilities having a high impact on the economy of the host country. Here, the issues centered around the political-legal constraints and the contribution that the facility would have on the development objectives of the host country or region (particularly in the case of LDCs).

Surprisingly, none of the executives interviewed placed a high level of emphasis on exchange rate relationships in the determination of facility location or in purchasing strategies. For Liz Claiborne Inc., the maintainance of long-term relationships with suppliers was critical. Thus, exchange rate relationships were not regarded highly in sourcing strategy. The other two firms felt that the problems involved in rebalancing supply sources when exchange rates changed were not worth the effort. The impression was that over the long-term, inherent exchange rate instability would negate any advantages to be had from shifting purchasing priorities as exchange rates fluctuated.

These case studies provide a broad overview of the issues salient to the design and management of international factory networks. The global manufacturing strategies of three firms operating in diverse industries illustrates the relationship between the industry and the relative impact of the environmental variables. Scope of operations, product technology, and production process requirements emerge as the three most critical company-specific variables shaping global operations.

## 6. CONCLUSIONS AND FUTURE DIRECTIONS

This paper has presented a modification to the Farmer-Richman comparative management matrix to reflect the increased importance of manufacturing configuration and coordination activities to the operations of the multinational enterprise and to assist MNE management in developing more efficient international manufacturing and logistics networks. The enhanced matrix offers a conceptual framework permitting a more careful and thorough evaluation of the global manufacturing alternatives open to the MNE.

Decision making performance is improved by allowing the rapid elimination of undesirable projects based on a lack of congruence between MNE requirements and host country endowments or policies. Viable projects can be emphasized or deemphasized based on the amount of modifications that need to be made to operations to facilitate the success of the investment. Also, a host country seeking to attract foreign direct investment can use the matrix as a means of taking stock of the assets the country has to offer to foreign firms. Where deficiencies are noted, progressive governments can implement programs and policy changes for their improvement. Finally, the matrix offers the academician a useful framework for the analysis of adaptations to management processes required in the development and management of international factory networks.

With respect to future research, more in-depth empirical and case study research at the plant level is needed to determine the nature and criticality of the variables impacting the manufacturing operations of a globally dispersed MNE. As the case studies were conducted by interviewing executives at the corporate level, the focus of the discussions centered around the long-term strategic configuration decisions with which, given their positions in the management hierarchy, these executives were most familiar. Detailed study of the manner in which the multiplant divisions of an MNE adapt operations at each manufacturing facility to host country requirements is required to permit a better understanding of the relationships between the environmental variables and manufacturing coordination decisions. Also, as labor content becomes a less important portion of the value-added of the product, the linkages between environmental variable impact and technology of the product and production process needs to be explored.

Further research may also lead to an expansion of the issues relevant to the manufacturing and technology support activity categories in the manufacturing strategy decision process (see table 5). Likewise, given the detailed disaggregation of the environmental constraints in the original presentation of the Farmer-Richman matrix, compression of these variables into fewer categories should be considered. A result of this research was the realization that not all of the variables in the matrix are critical to the manufacturing decision process. While these variables may be important to other functional areas of management, many of them are not critical to the management of the production function of the MNE.

ACKNOWLEDGEMENTS

The authors would like to thank Arthur Ortenburg, Larry McDonald, and John Conseline of Liz Claiborne Inc., Greg Deyonkers of General Motors Corporation, and Neil Jorgensen of NCR Corporation for their time and assistance in the completion of the case study portion of this research.

FOOTNOTES

[1] See Levitt (1983) for a discussion of the competitive forces at work to create new challenges for domestic competitors.

[2] Hout, Porter, and Rudden (1982) present details of the experiences of three firms that have succeeded in meeting the challenges of global competition.

[3] The original presentation of the framework appeared in Californioa Management Review in 1964. The framework was further extended and developed in book form in 1965.

[4] See Skinner (1969), Banks and Whellwright (1979), and Hayes and Abernathy (1977) for an overview of the salient issues.

[5] See Farmer and Richman (1965).

[6] Grunwald and Flann (1985) provide a detailed analysis of the use of this regulation in the rationalization objectives of the MNE and state that various versions of this regulation exist in other developed countries.

REFERENCES

Banks, R. and Wheelwright, S., "Operations versus Strategy: Trading Tomorrow for Today," Harvard Business Review, May–June 1979, pp. 112–120.

Bitran, G., Marieni, D., Matsuo, H., and Noonan, J., "Multiplant MRP", Journal of Operations Management, Vol. 5, No. 2, February 1985, pp. 183–203.

Calvet, A., "A Synthesis of Foreign Direct Investment Theories and Theories of the Multinational Firm," Journal of International Business Studies, Vol. 12, No. 1, Spring/Summer 1981, pp. 43–59.

Doz Y.L., "Managing Manufacturing Rationalizatin Within Multinational Companies," Columbia Journal of World Business, Fall 1978, pp. 82–93.

Farmer, R. and Richman, B., "A Model for Research in Comparative Management," California Management Review, (Winter 1964) pp. 55–68.

Farmer, R. and Richman, B., Comparative Management and Economic Progress, (New York: Irwin) 1965.

Flaherty, M.T., "Coordinating International Manufacturing and Technology" in Michael Porter ed., Competition in Global Industries: A Conceptual Framework (Boston, MA: Harvard Business School Press, 1987)

Gopal, C., "Guidelines for Implementing Global Manufacturing Systems," CIM Review, Fall 1986, pp. 25-32.

Grunwald, J. and Flann, K., The Global Factory: Foreign Assembly in International Trade, (Washington: The Brookings Institution) 1985.

Haas, E., "Breakthough Manufacturing," Harvard Business Review, March-April 1987, pp. 75-81.

Hayes, R. and Abernathy, W., "Managing Our Way to Economic Decline," Harvard Business Review, July-August 1977, pp. 67-77.

_____, and Wheelwright, S., Restoring Our Competitive Edge, (New York: John Wiley and Sons) 1984.

Hout, T., Porter, M. and Rudden, E., "How Global Companies Win Out," Harvard Business Review, September-October 1982, pp. 98-108.

Kogut, B., "Designing Global Strategies: Comparative and Competitive Value-Added Chains," Sloan Management Review, Summer 1985a, pp. 15-28.

_____, "Designing Global Strategies: Profiting from Operational Flexibility," Sloan Management Review, Fall 1985b, pp. 27-38.

Knickerbocker, F., Oligopolistic Reaction and Multinational Enterprise, (Cambridge MA: Harvard Business School Division of Research) 1974.

Levitt, T., "The Globalization of Markets," Harvard Business Review, May-June 1983, pp. 92-102.

Porter, M.E., Competition in Global Industries, (Boston MA: Harvard Business School Press) 1986.

Porter, M.E., "Changing Patterns of International Competition," California Management Review, Vol. 28, No. 2, Winter 1986, pp. 9-40.

Schmenner, R.W., "Every Factory has a Life Cycle," Harvard Business Review, March-April 1983, pp. 121-129.

Skinner, W., "Manufacturing-Missing Link in Corporate Strategy," Harvard Business Review, May-June 1969.

Starr, M., "Global Production and Operations Strategy," Columbia Journal of World Business, Winter 1984, pp. 17-22.

Wheelwright, S.C., and Hayes, R.H, "Competing Through Manufacturing," Harvard Business Review, January-February 1985, pp. 99-109.

MANAGING INTERNATIONAL MANUFACTURING
K. Ferdows (Editor)
© Elsevier Science Publishers B.V. (North-Holland), 1989

INTERNATIONAL MANUFACTURING AND DISTRIBUTION NETWORKS:

A NORMATIVE MODEL FRAMEWORK


Morris A. COHEN and Marshall FISHER

The Wharton School



Ramchandran JAIKUMAR

Harvard University


## 1. INTRODUCTION


The role of manufacturing as a key component in a firm's competitive strategy has only recently been recognized in certain segments of American industry. In other areas of the world (such as Japan, Korea and Europe), the operations function has long been viewed as critical for success in the market place. As global competition intensifies, it is now abundantly clear that the planning and control of activities associated with the design, manufacture and distribution of products must be part of a firm's competitive strategy. Moreover these activities must be managed on an international basis.

Recently, considerable progress has been made in the development of models and procedures for the analysis of manufacturing strategies (see Cohen and Lee [1] and Fine and Hax [7]). These methodologies allow management to consider decisions concerning production capacity, product and process technology, and policies for sourcing and distribution in terms of operations performance tradeoffs. Such performance is usually measured in terms of costs, quality, service and flexibility for each market segment being served.

Companies that produce and source globally face a variety of issues that have not been considered in the single country models noted above. The following list, while not exhaustive, serves to illustrate the range of factors which must be addressed in the formulation of an international manufacturing strategy.

    o    Manufacturers today need economies of scale to reduce raw material and production costs. The potential for economies of scale in manufacturing and sourcing can be maximized only if multinational plants and vendors are managed as a global system.

    o    Duties and tariffs are based on material flows and hence their impact must be considered as firms determine material input, intermediate product and finished product shipments across national boundaries.

    o    Currency exchange rates fluctuate randomly and affect profits in each country of operation.

    o    There are significant differences in corporate tax rates in each country.

    o    Global sourcing must be managed to account for tradeoffs between longer lead times, lower costs and access to new technologies.

o   Market penetration strategies, local content rules, counter trade and quotas all act to constrain the flow of product throughout the international chain of supply.

o   Product designs may vary by national market (especially for consumer goods).

o   Centralized control of operations is difficult in multi-national environments and hence appropriate incentives and transfer price mechanisms must be devised.

o   Cultural, language and skill differences are significant and must be accounted for in human resource management.

It is clear that there are significant gaps in our understanding of how firms should manage a manufacturing and distribution network in a manner that accounts for the issues noted above. The goal of this paper is to provide a preliminary framework for understanding many of these issues through the formulation of a normative model of certain key global manufacturing and distribution decisions. After a brief review of the relevant literature in Section 2, our model is developed in Section 3. The model is a mixed integer program concerned with the operation of a network of raw material vendors, plants and markets. We assume that the firm has specified its product mix, production technology, plant location and capacity and lower and upper limits on the amount to be supplied of each product to each market. The decisions considered in the model are the choice of which vendors to use, the amount of each product to be produced at each plant, the amount of each product to be supplied to each market and the optimal level of flows of raw materials from vendors to plants and finished goods from plants to markets. The model is a multi-period model that can consider a planning horizon of one or more years. As is common in long-range planning models, we assume that all inventories clear between periods. The objective of the model is to maximize after-tax profits in the numeraire currency of the firm subject to material flow constraints, plant capacity, market penetration strategies and local content rules.

The model incorporates many of the international issues raised above, including the impact of economies of scale, duties and tariffs, currency exchange rates, differences in corporate tax rates in each country, market penetration strategies, and local content rules. We also recognize that centralized control of operations may be difficult in a multinational environment and suggest in Section 4 possible incentives for promulgating the model output in a decentralized fashion. Section 4 considers other issues related to solution of the model, including coping with some nonlinearities through a two-stage analysis and the setting of transfer prices to minimize total corporate taxes.

In Section 5 we adopt the point of view that currency exchange rates and market prices for finished goods are random (and in general highly correlated) variables. In order to account for the firm's attitude towards risk, we will introduce both the mean and variance of after tax profit in the model's objective function. This will allow us to consider hedging and portfolio effects on global manufacturing strategies.

In Section 6 we offer some concluding remarks and suggestions for future research.

## 2. LITERATURE REVIEW

There is a vast literature on strategic planning, and a significant portion of it deals with the international context. Some authors differentiate among domestic, multinational and global firms. The operations of domestics is essentially contained within the national boundaries of one country. Multinationals operate fairly autonomous companies in different national markets. Finally, the global corporation attempts to coordinate the full range of its activities (including marketing, production and distribution) throughout the world. Our concern in this paper is with the global corporation.

Dyment [5] describes problems and issues of management control for these global corporations. Advances in communication and manufacturing technology now make it feasible for firms to effectively integrate the operations of their manufacturing and distribution facilites which are located in different countries. Everitt [6] points out some of the tradeoffs and opportunities associated with such worldwide manufacturing.

There have been a number of studies which address the linkage between manufacturing strategy and corporate strategy. Cohen and Lee [1] developed a paradigm for the manufacturing strategy problem which indicated the role of a model based system to support policy analysis. Fine and Hax [7] introduced a general managerial approach for manufacturing strategy development. As noted above, these and other past efforts have not explicitly considered the impact of global operations on manufacturing strategy.

In this paper, we introduce a normative model to analyze the management of operations for the global corporation. The model can be viewed as an extension of Cohen and Lee [2]. In that paper the authors develop a mathematical programming formulation and a solution algorithm for the design of the manufacturing and distribution network in a manner which considers fixed and variable cost tradeoffs throughout the supply chain. Cohen and Moon [3] recently extended the algorithm and report on its application. We note as well that the stochastic model framework introduced by Cohen and Lee [2] is also relevant, since it considers the cost/service tradeoffs associated with alternative material policies in a given supply chain network.

Our treatment of the currency exchange problem draws heavily on the work of Hodder and Jucker. In a series of papers ([10], [11] and [12]), they introduce a mechanism for dealing with random market prices and currency exchange rates in a model of international manufacturing planning. Our representation of the facility network associated with the manufacturing/ distribution system is more extensive. We also introduce the supplier explicitly into the analysis. In a more recent paper, Hodder and Dincer [9] develop a multifactor model of the price process. This model can account for the significant correlation between price movements in international markets.

The solution process proposed in this paper is hierarchical. The model developed by Dempster, Fisher, et al [4] is an illustration of the approach which is suggested here. They show how a hierarchical planning system can be analyzed as a multistage stochastic program.

## 3. MODEL FRAMEWORK

### 3.1. Features

The model is characterized by the following features:

o    There are three facility levels: vendors, plants, markets (see Figure 1).

o    There is a finite planning horizon (e.g., 12 quarters).

o    There are multiple products and input raw materials.

o    The firm is a price taker in each market. All prices are quoted in the currency of the source location.

o    Minimum and maximum demands are deterministic and differentiated by product, market and time period.

o    Vendor contract alternatives are available. Contract terms include costs, duration and volume limits.

o    There exist economies of scale in production at each plant and in raw materials acquisition.

o    Transfer prices between plants and markets are used.

o    Tariffs are charged for inter-country material transfers (including both plant inputs and outputs).

o    Corporate income tax is paid on profit in each country of operation.

o    We ignore intermediate products and plant-to-plant shipments.

o    Both plant locations and capacities are fixed.

o    There are no distribution centers, warehouses and other echelons in the distribution system.

o    Demand and supply clear in each time period and hence there are no inventory costs or variables.

o    Competitor actions and reactions are ignored.

o    The effects of national product design differences are not considered.

o    Local content restrictions are considered.


## 3.2. Decisions and Variables

The following subscripts are used:

$i$  =  product output
$j$  =  plant location
$k$  =  market region
$r$  =  raw material input
$v$  =  vendor location
$n$  =  vendor supply contract alternative
$t$  =  time period
$c$  =  country

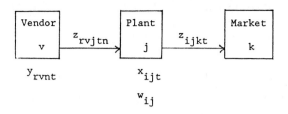

**FIGURE 1**

The operating decisions to be resolved in the model include which vendors will be used, which products will be produced at what levels in each plant, and the flow of raw materials and finished goods between vendors, lants and markets. The decisions are represented by the following variables, depicted schematically in Figure 1.

$$y_{rvtn} = \begin{cases} 1, & \text{if contract option n (for material r from} \\ & \text{vendor v) is selected in period t} \\ \\ 0, & \text{otherwise} \end{cases}$$

$$w_{ij} = \begin{cases} 1, & \text{if any amount of product i is produced in} \\ & \text{plant j} \\ \\ 0, & \text{otherwise} \end{cases}$$

$x_{ijt}$ = amount of product i produced in plant j during period t

$z_{rvjtn}$ = amount of raw material r shipped from vendor v to plant j under contract n in period t

$z_{ijkt}$ = amount of product i shipped from plant j to market k in period t

### 3.3. Details of Model Components

#### a) Vendor Supply Contracts

At time t, one or more possible supply contracts can be selected from vendor v with terms as defined below.

$\ell_n$         = fixed contract length

$C_{rvjn\tau}$    = unit cost for material r from vendor v for delivery to plant j in period $\tau$ (including transport, tariffs)

$F_{vnr}$     = fixed cost of opening contract

$\underline{Z}_{nrv}, \bar{Z}_{nrv}$ = lower and upper bounds on period shipments under contract n for material r from vendor v

We note that, through judicious choice of costs and upper and lower bounds, quantity discount price structures can be modelled. It is also possible to evaluate vendor contracts on the basis of their terms so as to eliminate all dominated alternatives. We will introduce some procedures for doing so in our discussion of the solution process.

#### b) Currency Exchange Rates:

Let

$$e_{ij} = \text{units of currency j per unit of currency i}$$

We assume that location 0 uses a numeraire currency and that all cash flows will be denominated in this currency. Since plants, vendors and markets can all be in different countries, it is necessary to use multiple exchange rate factors. We assume that

$$e_{ij} \, e_{jk} = e$$

in order to rule out possible currency arbitrage ploys.

c) Costs/Prices:

The following cost and price variables are used in the model:

$P_{ik}$   =   selling price of product i in market k

$v_{ij}$   =   unit cost of producing product i in plant j

$G_{ij}$   =   fixed cost of producing product i in plant j

$c_{ijk}$   =   unit cost, including tariffs, of shipping product i from plant j to market k

$M_{ijk}$   =   markup for product i from plant j to market k

$m_j$   =   fraction of vendor fixed costs allocated to plant j

We note that including a fixed cost for product production allows economies of scale in production to be represented in the model by defining several "pseudo products" corresponding to the various cost rates associated with different levels of production.

d) Local Content Rules:

In some countries, it is may be necessary to adhere to local content rules requiring a minimum expenditure on production and raw material acquisition within the country based on the level of sales in the country. This constraint will be based on the following parameters:

$K_c$   =   set of indices of market regions in country c

$V_c$   =   set of indices of vendors in country c

$J_c$   =   set of indices of plants in country c

$\alpha_c$   =   fraction of sales revenue in country c that must be spent in country c

## 3.4. Objective Function

Profit functions can be defined for each plant, each market (distribution center), and for the firm as a whole. Initially, we consider profits without taking into account currency or tax factors.

o  For each plant j:

$$
\Pi_{jt} = \sum_{i,k} (1+M_{ijk}) (v_{ij} + c_{ijk}) z_{ijk} - \sum_{i} v_{ij} X_{ijt}
$$

$$
- \sum_{i,k} c_{ijk} z_{ijkt} - \sum_{r,v,n} C_{rvjnt} z_{rvjt}
$$

$$
- m_j \sum_{r,v,n} F_{vnr} y_{rvtn} - \sum_{i} G_{ij} w_{ij}
$$

$$
= \sum_{i,k} M_{ijk} (v_{ij} + c_{ijk}) z_{ijkt} - \sum_{r,v,n} C_{rvjnt} z_{rvjtn}
$$

$$
- m_j \sum_{r,v,n} F_{vnr} y_{rvtn} - \sum_{i} G_{ij} w_{ij}
$$

o  For Market k:

$$
\Pi_{kt} = \sum_{i,j} P_{ik} z_{ijkt} - \sum_{i,j} (1+M_{ijk}) (v_{ij} + c_{ijk}) z_{ijkt}
$$

o The overall profit for the firm is computed by summing plant and market profits. Note that firm profits are independent of the transfer prices.

$$\sum_{i,j,k,t} [P_{ik} - (1+M_{ij})(v_{ij} + c_{ijk})] z_{ijkt} + \sum_{i,k} M_{ijk}(v_{ij} + c_{ijk}) z_{ijkt}$$

$$- \sum_{r,v,k,j} C_{rvjnt} z_{rvjtn} - \sum_{r,v,n} F_{vnr} y_{rvtn} - \sum_{i,j} G_{ij} w_{ij}$$

$$= \sum_{i,j,k} [P_{ik} - v_{ij} - c_{ijk}] z_{ijkt} - \sum_{r,v,n,j} C_{rvjnt} z_{rvjtn}$$

$$- \sum_{r,v,n} F_{vnr} y_{rvtn} - \sum_{i,j} G_{ij} w_{ij}$$

where we use the fact that $\sum_{j} m_{j} = 1$.


o Firm Profit in Numeraire Currency:

We now introduce the impact of currency fluctuations on the profit functions. The total firm profit in units of numeraire currency is given by:

$$\sum_{i,j,k,t} [P_{ik} e_{ok}] z_{ijkt}$$ 
sales revenue

$$- \sum_{i,j,k,t} [c_{ijk} e_{oj}] z_{ijkt}$$ 
outbound transport and tariff

$$- \sum_{i,j} \left[ \sum_{t} [v_{ij} e_{oj}] X_{ijt} + \sum_{i,j} G_{ij} w_{ij} \right]$$ 
production

$$- \sum_{r,v,n,j,t} [c_{rvjnt} e_{ov}] z_{rvjtn}$$ 
inbound purchase, transport and tariff

$$- \sum_{r,v,n,t} [F_{vnr} \, e_{ov}] \, y_{rvnt} \qquad\qquad \text{fixed supplier contract}$$

Recall that all cash flows are charged in source currencies. As we shall note below, product mix variables can be eliminated from the objective function since they are completely determined by the inbound and outbound flows.

Let $T_n$ be the corporate tax rate in market n. The firm's after-tax profit function must now be written as a sum of country specific profits. The transfer prices, which were eliminated in the before-tax calculation, become relevant once again.

The firm, after tax profit is,

$$
Z = \sum_{j,t} e_{oj}(1-T_j) \left[ \sum_{i,k} M_{ijk} \, (v_{ij} + c_{ijk}) \, z_{ijkt} \right.
$$

$$
- \sum_{r,v,n} e_{jv} \, (C_{rvjnt} \, z_{rvjtn} + m_j \, F_{vnr} \, y_{rvtn}) - \sum_i G_{ij} \, w_{ij} \Bigg]
$$

$$
+ \sum_{k,t} e_{ok}(1-T_k) \sum_{i,j} \left[ P_{ik} \, e_{kj}(1+M_{ijk}) \, (v_{ij} + c_{ijk}) \right] z_{ijkt}
$$

## 3.5. Constraints

Material Supply Contract:

The selection of vendor contracts acts to open a "time window" during which a plant can source material from the vendor. The flow limits are defined by the terms of the contract.

$$\bar{z}_{nrv} \, y_{rvn\tau} \leq \sum_{j} z_{rvj\tau n} \leq \bar{z}_{nrv} \, y_{rvn\tau}$$

$$t \leq \tau \leq t + \bar{t}_{n}$$

(for all t, r, v, n)

Material Requirements:

The material requirements associated with the production of finished goods is governed by the Bill of Material parameters:

$U_{ri}$ = units of raw material r required to make one unit of product i

The balance constraint is

$$\sum_{v,n} z_{rvjtn} = \sum_{i} U_{ri} \, X_{ijt} \qquad \text{(all r, j, t)}$$

Plant Shipments:

Since inventory is cleared each period, the plant output equals total shipments. This constraint can allow us to eliminate the $X_{ijt}$ variables from the problem.

$$X_{ijt} = \sum_k z_{ijkt} \qquad \text{(all i, j, t)}$$

Market Demand (units):

Outbound (plant to market) flows are constrained by volume limits.

$$\underline{D}_{ikt} \leq \sum_j z_{ijkt} \leq \bar{D}_{ikt} \qquad \text{(all i, k, t)}$$

Market Cash Flows:

The currency flows generated by shipments from plants to markets may be constrained as follows:

$$\underline{R}_{kt} \leq \sum_{ij} c_{ijk} z_{ijkt} \leq \bar{R}_{kt}$$

We note that the min (max) unit and cash flows for each market can be considered to be policy decision variables. Both market strategy and counter trade requirements can affect the selection of these constraint parameters.

Plant Capacity:

There are two types of production capacity constraints, based on the overall product mix and on a per item basis. In the constaints below, $\underline{X}_{ijt}$ and $\bar{X}_{ijt}$ are lower and upper limits on product i in plant j, $\bar{X}_{jt}$ is total plant capacity, and $a_{ij}$ is the amount of total plant capacity required to make one unit of product i.

$$\text{(mix)} \quad \sum_i a_{ij} X_{ijt} \le \bar{X}_{jt} \qquad \qquad \text{(all j, t)}$$

$$\text{(item)} \quad \underline{X}_{ijt} \le X_{ijt} \le \bar{X}_{ijt}$$

Local Content Rules:

The requirement that we must spend in country c at least a fraction of the sales revenue is expressed as

$$\sum_{v \varepsilon V_c} \sum_{rtnj} (C_{rvjnt} Z_{rvjtn} + m_j F_{vnr} y_{rvtn})$$

$$+ \sum_{j \varepsilon J_c} \left[ \sum_{ikt} (v_{ij} + c_{ijk}) z_{ijkt} + \sum_i G_{ij} w_{ij} \right]$$

$$\ge \alpha_c \sum_{ijt} \sum_{k \varepsilon K_c} P_{ik} z_{ijkt}$$

$$\text{(all c, t)}$$

Constraints on Financial Variables

$$M_{ij} \ge 0 \qquad \qquad \text{(all ij)}$$

$$m_j \ge 0 \qquad \qquad \text{(all j)}$$

$$\sum_j m_j = 1$$

In addition, all variables are nonnegative and $y_{rvtn}$ and $w_{ij}$ are 0 or 1.

## 4.  SOLUTION PROCESS


Figure  2  illustrates  a  hierarchical  solution process  for  the  global
manufacturing strategy problem.  The environment of the firm  is  determined  (for  our  purposes)  by:  1) the set of products, 2) the national
markets, 3) the facility/process technology infrastructure.  Based  upon
a strategic policy analysis, the firms will develop a global competitive
strategy for the medium term (2–5 years), which  is  consistent with  this
environment.   The  impact of this competitive strategy on international
manufacturing is captured through a manufacturing strategy specification
step  (box 1).  The output of this step is a set of market volume limits
(to capture market priorities and international trade factors) and a set
of qualified supplier contract alternatives.

In order to reduce the computational burden,  it  is  possible  to  pre-
screen  the  vendor  contract  choices  (box 2).  As  noted  in  our
formulation, such choices are characterized by fixed and variable costs,
a  duration  and (upper/lower) volume limits.  All dominated choices can
be eliminated.  A vendor contract option is dominated  if  there  exists
another  contract  with lower fixed and variable costs and with an upper
limit on the amount supplied sufficient to accommodate all  requirements
for that raw material.

The global manufacturing strategy solution is  generated  by  solving  a
version  of  the  mixed  integer,  nonlinear program appropriate for the
industry of interest (box 3).  The variables $M_{ij}$ and $m_j$ which  determine

SOLUTION PROCESS

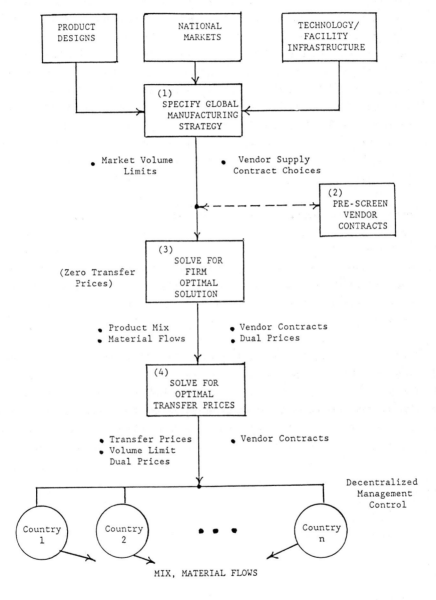

FIGURE 2

transfer prices and allocate overhead to the plants are interesting for several reasons. First of all, their presence makes the model nonlinear and therefore much more complicated to solve. However, their role in the model is of a secondary nature since they only impact the profit taxes paid in each country. For this reason, we suggest a solution approach in which these variables are initially fixed at nominal values. For example, set all $M_{ij} = 0$ and all $m_j$ to equalize allocation of overhead. The resulting model is now a linear mixed integer program and can be solved using standard procedures to obtain optimal values for the operational variables $X_{ij}$, $w_{ij}$, $z_{ijkt}$, $z_{rvjn}$, and $y_{rvtn}$. Then solve for optimal values of the financial variables $M_{ij}$ and $m_j$ to minimize taxes. Although the resulting solution will not in general be optimal to the overall problem, we could iterate on this process by reoptimizing the operational variables with respect to the values of the financial variables just obtained, etc. This iterative process could lead to very aggressive minimization of taxes in some countries and might be challenged as unreasonable by some taxing authorities. Therefore, it may be necessary to constrain the financial variables, such as requiring some minimal amount of overhead to be allocated to each country, perhaps in proportion to the level of business conducted there.

Another issue to be addressed as part of the solution process is how to implement the plan derived from the model. The most obvious approach would be a completely centralized implementation in which the actions required by the plan are transmitted to the various plants and markets. However, fully centralized control is difficult in any setting, and it is doubly difficult in an international context. For this reason, it is desirable to consider creating an incentive structure that would encourage each plant or country to make decentralized decisions that collectively agree with the plan. Another reason for the decentralized approach is that the model produces a long-range plan based on average conditions that would need to be "fine tuned" based on short-range contingencies. This fine tuning is best done at the local level through a decentralized control structure.

The incentive structure could be implemented using the transfer prices $M_{ij}$ , although in general the transfer prices that provide an incentive that supports the plan would not agree with those that minimize total taxes for the corporation. Dual variable values obtained as part of the solution process would also be useful in developing a decentralized control mechanism.

## 5. COPING WITH CURRENCY FLUCTUATIONS

Although we have treated currency exchange rates as deterministic, in reality these exchange rates will fluctuate randomly during the planning horizon of the model. A firm could insulate itself against the risk of the currency fluctuations by balancing cash expenditures with revenues in each country or in a group of countries whose currencies tend to move in a correlated fashion. Obviously, doing this would deviate from the optimal plan and introduce a higher expected cost. More generally, the firm would wish to optimize on some combination of expected cost and the variance in cost due to uncertainty.

In this section, both market price and currency exchange rates are treated as random variables. We let $\lambda$ be a constant risk aversion coefficient, and rewrite the firm's objective function as

$$V = E(Z) - Var(Z)$$

It is necessary to specify the stochastic processes of currency and price fluctuations in order to define the random profit process.

Hodder and Jucker [9, 10] introduced a model which links currency fluctuations and market prices and is based on the Law of One Price This law asserts that prices for identical commodities are equal in different national markets. This implies that

$$P_{ik} = e_{kj} P_{ik} \qquad \text{(for all i, j, k)}$$

In practice, this relationship does not always hold, due to a variety of factors. Consequently, Hodder suggests the following model,

$$P_{ij} e_{oj} = b_j (P_{io} + j)$$

where $b_j$ is an adjustment parameter that represents derivations from the Law of One Price levels. $P_{io}$ is the random price for product i in umeraire currency, and $\varepsilon_j$ is a (independent) country specific random currency disturbance term. We define

$$E(P_{io}) - \bar{P}_{io}$$
$$Var(P_{io}) - \sigma_{ip}^2$$
$$E(\varepsilon_j) - 0$$
$$Var(\varepsilon_j) - \sigma_j^2$$

With this model one can generate tractable expressions for the variance of global firm profit. It is well known, however, that the assumed independence of $\varepsilon_j$ ad $P_{io}$ in the model is unrealistic. Moreover, it is clear that $\varepsilon_j$ and $\varepsilon_k$ are not independent for any pair of countries j and k.

Note that if we assume that the currency exchange rate random variables are linear combinations of a set of orthoginal factors, then correlation can be introduced into the exchange rate process. The computational requirements will increase dramatically, however (see Hodder and Dincer [9]).

## 6. CONCLUSIONS

This paper presents a preliminary formulation of a complex managerial problem. The coordination of activities in manufacturing, procurement and distribution for the global corporation has been modelled in terms of a stochastic, dynamic optimization problem. A variety of issues associated with international manufacturing strategy has been included in the model. We note, in particular, that the model considers currency fluctuations, economies of scale in manufacturing and sourcing, market volume constraints, tariffs, global corporate taxes, and local content rules.

The model and solution procedure we have developed lends itself to decomposition into a two-level hierarchy for the purpose of evaluating solution and control mechanisms. The first level would be concerned with global corporate strategic planning. Policies for procurement, marketing and transfer prices are all addressed at corporate headquarters. Divisional managers are concerned with the control of manufacturing and distribution operations at the second level of the

hierarchy. Their decisions are constrained by the corporate policies
which are communicated via transfer prices, volume constraints, cash
flow constraints and vendor contract alternatives.

Work is ongoing to validate the concepts and tradeoffs presented in the
model. The authors are currently working with firms in the computer,
automobile and paper industries who operate as global corporations. The
formulation will be specialized to the operations of these firms and
tested against the reality of global manufacturing planning in these
company situations. Cohen and Hau Lee, of Stanford University, have
implemented a simplified variant of the model. Preliminary results
indicate that the tradeoffs, decisions and constraints presented here
are consistent with the realities of planning for international
production, sourcing and distribution. The impact of taxes, tariffs and
market content requirements, in particular, were shown to be especially
relevant. Validation of the model was also achieved.

We also plan to extend the model and the solution process. A number of
structural issues and algorithmic questions need to be addressed before
the model framework introduced here can be implemented and used.

The paper is designed to provide a platform for a number of issues in
international manufacturing and distribution that deserve further
research. First of all, how to develop transfer prices or other
incentive mechanisms that would enable decentralized implementation of a
globally optimal solution is a fascinating research question that lies
at the intersection of economics and mathematical programming. In the
area of currency fluctuations, an interesting question is to what extent
a firm should have excess capacity in various countries to allow
shifting of operations as currency exchange rates fluctuate. Finally,
in many industries different countries will have regulations that
require different product specifications. This raises a number of

interesting questions. Is it profitable to operate in a country with low demand that requires a highly specialized product? More generally, what mix of products achieves our market strategy at least cost. At one extreme, we might have one "mega-product" that meets the required specifications in every country. This would simplify manufacturing and allow economies of scale, although the single product would typically be "overspeced" in any one country. At the other extreme, we could have a separate product for each country. Usually, the answer will lie somewhere in the middle and it would be interesting to develop a model that would find that answer.

**ACKNOWLEDGEMENTS**

This research was supported in part by ONR Contract N00014-78-C-0302 P 000 10 and NSF Grants INT 84-08554 and OMC 86-0984, as well as a grant from the International Business Machines MOIS Project, to the University of Pennsylvania.

**REFERENCES**

[1] COHEN, M.A. and H.L. LEE, "Manufacturing Strategy: Concepts and Methods" in: Kleindorfer, P.R. (ed.), The Management of Productivity and Technology in Manufacturing (Plenum Press, 1985), 153-188

[2] COHEN, M.A. and H.L. LEE, "Strategic Analysis of Integrated Production-Distribution Systems: Models and Methods", Operations Research, in print.

[3] COHEN, M.A. and S. MOON, "An Integrated Model for Manufacturing and Distribution Systems Design" <u>Decision Sciences Working Paper</u> The Wharton School, University of Pennsylvania (1987).

[4] DEMPSTER, M.A.H., M.L. FISHER, L. JANSEN, B.J. LAGEWAG, J.K. LENSTRA, and A.H.G. RINNOOY KAN, "Analytical Evaluation of Hierarchical Planning Systems", <u>Operations Research 29.4</u> (1981), 707-716.

[5] DYMENT, J.J.,"Strategies and Management Controls for Global Corporations" <u>Journal of Business Strategy</u> (1987), 20-26.

[6] EVERITT, L.H.,"Worldwide Manufacturing -- A Multinational's Perspective", <u>Manufacturing Issues</u> (Booz-Allen & Hamilton, Inc., 1986), 22-23.

[7] FINE, C.H. and A.C. HAX, "Manufacturing Strategy: A Methodology and Illustration" <u>Interfaces 15.6</u> (1985), 28-46.

[8] HAX, A.C. and H.C. MEAL, "Hierarchical Integration of Production Planning and Scheduling" in: Geisler, M.A. (ed.), Logistics Vol. 1 (North Holland-American Elsevier, 1975).

[9] HODDER, J.E. and M.C. DINCER, "A Multifactor Model for International Plant Location and Financing under Uncertainty, Computing & Operation" Research 13.5, (1986), 601-609.

[10] HODDER, J.E. and J.V. JUCKER, "Plant Location Modeling for the Multinational Firm", Proceedings of Academy of International Business Conference on Asia-Pacific Dimension of International Business, Honolulu (1982).

[11] HODDER, J.E. and J.V. JUCKER, "International Plant Location under Price and Exchange Rate Uncertainty", Engineering Costs and Production Economics 9 (1985), 225-229.

[12] HODDER, J.E. and J.V. JUCKER, "A Simple Plant-Location Model for Quantity-Setting Firms Subject to Price Uncertainty", European Journal of Operational Research 2 (1985), 39-46.

[13] JAIKUMAR, R.,"An Operational Optimization Procedure for Production Scheduling", Computing and Operations Research Vol. 1 (1974), 191-200.

MANAGING INTERNATIONAL MANUFACTURING
K. Ferdows (Editor)
© Elsevier Science Publishers B.V. (North-Holland), 1989


INTERNATIONAL SOURCING: BEYOND CATALOG SHOPPING AND FRANCHISING


Therese FLAHERTY

Harvard University


## 1. INTRODUCTION


During the late 1970s and early 1980s, serious competitive difficulties
prompted managers of many U.S. manufacturing companies to reevaluate
their international sourcing policies, that is, their use of internal
and external manufacturing resources located around the world. Many of
these efforts resulted in dramatic improvements in the efficiency of
purchasing and manufacturing. But widespread outsourcing, plant clos-
ings, and the so-called hollowing out of U.S. manufacturing also ensued;
the international economy remained in flux.

Managers of U.S. companies had generally managed international sourcing
at arm's length, and it had fallen into one of two categories. First,
sourcing from independent, foreign vendors had typically been handled by
purchasing organizations, and contracts were awarded on the basis of
cost, specifications, and the ability to deliver. Inventory buffered essential operations from the unplanned effects of distant sources. I call
this category international catalog sourcing. Second, essential manufacturing was frequently dispersed internationally, located close to
customers, and managed almost completely by local general managers who
focused on serving their local customers. I term this international
franchising. In both cases input from corporate management was generally
limited to intermittent oversight of the budgeting process and oc-
casional new product introductions.

In this paper, I argue that during the 1990s managers of all world-class
companies, regardless of their base of operations, in technology- and
design-intensive industries who face international competition will have
to engage in international sourcing. And their international sourcing
will have to extend beyond catalog shopping and international franchising. They will not safely be able to assume that locating manufacturing
in developing countries assures relatively low cost products or that
locating manufacturing in one industrialized country assures local customer loyalty or innovation. Many must serve global customers with some

global products or components. Without access to international operations, they shall no longer be assured that they are familiar with the
best products and processes, materials and technology.

Rather, world-class managers will have to operate in all three major industrial centers of the Triad -- Western Europe, North America and Japan
and the newly industrializing countries of the Far East. The fundamental
reason for this is that in these centers companies with technology and
employees of comparable sophistication will simultaneously and indpen-
dently be generating new products and innovations as byproducts of doing
business in their local environment. By combining the three sources of
improvement, managers can almost surely achieve products and operations
superior to those of companies accessing only one. Conversely, without
access to the new technological directions and products emerging in each
location, a company operating in only one or two of the major industrial
centers could easily be blindsided when confronted with the mature version of a technology developed elsewhere.

Effectively combining innovations from the three industrial centers to
result in a sustained competitive advantage shall require much closer
contact between the management and technical employees of geographically
distant operations than international catalog sourcing or franchising
allows. The experiences of several pioneering U.S. companies already
demonstrate the large potential of this new approach. But they also suggest the difficulties in coordinating such international operations
effectively. Thus, those companies whose managers succeed in implementing international sourcing efforts beyond catalog sourcing and
franchising will be likely to sustain their competitive advantage.

This paper begins by describing the traditional patterns of U.S. companies' international sourcing. Section 3 discusses the decreasing
international cost differentials. Section 4 considers the rise of the
Triad and its effects on international sourcing in technology- and
marketing-intensive industries in international competitive industries.
Section 5 introduces the newer variations of international sourcing
which are particularly useful in globally competitive industries. The
final section suggests several managerial and research implications of
the paper.

## 2. PAST INTERNATIONAL SOURCING BY U.S.-BASED COMPANIES

U.S. managers have historically balanced technology, competitive, and
cost considerations [1] in deciding on the international locations of
their manufacturing. They generally began by sourcing the core products
and components they considered essential to the success of their

businesses close to their headquarters, R&D, and marketing. They purchased peripheral components and services from outside vendors and
managed at arms' length. But they carefully controlled and watched over
their core manufacturing. This included the manufacturing of new
products (which might require engineering and design changes) as well as
manufacturing processes (which might require frequent improvement or
significant engineering support). Because they developed most products
and processes in the United States, they also located most "core"
manufacturing in the United States.

Of course, after World War II many U.S. managers extended their operations to other industrialized countries. In order to meet competition
and satisfy local customers' demands for service, commitment, local
manufacturing content, low transport costs, and/or customized products,
they established local marketing, sales, and core manufacturing organizations very much like their original operations in the United
States. [2,3] These subsidiaries typically began with products
developed in the United States along with considerable capital and technical assistance. But, after start-up, local general managers had broad
authority to develop the business as they saw fit. [4] They managed
their product development and core manufacturing much as their U.S.
counterparts did and focussed on their local customers. Because of their
resemblance to their U.S. parent and their arm's length management relations with the parents, I use the term international franchise for these
subsidiaries and their manufacturing. In some cases, these subsidiaries
eventually developed new products and technologies that rivalled those
of their U.S. parent. Some subsidiaries even became the worldwide source
of a key product family or technology for the entire company, though
such developments required international management interdependence far
beyond that required by most international subsidiaries. [5]

Cost considerations dominated the choice of manufacturing location for
some products. For those products whose manufacturing operations were
stable enough, local service requirements low enough, and international
cost differentials great enough, manufacturing could be located in the
lowest cost location worldwide with great benefit to customers. Most
shoes for U.S. women, for example, are made in the Far East, Spain,
Italy and Brazil. Other products -- for example, assembled electronics
products and some printed circuit boards -- benefit from having their
early manufacturing located in core factories close to the R&D organization which developed them; but the manufacturing for a successful
product of this type is frequently relocated to the periphery after its
design is standardized, its manufacturing process is stabilized, and its
maximal sales volumes is reached. In still other product categories,
some manufacturing processes -- fabrication of advanced integrated circuits, for example -- are so unstable that they are always located in
core factories in the United States or other industrialized countries,
while other manufacturing processes on the same products -- assembly and

test -- are so stable that they are generally located in low labor cost
"peripheral" factories.

U.S. managers generally used relatively low cost foreign sources only
for the products and processes they considered to be standardized and
not critical to their business. When a product's manufacturing was
transferred to low-cost foreign factories, engineering support for its
design and its manufacturing process diminished. Furthermore, the dis-
tances between such sources and their customers were so great that face-
to-face contact, telephone conversations, and written communication were
difficult. Product specs, volumes shipped, and prices were therefore the
only feasible subjects of communication. And relations between customers
and foreign vendors were usually arm's length, even when both were part
of the same company. Thus, it was unlikely that a product would be enhanced by improvements in its manufacturing process or in its design
after its manufacturing was relocated to the periphery. [6] I use the
term catalog source for foreign sources -- both independent vendors and
subsidiaries -- whose use is justified on the basis of their relatively
low costs (given that product specifications and delivery requirements
are met), whose manufacturing operations are peripheral to the business
of their customers, and who have arm's length relations with their customers.

Each multinational company's international sourcing strategy, then, lo-
cates a number of specialized sources -- core and peripheral
manufacturing -- around the world so that together they form an effective network to deliver final products to customers. In the past,
peripheral manufacturing might have been located anywhere; but, whenever
direct labor costs accounted for a large part of manufacturing costs, it
was likely to be located in a relatively low labor cost region, such as
the Far East. Core manufacturing with its accompanying engineering,
marketing, and R&D was generally located in the U.S. or an industrialized country within a well-developed local business. I call the
structure of the resulting network an international manufacturing configuration. [7]

Figure 1 illustrates a typical international sourcing strategy based on
international catalog sourcing and franchising relations among the
manufacturing units. It also indicates the roles of core and peripheral
manufacturing within the configuration. In the figure, material
progresses through the value chain from top to bottom, with peripheral
operations performed at the top, [8] and core manufacturing operations
performed below, close to customers.

As Figure 1 indicates, the product flows in the configuration of the
typical U.S. multinational were fairly simple, linear, and clearly
directed, moving from the geographic periphery toward the major industrial centers where advanced industry and customers were

concentrated. Likewise, there was little information passed among the operations in the configuration, aside from that required to make material flow. What information did flow from headquarters generally concerned new products and processes or approval for large capital expenditures. Information flowing from core manufacturing to headquarters generally consisted of reports and requests for capital budgeting or engineering help.

Figure 1

International Manufacturing Configuration:

Catalog Sourcing and Franchising

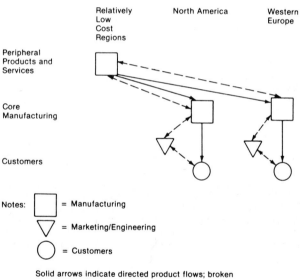

Notes:
☐ = Manufacturing

▽ = Marketing/Engineering

◯ = Customers

Solid arrows indicate directed product flows; broken arrows indicate directed information flows.

U.S. managers made numerous incremental changes in their international sourcing configurations in response to changes in demand patterns and the entrepreneurial zeal of their managers; there were also periodic network restructurings to accommodate world demand and product line changes. For example, during the early 1980s many products which had been sourced from the United States were sourced instead more at arm's length from relatively low cost sources in the industrial periphery.

But, by the late 1980s the widespread use of arm's length management to source from relatively low cost operations in the periphery and the independent management of core manufacturing operations in the industrial countries appeared to be inadequate for many companies competing in the global industries. The world had changed. This was due to three significant changes in the world business environment. First, the international cost differentials that drove increased catalog shopping were following a long term declining trend. Second, the industrial prowess of Japan and Western Europe -- especially the Federal Republic of Germany -- had caught up with and, in some cases, surpassed that of the United States. As a result, by the mid-1980s U.S. managers of multinationals had incentives to access technology as well as customers throughout the industrialized world. Furthermore, technology for travel, data processing, and communication made it possible and competitively advantageous for them to manage their international sources with much greater interdependence both among manufacturing sites and between headquarters and themselves.


## 3. DECLINING INTERNATIONAL MANUFACTURING COST DIFFERENTIALS

International factor cost differentials between the United States and most other countries were very large during the middle decades of the twentieth century. Despite this, most manufacturing remained in the United States through the 1970s. There were several reasons for this. First, the country was capable of satisfying most of its own needs for manufactured goods. Second, the countries with relatively low factor costs lacked the skilled labor, scarce capital, and the infrastructure needed to manufacture the products U.S. customers demanded at appropriate quality levels. Thus, even though the costs for direct labor were relatively low, in many countries skilled labor and an adequate infrastructure were absent; and to provide them for just one operation was expensive, so it was not possible to make many products which the U.S. market demanded at an acceptable total cost. Finally, U.S. managerial expertise to acquire products from abroad was not well-developed. Thus, U.S. efforts at sourcing manufactured goods and services from relatively low cost countries proceeded slowly.

By the late 1970s and early 1980s, infrastructures had been developed and employees trained in many relatively low factor cost countries. Many countries had developed the capability to manufacture products at a quality suitable for export to the world market. Finally, international communication and travel technology had been improved. These trends supported economic development and the long term decline in international labor cost differentials.

Between 1970 and 1985 the real wages of U.S. manufacturing workers declined relative to the wages of their counterparts in almost every other country in the world. This decline is reflected in the statistics in Table 1. For the electrical machinery [9] and shoe [10] manufacturing industries the wages of direct workers in a number of countries are compared with those in the United States in 1970, 1985, and 1988. In 1970 in the electrical machinery industry, in each country except Canada manufacturing wages were less than half those in the United States. But, by 1988 three countries had wages at least 90 percent of those in the United States, those in the United Kingdom were 69 percent of those in the United States, and wages in all countries had increased relative to those in the United States. In 1970 in the shoe industry, wages in three countries were more than half as large as their U.S. counterparts. The same long term trend of diminishing international labor cost differentials prevailed. [11]

While factor price differentials declined and capability in the developing countries increased, many U.S. managers had learned the practical aspects of international sourcing. During the early to mid-1980s, international sourcing to reduce manufacturing costs became feasible for the first time for many U.S. companies. Encouraged by the temporarily high exchange rate, U.S. managers increased their catalog shopping dramatically. Imports reached unprecedented levels. (In fact, some observers contend that many U.S. managers used catalog sourcing for products and components that should have been manufactured in core factories, thus forfeiting the potential competitive advantage of future process improvements.)

Just how big international manufacturing cost differentials could be is illustrated by the analysis of the International Trade Commission of international shoe manufacturing in 1984. At that time, the International Trade Commission [1985] estimated, the typical unit factory cost for making a pair of leather shoes in the United States was $3.14, of which $.99 was direct labor and $2.15 was materials and capital services. The delivered (in the United States) unit cost of a comparable pair of shoes made in Taiwan they estimated at $2.83, of which only $.33 was direct labor, $2.15 was materials and capital services, and $.35 was duty and transportation charges. That is, a profit of 30 cents a pair could be

TABLE 1

DIMINISHING INTERNATIONAL LABOR DIFFERENTIAL (1970–1985)
(RATIO OF WAGES IN A COUNTRY TO THOSE IN THE UNITED STATES)

| | Electrical | | | Shoes | | |
|---|---|---|---|---|---|---|
| | 1970 | 1985 | 1988 | 1970 | 1985 | 1988 |
| Canada | .84 | .87 | .97 | .75 | .90 | 1.0 |
| France | .44 | .42 | .50 | .44 | .62 | .74 |
| Ireland | N/A | .43 | .49 | .49 | .63 | .72 |
| Japan | .22 | .48 | .92 | .26 | .70 | 1.3 |
| Korea | .06 | .13 | .15 | .06 | .16 | .19 |
| Mexico | N/A | .13 | N/A | .25 | .26 | N/A |
| Singapore | .07 | .15 | .16 | .09 | N/A | N/A |
| United Kingdom | .45 | .50 | .69 | .60 | .80 | 1.11 |
| West Germany | .45 | .53 | .90 | .52 | .76 | 1.29 |

Notes: The entries are the ratio of the hourly wages of direct workers
in a given industry and country translated to 1985 U.S. dollars with the
corresponding hourly wages of U.S. direct workers in the same industry.
Source of data is the International Monetary Statistics published by the
International Monetary Fund and statistics published by the
International Labor Organization. Because 1988 wage rates were not
available, the 1988 statistics are based on 1985 reported wages adjusted
for June 1988 exchange rates. This seems a reasonable approximation for
most countries; Mexico, however, had experienced considerable inflation
making these computations particularly poor; thus the Mexican rates for
1988 are not reported. The statistics for France are based on 1972, not
1970 comparisons because data was not available for 1970.

made by importing shoes from Taiwan rather than making them in the United States. This analysis is consistent with the judgement of the U.S. purchasing managers I have interviewed from a wide variety of industries who typically explain that they expect to save 20 percent by sourcing internationally from low cost countries. [12]

By 1988, when imports were at an all-time high, many managers found that their international catalog shopping bargains had become relatively expensive. The shoe example above illustrates the problem. The Taiwanese dollar had appreciated by more than 35 percent against the U.S. dollar. Since there was not an offsetting decrease in wages, and many Taiwanese companies were interested in moving out of shoe manufacturing and into electronics assembly, they passed most of the exchange rate appreciation on to their U.S. customers. That pass through would raise the price of a pair of shoes imported from Taiwan to $4.82, or a $.42 a pair loss relative to U.S. production. Indeed, what U.S. shoe factories remained in 1988 were increasing their output.

One reason that the exchange rate movement had such an impact on the cost-minimizing location for products like shoes is that direct labor did not account for a large fraction of their manufacturing cost. Yet direct labor accounted for all the cost advantage from sourcing shoes outside the United States. For shoes sourced from independent vendors in Taiwan or Korea, the exchange rate was applied to the entire manufacturing cost since materials were procured locally. Of course, managers might find that the cost of materials was less affected by the exchange rate reevaluation because materials were internationally traded, but industry sources suggest that the exchange rate premiums were typically applied to the entire manufacturing cost. Alternatively, managers might find that they could provide materials from the United States or other low cost regions to their low labor cost sources. But this would mean incurring additional transport and managerial "grief costs" in order to coordinate international manufacturing and transportation. [13] These costs could easily outweigh the remaining cost differential.

This observation that direct labor does not account for a large portion of manufacturing costs, applies to most U.S. manufacturing industries. This fact derives from a long term trend to lower labor requirements in most manufacturing technology. [14] It means that manufacturing cost differentials will decline even more rapidly than the decline in international labor cost differentials because the other components of manufacturing cost -- capital, materials, indirect labor and management -- are more mobile internationally than immobile direct labor. Furthermore, they already had smaller international cost differentials than direct labor. [15]

Finally, the magnitude of the cost advantage a U.S. manager could expect
to gain over a competitor by relocating the manufacturing facilities for
materials and components had also diminished because most competitors
could easily duplicate the cost advantage by working with a similar
source in the same location. This was particularly feasible for companies that sourced products from peripheral factories with very little
engineering support: their processes and consequently their products
were easily duplicated by any manager with access to similar factor
costs.

This long term decline in international manufacturing cost differentials
based on international sourcing [16], of course, runs counter to the
motivation of many U.S. managers who increased their international
catalog shopping during the early and mid-1980s. By the late 1980s their
cost motivation for international catalog sourcing had declined substantially. There were still advantages to international sourcing,
including cost advantages in some cases. But they had to confront the
fact that their competitive advantage based on lower cost was probably
declining and would continue to do so. They had to wonder whether there
were other more effective ways of creating competitive advantage.

It appears, for example, that the magnitude of cost saving available
through improved process and product design can outweigh the cost
savings from international sourcing. The Sunbeam global iron [17] is a
case in point. GE/Black & Decker had designed a world iron and manufactured it in Singapore, presumably to take advantage of relatively low
cost labor. Sunbeam's estimates in 1984 of the delivered unit cost of
the Singapore-made iron in the United States was $5.98: $.65 higher than
their cost of manufacturing the Sunbeam global iron in Louisiana. The
reason for the low U.S. cost was a design that required both very little
labor and very little automation. Furthermore, by 1988 the cost advantage of sourcing from Singapore had diminisheded due to the exchange
rate reallignment, but the low U.S. costs based on process and product
design persisted.

Although this example seems to suggest that it is wise to enhance
products and operations and to retreat from international sourcing locations to a single location for marketing, R&D, and manufacturing. I
believe that this would be a mistake for companies in technology- and
marketing-intensive industries facing international competition. Rather,
it appears that because of the rise of the industrial Triad it will be
critical for companies in these industries and to become more global in
their international sourcing, to access innovations developed throughout
the industrialized world in order to compete on an equal basis with
their global competitors.

## 4. THE RISE OF THE INDUSTRIAL TRIAD

The very forces of economic development that worked to diminish international manufacturing cost differentials also fostered economic
development in many countries. By the late 1980s, the economies of a
number of countries in Western Europe and the Far East were effectively
equal with that of the United States. The term Triad came to be used increasingly to denote the commercial parity of the three regions.

The regions of the Triad were equal in several ways. First, they were
similar in the size and buying power of their consumer and industrial
markets. Second, consumers in the three regions of the Triad were rich
enough and had similar enough lifestyles that many products they
demanded both at consumer and industrial levels were similar. This meant
that many similar products could be sold in all three regions. Third,
some companies based in each region competed directly and successfully
with the world's best companies in the dynamic marketing- and
technology-intensive industries. In industries as important and diverse
as electronics, automobiles, and pharmaceuticals, leading edge innovations were equally likely to come from companies in each region of the
Triad.

While recognizing the increasing similarity of the regions of the Triad,
it is also useful to recognize their differences. The regions differed
in their languages, their cultures, their ideologies, the customs, and
lifestyles of their people. They also differed in the approaches of
their people to problem-solving in business.

These aspects of the emerging Triad of commercial regions affected companies in marketing- and technology- intensive businesses on the demand
side through their customers and on the supply side, through their own
operations and those of their vendors. The demand side implications --
global products and global customers -- of globalization have been discussed and explored extensively elsewhere.[18] The supply-side effects
of the Triad have been less extensively explored, so they will be explored more in this section.

The emergence of the Triad brought two big changes on the supply side.
First, sources of manufactured goods which had previously had relatively
low cost, with little expertise and little engineering support, had increased their relative costs. As noted above, the international
manufacturing cost differential motivation for international sourcing
was diminishing. Second, many companies in formerly low cost countries,
as well as many companies which had previously served largely local
markets for goods of intermediate sophistication, had also developed

extensive   engineering support for their own manufacturing and for their
customers. This resulted in much <u>greater potential for innovation</u> in the
Triad   than   earlier   when the United States had been by far the primary
region for innovation.

When the three different, but equal, regions of the Triad   replaced   the
United   States   as   the main region where state-of-the-art knowledge was
generated, the potential for industrial innovation increased enormously.
There were then three, not one, regions to generate innovations. The innovations, of course, came from similar regions with similar business
problems,   so   the   innovations   were   likely   to be relevant to similar
businesses throughout the Triad. In fact, there was likely   to   be   considerable   duplication.   But there were also differences in the business
environments which provided problems whose solutions   led   to   different
innovations   among   the   regions.   Many, but not all, solutions could be
usefully adopted throughout the Triad. Thus, the rate of   innovation   in
Triad industries was potentially faster than that when the United States
economy dominated.

Evidence that the potential knowledge was relevant and   valuable   across
regions of the Triad is ubiquitous. The large and growing number of U.S.
patents awarded to   non-U.S.   citizens   suggests   that   there   was   considerable   geographical   dispersion   of   leading-edge technology and
manufacturing capability. The disparities in manufacturing and engineering capability likely to be built up through doing business in different
geographic areas were also well demonstrated by the   wide   emulation   of
Japanese   manufacturing methods by U.S. companies during the 1980s. Many
U.S. companies sourced high technology components and services, like advanced   integrated   circuits   or   flexible   machining   centers,   from
indepedent vendors in Japan or Europe, rather than from   others   in   the
United States.

It   was   possible   to   access these technological resources of the Triad
through wholly-owned manufacturing as well as   through   close   relations
with   independent   suppliers.[19]   But   it is easiest to gauge the magnitude of potential gain from accessing such technology by reference   to
multinational   manufacturing   companies that had operated their international subsidiaries as market-oriented international franchises for many
years.   Here, I   discuss   the   potential   found by the managers of one
specialty chemical manufacturer and by Sunbeam Appliance Company.

The specialty chemical company [20] had six international   plants   which
for   between   10   and 20 years had been independently making essentially
the same product within subsidiaries that were managed as   international
franchises.   The   worldwide   business   was   losing money, and there were
potential competitors. One approach to the problem involved   restructuring   the   network,   eliminating high cost plants and relying more on the
most efficient plants, taking into account transport costs duties and so

on. This would result in a roughly $4 million annual cost reduction, and would put the worldwide business in the black.

Transferring innovation and process knowledge among the plants would result in much greater savings. At the Japanese plant, employees had improved waste management and achieved unexpected improvements in raw material utilization; at the West German plant, a technician had improved the manufacturing process so as to reduce cost and enhance the properties of the product for local customers. If these potential improvements were made throughout, the cost impact alone would have moved the worldwide business from losses to profits and the product would be improved. A lower bound benchmark [21] of potential cost reduction is the annual total cost reduction that would ensue if all the plants had the average cost of the lowest cost plant: $18 million a year. This would transform an unprofitable business to one with a pretax profit of 22 percent of sales!

Sharing product ideas through the Triad could also be the basis of effective global innovation. Sunbeam Appliance Company [22] designed and marketed the first iron that automatically shut off when it electronically sensed no movement on the basis of a product idea from its Australian subsidiary. And the company introduced the first small food processor, the Oskar, to the U.S. market: a product designed and manufactured -- but not successfully marketed -- in Europe that the U.S. company's marketers heard about through their Australian subsidiary. These two products, when positioned and advertised in the United States, transformed both markets, earned the U.S. company a substantial portion of its sales during the mid-1980s, and contributed to the company's resurgence.

It is important to note two aspects of these examples. First, the innovative ideas in these cases probably would not and could not have been developed by an individual plant putting greater R&D investment into their own process. The innovative ideas in each case were generated by people who were actually doing business in the different regions. It suggests an extreme proposition that no individual company operating in one region can expect to be self-sufficient and world-competitive for long, regardless of how much it invests in R&D. This is because the operations in different regions will be pushed in different directions by their business partners, suppliers, and customers. No company alone can realistically expect to control a technology once it is used throughout the Triad.

This does not mean that every company that hopes to benefit by accessing innovations throughout the Triad must own subsidiaries and operate throughout the Triad. But it does mean that many companies -- because their business is innovative and they face competitiors based throughout the Triad -- need to access innovations in other regions. They must

either do business there and make the innovations themselves or they
must work closely enough with those who do business in each region to
stay aware of innovations that are being developed.

Second, it appears from these cases -- and, I believe, in most cases --
that identifying what should be transferred is a major task. Consider
the specialty chemical company example. The benchmark cost calculation
indicates how valuable a transfer can be, but it does not indicate what
particular manufacturing capabilities need to be transferred among the
different plants. It only indicates manufacturing performance, and is
measured in a universal business unit. In the specialty chemical company, the engineering study identified raw material utilization as the
manufacturing capability that was particularly good in Japan and raw
material utilization along with drying in Germany. Manufacturing
capability is a skill particular to a manufacturing operation; it is
measured in units specific to the operation.

Even the engineering study, however, went only so far as to indicate the
manufacturing capabilities on which to focus. Details of what aspects
of the methods, management and equipment from each plant should be incorporated in other plants only be done by line people aware of the
details of manufacturing at each plant. In the specialty chemical company the technical specialist from Germany was commissioned to work
personally and in detail with other plants. (The analogous point could
be made for product design and market positioning through the example of
the Sunbeam products. Without the work in those areas by the Sunbeam
Appliance Company in the United States, the resulting products would
likely not have been successful.) In general, a company seems to need
considerable internal development capability -- in manufacturing process
engineering and in product design and marketing -- in order to identify
what manufacturing capability or aspect of a product will be valuable in
other regions. Then, the company must have line people capable of
adapting just the valuable parts to existing opertions and products in
other regions.

What is new here is the need for globally competitive companies to have
internal product and process improvement skills IN ADDITION TO accessing
the business experience of sources in all three major industrial centers. Doing both requires considerably more management skill and
attention than simply doing either one. It is a major challenge in
creating a sustainable advantage in global competition. Managers must
decide what they need to depend on outsiders for, what they must work on
themselves (usually because it is core to their business), and how much
overlap there should be. They need to appreciate the capability and
potential of their sources in different parts of the world.

These effects are probably most important in industries in which design (based on technology or marketing) moves quickly and in which international competition is an important threat. Such a company can expect to be exposed to the innovations generated in the different regions. Equipment is a good example of such a business where technology moves quickly and companies develop new products by solving their customers' problems; innovations are made cooperatively with customers and at their request. Furthermore, advanced user companies are located throughout the Triad. Consumer electronics products were design- and marketing-intensive, and design concepts for them were increasingly applicable throughout the Triad (recall the toothpaste pump which originated in Europe and swiftly became a success in the United States). In such industries, where the rate of innovation is high and there is international competition, innovation strategies should be Triad-wide.

In contrast, the semiconductor industry during the 1950s and 1960s was located almost entirely within the United States, and there was little need for a company to look outside the country for innovation. There innovation strategies were U.S.-based (or national). In some industries, like large consumer durables (washing machines for example) there was rapid innovation in Europe and Japan as well as in the United States, but during the 1950s and 1960s there was little international competition. Companies' innovation strategies were reasonably multidomestic. By the late 1980s there was considerable international competition in the semiconductor industry; both business and innovation strategies were necessarily global.

There are also products for which design and technology changes little and for which international competition is effectively foreclosed, like cement manufacturing. In such industries, what little innovation there is can afford to be national.

Finally, in many industries the innovation rate has not been rapid, but there is stiff international competition. Businesses of this sort have been frequently in the bulk chemical and high volume food ingredients areas, for instance. Companies in these businesses have long recognized the need for innovation because the cost effects of even small innovations can affect their profitability and survival. These businesses have long had international engineering efforts, although these efforts did not have to be as extensive and large-scale as those needed in current marketing- and technology-intensive industries.

For many U.S. industries -- such as the specialty chemical business discussed above -- there were dramatic increases in technology and design innovation as well as in international competition during the late 1970s and 1980s. Industries were moving toward the upper right of Figure 2. This movement necessitates increased management consideration of accessing innovations made throughout the Triad.

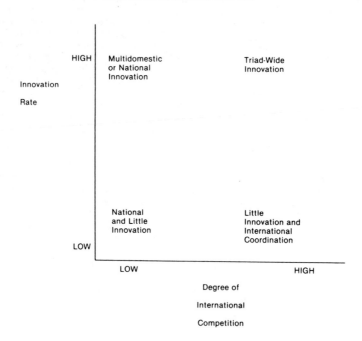

Figure 2

Requirements for Triad-wide Innovation

5. COORDINATION AND THE NEW INTERNATIONAL PLANT

Configurations

It appears that, for businesses in marketing- and technology-intensive industries facing international competition, there are large potential benefits to accessing innovations and serving customers in all three regions of the Triad. Capturing these benefits requires managers of many companies to change their traditional approaches to international sourcing.

First, there is a change in the markets to which they sell. In the extreme, customers throughout the Triad are eager to purchase exactly the same product. Such global products can be designed and manufactured and, in some cases, marketed centrally to take advantage of all possible economies of scale. In such cases when economies of scale are very large, the international manufacturing configuration is simple: one core or peripheral factory supplying customers worldwide with one product family. Figure 3 shows an international plant configuration in which several core manufacturing operations located in different countries provide the worldwide needs of different products. This contrasts with the market-oriented assignment of products used in the past by many U.S. companies and which I have called international franchises, where each international business provided the full product line needs for local customers. Note also that in the new configuration -- unlike in the past in Figure 1 -- core manufacturing and business units can be located throughout the Triad, including in the Far East.

Figure 3

Global Products

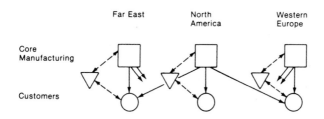

Such global products are, of course, very rare because the Triad regions are not homogeneous. Customers throughout the Triad demand many products which are similar, but not identical. So, economies of scale in their production processes are either less extreme or less exploited. And managers frequently choose to establish several similar plants in different regions. These plants were frequently managed independently within independent subsidiaries. Some companies have explored the possibility of combining the requirements of some components [23]. These are variants on the global product theme.

With the emerging Triad some global customers of component and material companies operate the same process in several parts of the world. They want to buy materials which function identically in their products regardless of the particular factory at which they were manufactured. The managers of a company supplying such a global customer have a choice about their international sourcing strategy: (a) continue to define each

plant's customers geographically, but then institute tight controls on
the manufacturing process between plants so as to ensure that their
products are identical [24]; (b) redefine the customers of each plant so
that customers who have worldwide requirements for a material always
receive it from the same factory. The former solution leaves the
manufacturing structure roughly as it is in Figure 1, but it also entails worldwide account management and coordination of manufacturing,
sales and marketing as in Figure 4. The latter solution changes product
flows as in Figure 3, and it entails extra transport costs and sub-
standard (because long distance) service to the global customer's sites
in most parts of the world; this sort of solution also may not offer the
economies of scale that compensate the managers of the global products
plants for their extra marketing, sales, and transport costs. Neither
solution is easy to implement nor entirely satisfactory. Many companies
opt for worldwide account management, but that is very difficult to
manage.

The first supply side issue accompanying the emerging Triad is the
diminishing international manufacturing cost differentials. They had not
dissappeared by the late 1980s, and they will doubtless be important for
quite some time. These sources are drawn as peripheral manufacturing in
Figure 1, and they perform mainly simple tasks. As their international
manufacturing cost advantage disappeared, their products and services
could no longer be sold on the basis of low cost. The cost savings also
had to be more carefully compared with possible foregone opportunities
for process and product improvement. One possibility is to eliminate
such suppliers whose expenses rise from their sources and to look for
lower cost sources. For some products this was surely the best thing to
do.

An alternative is for a company to upgrade the manufacturing operation
from a peripheral one to a more core facility with supporting engineering and marketing. This is sugggested by the configuration in Figure 3.
In this figure, in contrast with Figure 1, there is no peripheral
manufacturing particularly in the Far East, but there is core manufacturing capable of serving local customers. Some low cost peripheral
sources have become capable of core manufacturing. In fact, some previously low cost, limited commercial centers have already become world
leaders in certain areas. Singapore, for example, came to be thought of
by many electronics managers as the site for the world's best commercial
printing. The infrastructure there meant that many parts could be obtained quickly and in flexible volumes. Furthermore, many companies
which had established sources in the Far East on the basis of their
relatively low costs during the 1970s found that by the mid-1980s those
same operations were particularly valuable for their access to large
numbers of well-trained manufacturing engineers. [25] This meant many
catalog sources had much more to offer than just low cost.

The second change accompanying the emergence of the Triad is the need for companies in technology- and marketing-intensive industries that are subject to international competition to access innovation from each region of the Triad. In order to take advantage of the greater capability and innovativeness of such offshore sources, however, managers would not have to change the locations of their products and plants. But, they would have to manage their sources -- probably including independent vendors -- differently and acquire some close international sources if they did not already have them.

In these cases, internationally franchised operations retain their international plant configuration, product responsibilities and customer responsibilities but, at the same time, undertake some joint projects and communication. In Figure 5 the plants and product flows to local customers in the are unchanged from Figure 1. But information and additional product flows are added between the sister plants located in different countries and the Far Eastern core manufacturing is added. The change almost surely weakens the authority of country managers, but they retain primary control over the local manufacturing operations.

Figure 4

Global Customers

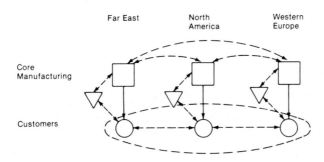

See Note on Figure 1.

What is dramatically changed, is that the operating level people in international plants talk to each other, work on joint products, and help each other. These interactions are represented by double dotted line information flows between the plants in Figure 5. As a result, the authority of manufacturing process experts within the company is typically strengthened, and the customers in each location are served by

Figure 5

Coordinated International Manufacturing

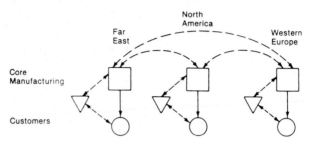

See Note on Figure 3.

the strength of several plants. In order to accomplish the kinds of process improvement transfer envisioned in the case of the specialty chemical company and the product redesign and transfer in Sunbeam Appliance Company, it is necessary that line people in different regions work together. It appears to be necessary that they time-share with their line work. The reason is that the international project rarely requires their full-time attention, and they are critical for their local business. Fortunately, the improvements in travel, telecommunications and data processing technology make it possible for operating people to be time-shared on international projects.

Accomplishing the innovation access, identification and transfer discussed above is a very difficult management challenge. This is reflected by the limited success most international manufacturing companies have had in the area. The question arises: why is there so little sharing of technology and knowledge among international plants that belong to the same company and between vendors and their international customers that work in related technologies. There appear to be several reasons that managing this type of cooperation is difficult.

(1) There are established regional organizations in most companies and consistent compensation systems. This means that managers are compensated by a system that reinforces an international franchising business strategy where every employee focuses on his local customers, and where there is no financial incentive to aid an employee of a different geographic division to increase the effectiveness of their

manufacturing or to identify an effective new product. Most compensation systems of U.S. companies, at least, reinforce the regional geographic focus of employees and discourage global cooperative thinking.

Many employees observe the opportunity to aid the company while injuring themselves under the current compensation system. In the short term most employees I encounter will aid the company in its global endeavors, but they are concerned with compensation and with the awareness of top managers of their selfless actions. If top managers do not acknowledge the sacrifice within a few years, the middle managers will leave. It is interesting to know that acknowledging the contribution top managers do not necessarily have to confer immediate financial rewards if business strategy and top management awareness reward them in the medium term. Furthermore, if this global sharing of knowledge issue is important enough, a manager might expect to be given more job responsibility in the future.

(2) Many employees confronted with the possibility that operating employees of another plant or a vendor can teach them something react with the NIH (Not Invented Here) resistance to learning more about the good ideas of the other. This can thwart good efforts to transfer technology.

(3) The ethnic, language and national differences among operating employees who might be members of an international project team could also erect difficult-to-surmount barriers. It seems to me that it would be very difficult for a plant manager to come from another culture for precisely this reason. Support staff, however, can usefully come from headquarters.

(4) To make the efforts effective it appears that line managers and technical people must be time-shared between their line work, which they know well and the international project. This requires people to work internationally, and it requires substantial travel budgets for people lower in the organization who did not travel before, as well as telecommunications investments. Of course, these budgets are commensurate with the overseas investment. A small company can be effective depending on the travel and communication of only a few key people.

It is difficult to know without much more research, but it appears that there are a number of steps that many companies go through as they work to attain manufacturing excellence. First, they do international competitive benchmarking. This was done early on by both the chemical company and by Sunbeam. Although this is typically not pleasant, it helps to set the standards for the team. In fact, this effort was essential in improving the deficient aspects of U.S. manufacturing. It is essential that top management be involved because the poorer performing organizations will always by discovered. If the attitude is taken that they must be punished or weeded out then there will be no cooperative atmosphere. If, on the other hand, the problems are to be cherished and the system improved, then everyone will be receptive. There must be a long run plan in view that makes it clear what the long-run effects of the system-wide improvements will be.

Second, they set up international manufacturing meetings. Line people from throughout the world get together and talk about their operations. Generally, some good ideas are fleshed out and transferred.

What is surprising about both these examples and other comparable ones discussed in Flaherty [1987] is that, despite problems, early efforts at international coordination were invariably quickly and richly rewarded. The potential for transferring knowledge among previously independent internationally franchised operations appears enormous. It also appears that getting receptive operating people from different locations together usually results in someone's learning something relevant to his or her own job.

The benefits to the company from these first two types of activities are large, but generally serendipitous. The specialty chemical company example suggested that there are very clear needs for sharing particular knowledge among international operations. In the meetings, the knowledge that gets shared is as much a function of which people happen to get along as of the benefit to be derived. Building interpersonal ties is critical early on. But, there should also be opportunities for managers to direct the sharing of particular knowledge about particular aspects of manufacturing capability or product design.

In the late 1980s, these efforts were just beginning. They had not yet generated many widely observed successes. Some were projects with particular goals. For example, the Sunbeam global iron that was developed by a global team with engineering and marketing critiques from each important subsidiary. Others were sister plants.

Clearly, there are many possible approaches to Triad-wide international sourcing and innovation. Only a few will be appropriate and cost-effective for a particular business. Managers will find it necessary to explore many possibilities. If they are in marketing- and technology-intensive businesses and facing international competition, they will likely find their efforts both necessary and rewarded.

## 6. MANAGERIAL ISSUES AND RESEARCH IMPLICATIONS

As managers attempt to go beyond international catalog shoppping and franchising, a number of unresolved and new issues arise. I have identified several concerns and some approaches to understanding them.

One salient issue is how the MANUFACTURING CAPABILITY of a company's sources compares with that of competitors. One research approach to the issue is a comparison of similar operations in several countries, like that presented in Schoenberger (1982) and Garvin (1983). These seminal studies, in part, demonstrate the magnitude of the disparities between U.S. and Japanese manufacturing. Further work by Abernathy, Clark and Kantrow (1984), and Hall (1987) have begun to address the reasons for the differences in performance of just-in-time and zero defects manufacturing approaches.

It would be useful to extend these studies. Managers need to understand what capabilities have been developed by their sources in countries like Singapore and Korea. They must learn about these sources' abilities to improve manufacturing processes, to alter product mix and volume, to introduce new products, and to design new products to serve their local customers. To appreciate these capabilities, however, it is necessary to extend the method of a manufacturing audit. Considerable work is needed to understand how different features of a manufacturing operation contribute to the non-cost and non-quality attributes of the product/service delivered by a company.

After the actual capabilities are better ascertained, how these capabilities are improved and enhanced must be documented. Doing business in different industrial regions apparently generates new capability. Because there are also considerable differences among companies' capabilities within countries, capability enhancement should be directed by managers. Field work in comparable companies should explore the importance of connections with vendors and customers, as well as the importance of having a local applications engineering group, their technology, their workforces, and their performance. There are questions of what measures are available, how meaningful they are, and their relation to the several performance measures. Case-based studies of individual plants would be a good first step at indicating which measures are likely to be useful. [26]

A second concern of many U.S. managers during the late 1980s was whether they were using enough international sources and whether they were using the best international sources for the best purposes. This is really a question of the STRUCTURE of the existing international sourcing network. During the 1960s and 1970s many U.S. managers whose companies had substantial offshore manufacturing had used rules of thumb which were no

longer valid during the late 1980s to guide their international sourcing
decisions. For example, formerly low cost sources in Singapore could introduce and develop even automated manufacturing processes capable of
introducing new products more quickly than some U.S. factories.
Conversely, some U.S. factories were more cost effective than many off-
shore factories for supplying the U.S. market. Managers had had similar
rules of thumb regarding their internal and external research and
development. But technology, international competition, and globalization made the simplistic approaches obsolete.

Research can be expected to improve these outdated rules of thumb. In
particular, it might focus on how to evaluate factories and the related
logistics systems on bases other than cost and yield. Factories must be
evaluated on their flexibility to new product introduction as well as to
mix and volume change and cost. Of course, these new approaches will be
considerably more complex. They will require a much more detailed ap-
praisal of the quality, reliability, service and location capabilities
of the sources. Similarly, the notion that a company can do all of its
own research and development will have to be replaced with considerations of how the research and input burden could be shared with sources.

A third issue is how much COORDINATION needs to be done and with which
sources. There are far too many potential sources worldwide to coordinate with them all. But, obviously working closely with "good" ones
could be very useful. Managers need to know how closely to coordinate
with each source. It is difficult to identify the useful ideas and
products from another foreign facility, even if the facility is part of
your own company. Doing this requires going considerably beyond the
price, product specs and delivery requirements of catalog shopping and
the annual budget process of international franchising arrangements.
Unfortunately, however, a research agenda for in-depth functional research in this area is not at all clear. This is an area where
exploratory descriptive work is in order.

Fourth are the managerial problems of IMPLEMENTATION. Effective operating managers have limited attention to devote to working with their
counterparts at foreign sources. Frequently incentive and evaluation
systems in U.S.-based multinational companies --because of the history
of success with their market-oriented approach to international business
-- penalize managers who cooperate with those located outside their organization. There are practical problems like language, time zone
differences, local customer and vendor idiosyncracies. There are even
political and national barriers, cultural differences, trade barriers,
prejudice, and the basic limitations of individual people to overcome.
Unfortunately, there are no simple remedies for these problems.

Nonetheless, whenever meetings of operating managers from related international sources are brought together with the intention of exchanging

knowledge, large and surprising benefits, nearly always, ensue. Good operating managers are in fact eager to learn from their counterparts, and they have the power to change their own practice very quickly. Of course, the benefits appear to be serendipitous, related to the ability of individuals to communicate. A major challenge for managers is to ensure that the most valuable coordination occurs, not merely the most fortuitous. There is a corresponding challenge for research.


## ACKNOWLEDGEMENTS

I wish to acknowledge the comments and suggestions of Edward Davis, Kasra Ferdows, David Garvin, Ruth Raubitschek, Robert Stobaugh as well as the participants at the Symposium on the Management of International Manufacturing, held at INSEAD in September 1987.


## NOTES

[1] They also considered governmental preferences and restrictions as well as a number of other factors. For a more complete discussion of international manufacturing location decisions, see Flaherty [1987].

[2] Many companies begin their manufacturing in foreign subsidiaries with peripheral tasks, such as assembly rather than fabrication of products, as a way to develop a manufacturing capability in the local market that could become core manufacturing. Tilton [1971], for example, illustrates just such an evolution of many manufacturing facilities for semiconductors in Europe.

[3] See Flaherty and Raubitschek [1987] for a theoretical explication of the competitive interplay that might result in such a situation.

[4] See Duerr and Roach [1973] for a survey which indicates that U.S. multinational headquarters exert their on-going influence on their European subsidiaries largely through the annual budgeting process. De Bodinat [1975] He distinguishes those companies which provide strict guidance on technology choice and policies such as compensation from those which are even less involved. His work in both cases is consistent with our observation that headquarters involvement with subsidiaries in industrialized countries is typically quite limited. Skinner [1961] provides similar support for the limited involvement of U.S. headquarters in subsidiary management in his description of production management in American subsidiaries in Turkey during the 1950s.

[5]  Stobaugh and Telesio [1983] use the term marketing-intensive for the first type of subsidiary and technology-intensive for the latter. They note that some companies use large foreign manufacturing facilities to obtain economies of scale for a region.

[6]  This separation of product design and process improvement from the manufacturing process -- and the consequent decline of process improvement -- appears to explain why the "hollowing out" of U.S. manufacturing alarms scholars like Cohen and Zysman [1987].

[7]  See Flaherty [1987] for a more extensive discussion of the development of this concept.

[8]  There are a number of cases, such as apparel and electronic components, where the core manufacturing is done in an industrialized country and some peripheral work, such as assembly and test, is performed afterwards in a less industrialized country. I categorize most of these situations as having hardly any more coordination of the sourcing than the simpler examples in the figure. For illustrative purposes, I ignore this more complex pattern in the figure.

[9]  Electrical machinery apparatus, appliances and supplies, or the industry designated in international trade statistics by number 383.

[10] Footwear, except vulcanized or molded rubber or plastic footwear. The industry is designated in international trade statistics by the number 324.

[11] The same long term trend appears to hold throughout manufacturing industries.

[12] This estimate of 20 percent cost savings appears to be a focal point for savings estimates across many industries. Sourcing from some countries appears to have been even more advantageous due to tax concessions and government subsidies.

[13] See Quick, Finan & Associates [1988].

[14] This is supported by Kaplan and Johnson [1987] who presented empirical evidence that the direct labor component of manufacturing cost is low and experiencing a long term decline throughout the world.

[15] In developing countries the wages of managers and technical staff are a higher multiple of those of direct workers than they are in the United States and other industrialized countries. For example, Amsden [1989] finds that the ratio of plant managers' salaries to those of production workers in Korea was on average 3.95 in 1980,

larger than a comparable estimate of 1.9 in the United States in 1977. In informal surveys of several hundred international participants in top management programs at Harvard Business School, Robert Hayes [1988] found that the compensation packages of U.S. top managers was generally a larger multiple of those of direct workers' than their counterparts in other industrialized economies. Nevertheless, he found that the multiple was still higher for developing countries like Korea.

[16] One possible counter to this trend would be improvements in manufacturing technology and capability that was not transferred throughout the world. Thusfar, while differences in manufacturing effectiveness and technology do arise, it appears that they also get transferred worldwide quickly enough to eliminate long term international cost dfiferentials based on manufacturing capability alone.

[17] See The Global Iron Proposal (A).

[18] See Competition in Global Industries [1987], Levitt [1983], and Ohmae [1987].

[19] See Shapiro [1985].

[20] Applichem (A).

[21] This neglects potential innovations from other than the lowest cost plant. For example, the lowest cost plant was German with the technologist's improved manufacturing process; this estimate neglects the improved waste management innovations from the Japanese plant which surely would reduce cost at other plants, even the lowest cost plant. This estimate also ignores the possibility that the product improvements accompanying cost reducing technology will enhance demand for the product. Finally, it should be noted that many of these improvements were not scale-dependent and could have been implemented in chemical plants of any size.

[22] See The Global Iron Proposal (A).

[23] See Lehnerd [1987] on the Black & Decker experience with designing global power tools.

[24] See Flaherty [1987] for a discussion of the operations problems that arise when apparently identical products do function alike in customers' manufacturing processes and products.

[25] My interpretation is that the number of manufacturing engineers in these countries is an order of magnitude greater than that in the

United States, their quality is high, and their wages are  somewhat lower.  It  appears that there are very few manufacturing engineers in the United States because the job is not prestigious and because universities have very few programs to train them.

[26] Professor Bill Fischer of the  University  of  North  Carolina  has begun work on just such a flexible plant audit procedure expecially with Chinese plants in mind.

**REFERENCES**

Harvard Business School Cases:

Applichem (A) (9-685-051) written M. Therese Flaherty.

Note on the U.S. Footwear Industry (9-687-034) written  by  Eric  Mankin under the direction of M. Therese Flaherty.

International  Sourcing  at  Intercon (9-688-055) written by Eric Mankin under the direction of M. Therese Flaherty.

Intercon Japan (9-688-056) written by Kazuhiro Mishina under the  direction of M. Therese Flaherty.

The Global Iron Proposal (A) (9-688-082) written by M. Therese Flaherty.

The Global Iron Proposal (B) (9-688-083) written by M. Therese Flaherty.

Articles and Books:

Abernathy, W. J., K.B. Clark, and A.M. Kantrow, Industrial  Renaissance, New York: Basic Books, 1983.

Amsden, Alice, Asia's Next Giant, New  York:  Oxford  University  Press, forthcoming 1989.

Caves, Richard E., Multinational Enterprise and Economic  Analysis,  New York: Cambridge University Press, 1982.

Cohen, Stephen S., and John Zysman, Manufacturing Matters, New  York: Basic Books, Inc., 1987.

Competition in Global Industries, editor Michael E. Porter, Boston: Harvard Business School Press, 1987.

De Bodinat, Henri Rene, "Influence in the Multinational Corporation: The Case of Manufacturing", Doctoral Dissertation, Harvard Business School, 1975.

Duerr, M. G., and J. M. Roach, Organization and Control of International Operations, New York: The Conference Board, 1973.

Fischer, William, Personal Communication, November 1987.

Flaherty, M. Therese, "Coordinating International Manufacturing and Technology," in Ed. Michael E. Porter, Competition in Global Industries, Boston: Harvard Business School Press, 1987.

Flaherty, M. Therese, "The Emerging Global Business Environment and Managerial Reactions to It", Prepared for the MITI Symposium on Globalized Business Activities and the International Economy, June 23-24, 1988.

Flaherty, M. Therese, and Ruth Raubitschek, "Rivalry and Global Resource Deployment," Manuscript, 1987.

Garvin, David A., "Quality on the Line," Harvard Business Review, September-October 1983, 64-75.

Grunwald, Joseph, and Kenneth Flamm, The Global Factory, Washington, D.C.: The Brookings Institution, 1985.

Hall, Robert W., Attaining Manufacturing Excellence, Homewood, Ill: Dow Jones-Irwin, 1987.

Hayes, Robert, Personal Communication, 1988. Jaikumar, Ramchandran, and Roger Bohn, "Production Management: A Dynamic Approach", Harvard Business School Working Paper 9-784-066, 1984.

Kaplan, Robert S., "One Cost System Isn't Enough," Harvard Business Review, January-February 1988, 61-66.

Kaplan, Robert S., and H. Thomas Johnson, Relevance Lost, Boston: Harvard Business School Press, 1987.

Levitt, Theodore, "The Globalization of Markets", Harvard Business Review, May-June 1983, 92-102.

Lehnerd, Alvin P., "Revitalizing the Manufacture and Design of Mature Global Products," in eds. Bruce R. Guile and Harvey Brooks, Technology and Global Industry, Washington, D.C.: National Academy Press, 1987.

Moxon, Richard W., "Offshore Production in the Less Developed Countries-," The Bulletin (New York University Graduate School of Business), (98-99), July 1974, 6-90.

Quick, Finan & Associates, "Contracting for Machining and Tooling: The Hidden Costs of Sourcing Abroad", Report for the National Tooling and Machining Association, September 1988.

Porter, Michael E., editor, Competition in Global Industries, Boston: Harvard Business School Press, 1987.

Ronstadt, Robert C., "International R&D: The Establishment and Evolution of Research and Development Abroad by Seven U.S. Multinationals," Journal of International Business Studies, Spring-Summer 1978.

Schoenberger, Richard, Japanese Manufacturing Techniques, New York: Free Press, 1982.

Shapiro, Roy D., "Toward Effective Supplier Management: International Comparisons", Harvard Business School Working Paper 9-785-062, 1985.

Skinner, C. Wickham, "Production Management of U.S. Manufacturing Subsidiaries in Turkey", Doctoral Dissertation, Harvard Business School, 1961.

Stobaugh, Robert, and Piero Telesio, "Match Manufacturing Policies and Product Strategy", Harvard Business Review, March-April 1983, 113-120.

Tilton, John E., International Diffusion of Technology: The Case of Semiconductors, Washington, D.C., The Brookings Institution, 1971.

U.S. International Trade Commission, Publication 17117, Non-Rubber Footwear, July 1985.

"U.S. Shoe's Manufacturing a Step Ahead," Cincinnati Enquirer, June 1, 1987.

PART TWO


INTERNATIONAL COMPARISONS OF MANUFACTURING MANAGEMENT

MANAGING INTERNATIONAL MANUFACTURING
K. Ferdows (Editor)
© Elsevier Science Publishers B.V. (North-Holland), 1989

OVERLAPPING PROBLEM SOLVING IN PRODUCT DEVELOPMENT

Kim B. CLARK and Takahiro FUJIMOTO

Harvard University

This paper examines management's impact on product development lead time. The empirical evidence comes from an ongoing study of product development in the world auto industry. Using data and interviews from European, Japanese and U.S. companies, we focus on the management of problem-solving and its impact on development lead time. Of particular interest is the way in which firms integrate problem-solving activities in adjacent phases of development. The evidence suggests that what we call "overlapping problem solving" characterizes the more effective projects.

1. INTRODUCTION

In a world of intense international competition, of increasingly sophisticated customers and markets, and of significant technological change, product development has become the focal point of competition in a wide variety of industries. The design of a product directly affects product cost and reliability.[1] With customers of increasing sophistication and discrimination, product content--concept, style, performance--is an important issue in product selection and differentiation. Moreover, the need to respond quickly to the moves of strong international competitors and the pace of technological change place a premium on the ability to develop products rapidly. Developing better products faster is thus at the top of the competitive agenda.

This paper examines management's impact on product development. We treat the development process as a set of information-processing activities that translate knowledge of customer needs and technical opportunities into information assets for production.[2] These activities involve recognizing, defining, and solving problems using technical capabilities.

The empirical evidence we use comes from an ongoing study of product development in the world auto industry. Using data and interviews from Japanese, European, and U.S. companies, we focus on the management of problem solving and its impact on development lead time. In particular, we examine the way in which firms integrate problem-solving activities in adjacent phases of development. To gain insight into problem-solving integration, we take an in-depth look at one aspect of the development process in microcosm: the design and production of body panels and associated production dies.

The paper begins with a brief discussion of the conceptual framework for our empirical work. We develop the notion of product development as a sequence of problem-solving cycles, and identify different ways in which firms integrate them. In the second section of the paper, we describe the auto study and present empirical evidence on lead time and modes of problem solving in Japanese and U.S. firms. The evidence suggests that what we call "overlapping problem solving" characterizes high-performance development projects. The third section of the paper discusses the managerial and operating conditions associated with "overlapping problem solving." The paper concludes with a brief summary and suggestions for further work.

## 2.  PRODUCT DEVELOPMENT AS INFORMATION PROCESSING

The development of a product involves various activities and can be examined from several vantage points. In this paper we use the notion of information processing to organize our analysis of product development. In essence, we treat product development as a set of information-processing activities that translate knowledge of market needs and technological opportunities into information assets for production. The information stock created through the development process includes product concepts, styling models, specifications, layouts, prototypes, engineering drawings, process designs, tools and dies, equipment, and software. In this framework, the product itself is a bundle of information embodied in materials.

Figure 1 shows the sequence of activities involved in a development project and the relationship between upstream and downstream activities. In our framework a project creates new information assets for production of a new model or model family in four stages -- concept generation, product planning, product engineering, and process engineering.[3] The four stages are linked in tandem, so that output information of one stage becomes the input information of the next stage. This is a simplified view of the process; as we note later, feedback and overlap among the stages may be important.

At each stage of the development process, the firm (and the relevant departments and organizations within it) is presented with a set of objectives and alternate ways of meeting them. Although some alternatives are well defined, and some choices are obvious, many objectives cannot be met with obvious alternatives. When this happens, the designers and engineers have a problem and the problem-solving cycle begins. A generic model of a problem-solving cycle is presented in Figure 2.[4] In our framework, problem solving involves a search for alternatives and a procedure for testing them to find one that provides a solution.

Cycles of problem solving occur on a small scale, such as the work of an individual engineer or small engineering group and on a large scale, such as the work of an entire department. At the product engineering stage of a car development project, for example, target performance specifications, styling models, and layouts (output information of the previous stage) are input as goals (stage 1 in Figure 2); alternative drawings are then generated (stage 2); prototypes are then built according to the drawings (stage 3); and are tested in proving grounds or laboratories (stage 4). At this point, the process may cycle again until the best possible design according to the test results, is chosen, (stage 5).

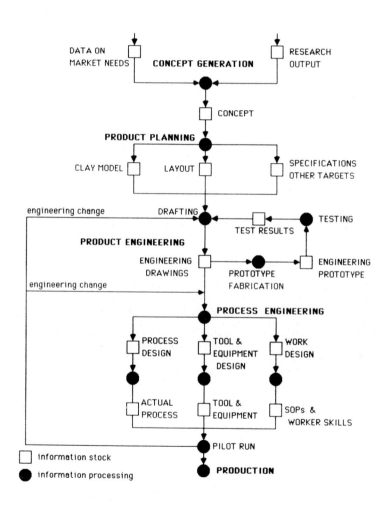

FIGURE 1    PRODUCT DEVELOPMENT AS INFORMATION PROCESSING

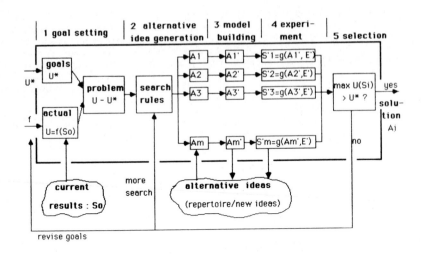

FIGURE 2    GENERIC MODEL OF PROBLEM-SOLVING CYCLES

## 2.1  Problem Solving and Product Development Performance

Within an information-processing framework, problem-solving is the dominant activity in product development. Thus, the performance of a product development project depends on the way in which the organization executes and integrates numerous problem solving cycles in each stage of development. Three interrelated dimensions of performance are critical.

**Design Quality:** This is the most important dimension in evaluating the effectiveness of product development. In a broad sense, design quality measures how well the information output of product development meets the demands of the target customer.

**Cost:** The resources used in development determine the project cost. Although the direct impact on product cost is not large, development cost affects the number of projects (and the content of a specific project) given a budget constraint.

**Lead Time:** We define overall lead time as the length of time from the initiation of concept generation to the market introduction. Stage-level lead time (concept study, product planning, advanced engineering, product engineering, process engineering, pilot run) and some step-level lead times (e.g., first prototype, body die development) are important in assessing development performance.

Our focus in this paper is on the effect of differences in problem solving on development lead time. Lead time is an important dimension in its own right, and reducing it is a point of significant management attention. But the interrelated nature of the three dimensions of performance suggests that the issue is not reductions in lead time per se, but reductions in lead time for a given level of resources and design quality.

The literature on product development and our own field experience suggest that, for a given design quality and resource base, lead time is strongly influenced by the way problem-solving cycles are linked.[5] To illustrate the choices firms face in linking problem-solving cycles, we consider two quite different approaches. The first is the "phased approach," which involves a sequential linkage; The second is the "overlapping approach," which involves parallel and integrated activity.[6)] The two approaches differ not only in timing, but also in the way information is processed. In the "phased approach" for example:

1. The upstream stage releases information to the downstream stage only after completing its activities and finalizing its output (batch transmission of information).

2. The downstream stage starts its activities only after it receives complete information from the upstream stage. Thus, the downstream group assumes the information it receives from the upstream group is certain.

3. Information flows from upstream to downstream; upstream influences downstream, but not vice versa.

Information processing in the "overlapping approach" is quite different:

1. The upstream stage gradually releases preliminary output information to the downstream stage before the information is finalized (piece-by-piece transmission of information).

2. The downstream stage uses the preliminary information as clues to forecast the final outcome of the upstream activities. The downstream group thus starts its activities before upstream output is complete, and provides the upstream group with timely feedback.

Overlapping may be observed at various levels. There may be "large" overlapping between major problem-solving cycles, such as starting production preparation before product engineering is complete. There may also be "small" overlapping within a particular cycle, such as starting

prototype fabrication before engineering drawings are done. The two
approaches are illustrated in Figure 3. Each bar chart represents a
particular problem-solving cycle or step, one in the upstream and the
other in the downstream. The blackened portion of each bar chart shows
the level of certainty (level of knowledge) about the upstream output from
the upstream and downstream points of view respectively.

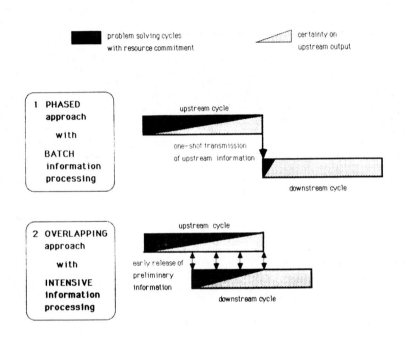

FIGURE 3    ALTERNATIVE APPROACHES OF LINKING PROBLEM SOLVING CYCLES

As Figure 3 makes clear, overlapping may reduce overall lead time if the
lead time of each individual cycle (length of each bar) does not increase
with overlapping. To realize that potential involves more than simply
operating in parallel. For effective operation of overlapping, problem
solving must be integrated through dense, reciprocal flows of information.
Effectiveness is not only a matter of timing of activities; management of
information flows during the overlapped period is also critical.

## 3.  MEASUREMENT AND EMPIRICAL EVIDENCE

In this section of the paper, we use data and evidence from our study of product development in the world auto industry to examine the relationship between development lead times and the management of problem solving. The auto industry study is focused on the management of product development and its impact on performance. The study is international in scope; participating firms come from Japan (8), Europe (9), and the United States (3). In each firm, we study one or two development projects using both in-depth interviews and a questionnaire to develop data on the project and its management. These projects are major model changes involving extensive design of components and systems.[7]

The framework outlined above suggests that variations in lead time (for a given level of resources and design quality) may be affected by the degree and nature of "overlapping" in problem solving between upstream and downstream activities. To examine this hypothesis, we first present data on lead times from our sample of projects. We then explore the relationship between lead time and two aspects of problem solving: 1) the degree of parallelism in the timing of activities; and 2) the nature of information processing. We examine the first aspect using timing data on the projects as a whole and in specific stages. We examine patterns of information processing through an in-depth comparative analysis of the development process in microcosm: the design and development of body panels (e.g., fenders) and associated dies.

### 3.1  Lead Time in Car Development Projects

Table 1 presents data on lead time, measured in months from market introduction, as well as length of development stages for auto projects. Besides the four major stages outlined in our basic framework (concept, planning, product engineering, and process engineering), we have added data on advanced engineering and pilot production. The projects in each region cover a similar range: from micro-mini cars to mid-sized sedans, including small vans. However, the data in Table 1 are raw averages with no adjustment for differences in project content, resources, or design quality.

Table 1

Average Project Lead Time and Stage Length
European, U.S., and Japanese Automakers

| DEVELOPMENT PHASE | JAPANESE | | | UNITED STATES | | | EUROPE | | |
|---|---|---|---|---|---|---|---|---|---|
| | begin | end | stage length | begin | end | stage length | begin | end | stage length |
| concept study | 42.6 | 34.3 | 8.3 | 61.9 | 44.0 | 18.0 | 62.6 | 49.6 | 13.1 |
| product planning | 37.8 | 29.0 | 8.8 | 57.0 | 39.2 | 17.8 | 58.2 | 40.8 | 17.4 |
| advanced engineering | 41.8 | 26.6 | 15.2 | 56.4 | 29.9 | 26.5 | 54.9 | 41.5 | 13.5 |
| product engineering | 29.6 | 5.8 | 23.8 | 40.1 | 11.6 | 28.6 | 41.8 | 18.6 | 23.2 |
| process engineering | 27.7 | 6.1 | 21.6 | 30.9 | 5.5 | 25.4 | 36.6 | 9.7 | 26.8 |
| pilot run | 7.1 | 2.7 | 4.4 | 9.2 | 2.7 | 6.5 | 9.8 | 3.5 | 6.4 |
| TOTAL | | | 82.2 | | | 122.6 | | | 100.3 |

NOTE:   data in months
        sample size:  Japan          12
                      United States   6
                      Europe         11

The data suggest sharp differences between Japanese and other producers in the timing of activities and the overall pattern of development. Except for process engineering and pilot run, which begin about the same distance from market introduction, the U.S. and European firms begin activities much earlier. For this sample of projects, overall lead time is 19 months shorter in Japan, and detailed product planning begins about 20 months later on Japanese projects for a car introduced at the same time.

When one looks, however, at the total stage time, the differences are even greater: 81 months in Japan, 100 months in Europe, and 117 months in the United States. The difference between the U.S. and Europe largely is due to differences in advanced engineering. The differences with the Japanese suggest that there is a significant amount of parallelism (in the timing sense) in the U.S. development cycle. The data show that parallel timing is most significant in the early stages of development, and that the early stages account for much of the difference in total stage time. Long stage length and significant overlap in concept study and product planning are probably connected; without overlap, the long stage length would make the program untenable.

A look at the engineering of the product and the process shows much less difference in stage length, but also more parallel activity in the Japanese case. Although process engineering starts at about the same time in the U.S. and Japan, product engineering begins and ends about seven to nine months closer to the market in Japan. The European data show that product and process engineering start about ten to twelve months earlier than the Japanese and a few months earlier than projects in the U.S. The data suggest that the product and process engineering are somewhat more "phased" or sequential in the U.S. and Europe. Thus, although the actual engineering stage lengths are quite similar, the overall lead time is much shorter in Japan.

### 3.2 Overlapping and Lead Time: The Case of Parallel Timing

The data in Table 1 suggest that parallel timing of activities may explain some of the advantage in lead time one observes in the Japanese projects. This seems to be the case in the timing of product and process engineering. However, these data are raw averages. Differences in the nature of the products may affect the impact of parallel timing. To examine the timing issue more carefully and to examine its impact within each country, we have developed a measure of the simultaneity in adjacent project phases and applied it to the project data. We define the simultaneity ratio as follows:

$$SR_i = \frac{\sum_{j=1}^{N} t_{ij}}{T_i}$$

Where SR$_i$ is the simultaneity ratio of the i-th project; t is the lead time of the j-th development stage in the i-th project; T$_i$ is the total project lead time (from concept study to market introduction); and N is the number of stages in one project.

The simultaneity ratio is unity in the phased approach and equals N when N stages achieve complete simultaneity. From the above formula, we also have the following:

$$SR_i = \frac{\sum_{j=1}^{N} t_{ij}}{SR_i}$$

This equation makes it clear that the observed relationship between the simultaneity ratio and lead time will depend on how stage length and simultaneity are related. In a cross-sectional data set, such as the one we examine, there are two extreme cases.

If regulatory action or collusion or some other means creates a standard lead time in the industry, simultaneity will vary directly with stage length. In this situation, firms use simultaneity to compensate for changes in stage length to meet industry standards on total lead time. If, in contrast, industry norms on simultaneity have been established, so that firms choose a degree of simultaneity independent of stage length, lead time will vary directly with stage length. Simultaneity, however, will have no effect on lead time.

Between the two extremes lie a range of possibilities. For example, a higher degree of simultaneity will reduce total lead time if stage lengths are fairly stable and are not affected by simultaneity. However, if parallel timing increases stage length (e.g. perhaps because of premature commitments or confusion because of poor information), or if parallel timing occurs because of difficult problems in development, then a higher degree of simultaneity may be associated with longer lead times. Thus, the impact of parallel timing is an empirical question. Moreover, assessment of the impact of simultaneity on lead time requires that we take into account differences in project characteristics.

Table 2 presents data on the simultaneity index in the sample, and examines the relationship between the degree of simultaneity and selected project characteristics. Data are presented for the project as a whole and for the engineering phase of development. The mean values of SR show more simultaneity in the Japanese projects, while the timing is least parallel in the European projects.

Table 2

Simultaneity and Project Characteristics

| | | Mean Values | | | | Regression Analysis | | | | | | | |
|---|---|---|---|---|---|---|---|---|---|---|---|---|---|
| | | Japan | Europe | U.S. | Total | CONS | PRICE[a] | MICRO | BODY | NH | JAPAN | $R^2$ | SEE | d.f. |
| 1. | Simultaneity Ratio - overall | 1.63 | 1.37 | 1.54 | 1.51 | .58 (.35) | .14 (.07 | -.06 (.20) | .06 (.06) | 1.02 (.42) | .43 (.14) | .35 | .29 | 22 |
| 2. | Simultaneity Ratio - engineering | 1.76 | 1.55 | 1.58 | 1.64 | 1.13 (.26) | .13 (.05) | .25 (.15) | .04 (.04) | .24 (.31) | .26 (.10) | .38 | .21 | 22 |

[a]Coefficient has been multiplied by $10^4$.

Note:

    CONS - constant term
    PRICE - retail price of vehicle in 1987 U.S. dollars
    MICRO - dummy variable = 1 if vehicle is micro-mini car
    BODY - number of body types developed on the project
    NH - new, in-house ratio -- function of engineering effort done in-house by the project team
    JAPAN - dummy variable = 1 if project developed by Japanese company

To examine the impact of differences in project characteristics on parallel timing we estimate a simple regression with SR as the dependent variable. In addition to a dummy variable for Japan, the regression includes a set of control variables measuring differences in engineering activity in the project (fraction of parts that are new and developed in-house) and the complexity of the product (body size, number of body types, price).

The results in Table 2 show a significantly higher degree of simultaneity in the Japanese projects, while the evidence on engineering activity and product complexity is mixed. In the overall results, a higher price (implying more complex engineering) and more in-house engineering are associated with a higher degree of simultaneity, although the association is not strong. In the engineering results, price has a positive effect, while the in-house engineering variable is insignificant. There is thus some evidence of a relationship between SR and the scope and difficulty of a project, but the data is weak on this issue and strong conclusions are not warranted. Indeed, much of the variation in SR is not explained by these variables. This is consistent with evidence we uncovered in our interviews that the degree of simultaneity in timing is often a matter of policy or standard procedure and is determined independent of the content of the project.

The impact of simultaneity on lead time is examined in Table 3. We use both overall lead time and engineering lead time -- defined as the time from beginning of detailed engineering (either product or process) to final engineering release -- as dependent variables, and include the same

Table 3

Simultaneity and Lead Time
(standard errors in parentheses)

| Dependent Variable | CONS | PRICE[a] | MICRO | BODY | NH | JAPAN | SR | J*SR | $R^2$ | SEE | d.f. |
|---|---|---|---|---|---|---|---|---|---|---|---|
| 1. Overall lead time | | | | | | | | | | | |
| a) | 38.3 (11.6) | .58 (.25) | -2.9 (6.3) | .43 (1.94) | 33.2 (14.6) | -9.6 (5.2) | -2.0 (6.6) | -- | .68 | 8.9 | 21 |
| b) | 30.5 (12.4) | .57 (.24) | -4.3 (6.2) | .48 (1.89) | 29.1 (14.5) | 18.0 (19.1) | 4.9 (7.9) | -17.9 (12.0) | .71 | 8.7 | 20 |
| 2. Engineering lead time | | | | | | | | | | | |
| a) | 32.4 (9.4) | .21 (.16) | -5.8 (4.2) | -.78 (1.23) | 9.7 (8.3) | -.23 (3.13) | -3.9 (5.7) | -- | .43 | 5.6 | 21 |
| b) | 31.5 (10.7) | .21 (.17) | -5.6 (4.5) | -.78 (1.26) | 9.6 (8.5) | 3.5 (20.2) | -3.3 (6.8) | -2.2 (12.1) | .43 | 5.8 | 20 |

[a]Coefficient multiplied by $10^3$

Note: CONS - constant term
PRICE - retail price of vehicle in 1987 U.S. dollars
MICRO - dummy variable = 1 if vehicle is micro-mini car
BODY - number of body types developed on the project
NH - new, in-house ratio -- function of engineering effort done in-house by the project team
JAPAN - dummy variable = 1 if project developed by Japanese company

control variables as before. In both the overall and the engineering results, we find a negative relationship between lead time and parallel timing, but the estimates are neither substantively nor statistically significant.

There is some evidence in the data that the weak estimates are due to very different behavior in the U.S., Europe and Japan. At least in terms of overall lead time, the relationship between SR and lead time is much stronger in Japan. To illustrate this point, we added to the regression a variable measuring the interaction between the Japan dummy and SR. The coefficient on this variable captures the difference between Japan and the rest of the sample in the impact of simultaneity on lead time.

The interaction term is negative in both the engineering and overall results, but it is significant only in the latter. Thus, in the development process as a whole, it appears that a higher degree of simultaneity is associated with shorter lead times in Japan. In detailed engineering, however, no strong relationship between simultaneity and lead time emerges, although the coefficient is negative in both Japan and the U.S. and Europe. The problem in finding any strong relationship between parallel timing and lead time is evident in Figures 4 and 5, which graph the relationship between SR and lead time, after both variables have been adjusted for differences in project characteristics.

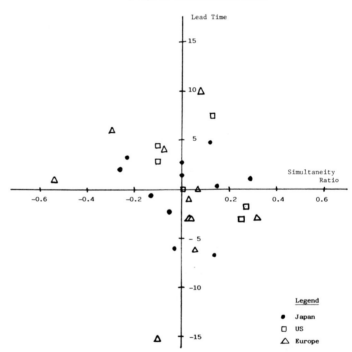

FIGURE 4    LEAD TIME VERSUS SIMULTANEITY RATIO--ENGINEERING

In Figure 4, the moderate negative relationship in Japan is apparent in the overall Japanese data, while the overall data for U.S. and Europe is scattered in a random pattern. In the engineering results, we see a negative pattern for much of the Japanese sample, but a few Japanese firms appear to have a policy that product and process engineering starts at the same time (i.e. SR=2), irrespective of project content. The result is a weak negative estimate in Japan. A similar conclusion emerges for the U.S. and European data. For some part of the sample one can find a negative relationship, but there are a few cases that do not conform to that pattern, leading to an overall weak negative estimate for the U.S. and Europe.

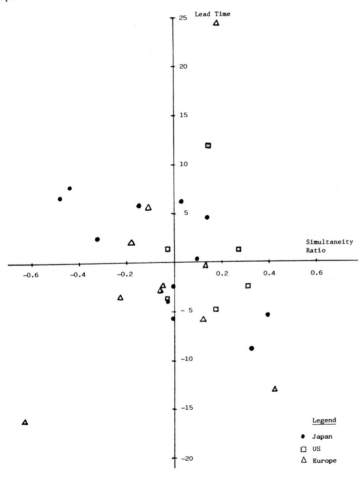

FIGURE 5    LEAD TIME VERSUS SIMULTANEITY RATIO--OVERALL

Taken as a whole, the evidence suggests that parallel timing may bear a different relationship to lead time in Japan than is true in the U.S. or Europe. However, we did not find a strong relationship between the degree of simultaneity and lead time. As noted above, part of this may be due to the different relationships between stage length and parallel timing that may arise in a given project. But it may also be due to the fact that we have examined the problem at a very high level of aggregation (e.g. overall product and process engineering). There may be important effects ofpparallel timing on lead time within the numerous activities that make up the aggregate project phases. It may be the simultaneity of such activities within the larger stages of development that is important for overall lead time.

Furthermore, we have examined simultaneity in timing without taking into consideration the second important aspect of problem solving: the nature of information processing. Without effective communication, simultaneity in timing may be dysfunctional. Thus, the important issue may be less the degree of simultaneity per se, and much more the effectiveness with which simultaneity is managed. In order to pursue these issues in a specific case, we turn to the problem of designing body panels and associated dies.

### 3.3  Integrated Problem Solving in Die Design and Die Making

The framework developed in Section II identified two distinguishing features of the information processing that integrates upstream and downstream activities in "overlapping problem solving." The first is that many small bits of "early" information -- i.e., incomplete, possibly fragmentary -- move up and downstream; and second, that the information bits are an integral part of the problem-solving process in both domains. To examine these propositions and to study how information processing may affect lead time development performance, one needs specific and detailed data about upstream and downstream problems and their solutions. Although overlapping may occur at several levels in development, we have chosen to pursue the detailed and specific data in one particular set of activities where product and process engineering are intimately connected: designing body panels and dies for their production.

Although the design and development of body panels and dies fits the requirements for data, there are several other reasons that make this activity attractive for study. Die development for body panels is a major component of process engineering in car development. Die design/making is on the critical path in product development projects. Shortening this step would shorten the total lead time. Overlapping die development with product engineering, the upstream process, could also further shorten the total lead time.

There are two kinds of dies in automobile development: prototype dies and production dies. Although the former is no less important in performance of product development, we will focus on production dies. Die design/

making consists of very complicated information processing, from line
drawings of the body (exterior and structure) all the way to a set of
stamping dies. An example of this process, based on evidence from a
Japanese die maker, is sketched out in Figure 6.

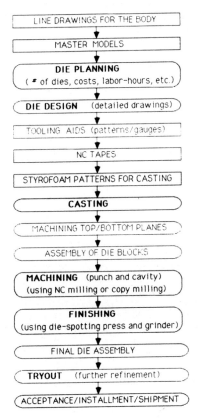

NOTE: Actual activities are not always sequential as the diagram suggests.

**FIGURE 6    DIE DEVELOPMENT PROCESS IN A TYPICAL JAPANESE DIE MAKER**

The companies in our sample were asked to provide data on the time
required to design and fabricate the dies for a major body panel, such as
a fender. We divided the total die lead time into three phases:

1. From the first release of rough part drawings to the final
   detail drawing release. (The former triggers the basic die-
   planning process and the latter means official commitment for
   tooling orders.)

2. From the final part release to the delivery of the dies. (Part
   of the design and most of the manufacturing process occur in
   this period.)

3. From die delivery to the completion of tryouts. (Dies are
   ready for pilot production at this point.)

Averages for the U.S. and Japanese projects are presented in Table 4. The
data show that the U.S. firms take almost twice as long to go from initial
release of the body panel drawing (and start of die planning) to a

Table 4

Die Lead Time (Months)

|  | Japan | United States | Europe |
|---|---|---|---|
| First to last release | 3.2 | 8.5 | 6.0 |
| Release to delivery | 5.6 | 14.3 | 15.6 |
| Delivery to finished die | 4.2 | 4.4 | 6.0 |
| TOTAL | 13.8[a] | 24.8 | 27.6 |

[a]The total for Japan includes an observation that is not included in
the sub-categories; the sub-categories, therefore, do not add to the
total.

Note: Sample size:  Japan  11
                    U.S.   6
                    Europe 8

production die ready for pilot production. To understand this radical difference and the role of overlapping problem solving, we conducted a series of interviews on the details of this process. A schematic summary of the process for the Japanese firms is presented in Figure 7, and for the U.S. firms, in Figure 8.

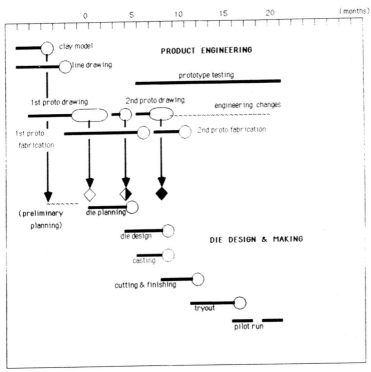

FIGURE 7   HYPOTHETICAL TIMING CHART OF DIE DEVELOPMENT

A TYPICAL JAPANESE CASE

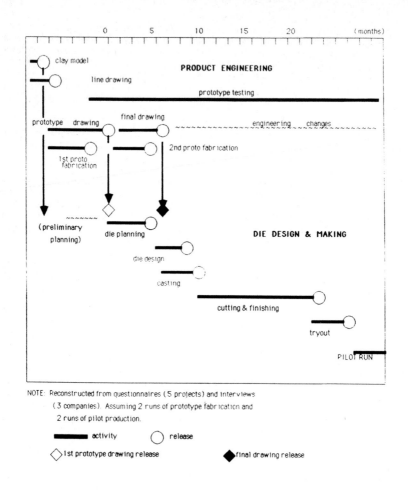

FIGURE 8     HYPOTHETICAL TIMING CHART OF DIE DEVELOPMENT

A TYPICAL U.S. CASE

The patterns in these figures are quite different. We look first at the Japanese process and describe the typical pattern of overlapping information release from product engineering (upstream) to die design/fabrication (downstream). Following are the main features of the process.

1. As the upstream activities, such as product planning, prototype drawing, prototype fabrication, and prototype testing make progress, preliminary information on body designs is gradually released to die people. Early information release at product planning stages includes clay models, line drawings, and digitized styling data. At this stage, die engineers start preliminary planning.

2. Full-scale die planning starts with the first prototype drawing release. Planning includes the estimation of die costs and labor-hour requirements.

3. The next milestone is a drawing release for tooling orders. This is separate from and earlier than the final engineering drawing release. The tooling order release comes even before the completion of the first-generation prototype. At this point, die engineers start detailed die designs, especially for dies with longer lead time, such as those for rear fenders.

4. Final release occurs before the last generation of engineering prototypes are complete. Final release is the go-ahead for cutting dies.

Even after final release, engineering changes linger on, in response both to prototype testing and pilot runs. At the peak time, hundreds of changes are ordered per month. Die people try to absorb these changes at minimum cost by using cutting margins, build-up welding, and replacement blocks. Scrapping a whole die is rare and depends on company policy.

The diagram of the Japanese process underscores the importance of early information and its integration into downstream and upstream work. The process is not just a paper exercise; the die engineers act on the information they receive and begin to make commitments (design tools, cut metal) before upstream work is officially complete. There is something of an art involved. Information is gradually released from upstream, while downstream engineers process that information step by step, making subtle trade-offs between the risk of change and the benefit of starting early.

There are several contrasts with the U.S. process, particularly in the commitments the die engineers make based on upstream information. Looking at Figure 8, we note the following about the U.S. process:

(1) Die planning starts with the first prototype drawing release, but few commitments are made.

(2) There is no formal release for tooling orders, separate from the final drawing release.

(3) Final release comes only after the completion of the last generation of prototypes. This, combined with longer prototype lead time, may push up the final release time.

(4) Japanese makers start die design on tooling order release, while the U.S. makers seem to start on final release. The U.S. engineers thus cut metal a few months after final release, which means further delay.

(5) Die manufacturing lead time is significantly longer in the U.S. process.

(6) Tryout and finishing are significantly shorter in the U.S. process.

Two aspects of the United States – Japan comparison deserve further comment: 1) the die-making process and 2) the timing of commitments. One of the most striking differences between the U.S. and Japanese processes is the time required to manufacture the dies. Our investigation of this difference suggests that it stems from fundamental differences in the way the production process is organized. Traditionally, dies have been produced in a classic "job-shop" process.[8] In this set-up, various types of machine tools are grouped together, and the work pieces (dies in process) move back and forth around the shop in a jumbled flow depending on the particular set of operations required. To maintain a high utilization rate of people and machines, job shops typically create a sizeable queue of work pieces in front of each operation. In this way, individual operations are kept fairly independent and problems or delays in one area will not spill over into other areas.

These policies create a very flexible process, but one in which throughput time is quite high. Although the actual metal-cutting time may only be a matter of hours, a work piece may spend several weeks in a job shop because of waiting and transportation time. This seems to explain the long manufacturing time in the U.S. process. The die manufacturing step in the Japanese process, outlined in Figure 7, is organized differently. Using "just-in-time" manufacturing concepts (e.g., low work-in-process inventory, multifunction workers) the Japanese die producers have substantially reduced the amount of waiting time, and thus the throughput time for dies.[9]

The timing of commitments provides another example of sharp contrast between the U.S. and Japanese processes. The Japanese firms use an "early design, early cut" paradigm, which seems to imply a long tryout period, and many engineering changes. This is in fact what we observe: the tryout period is twice as long as in the U.S. process (i.e., 4 months vs. 2 months.) We also uncovered a good deal of qualitative evidence of large numbers of engineering changes after final release. In contrast, the U.S. paradigm seems to be "wait to design, wait to cut." It appears that the strategy behind waiting is to avoid extensive changes and the possible risk of obsolete dies. We find, however, that the cost of engineering changes accounts for a relatively large fraction of the budget for die design and construction in U.S. firms. Japanese auto companies typically include a 10 to 15 percent margin for engineering changes, while firms in the United States often allow margins for engineering changes that are 3 to 4 times as great.

The higher relative share of engineering change costs suggest that the number and/or magnitude of changes may be higher in the United States. But it may also be true that the cost of making a given kind of change is relatively lower in Japan. The hypothesis is that the kind of problem-solving capability that allows the Japanese firms to adopt a paradigm of "early design, early cut" also allows them to make subsequent engineering changes at lower cost. We plan to examine this hypothesis in our subsequent work.

## 4.  THE MANAGERIAL PROCESSES FOR OVERLAPPING

The previous section has documented the very different levels of performance and the very different processes of die design/making in U.S. and Japanese auto firms. We have sketched out the relationship between the timing of activities and the structure of information processing. It seems clear that what we have called overlapping problem-solving may explain an important part of the performance differences.

Yet the introduction of overlapping without the appropriate managerial or organizational conditions may cause serious side effects, such as lower design quality, unintended schedule delay, and loss of motivation. These conditions are all related to management of information, uncertainty and risk between upstream and downstream. Moreover, effective overlapping also clearly depends on a different set of skills and operating capabilities.

We consider four aspects of management and capability:

(1) downstream skill in, and a willingness to, forecast upstream changes and to cope with them flexibly.

(2) upstream skill in, and a willingness to, forecast consequences of its output to downstream and to cope with them.

(3) integration mechanisms to handle increased information load between upstream and downstream; and attitudes which facilitate integration.

(4) operating capabilities in short-cycle production systems.

### (1)   Downstream Conditions

Forecasting:  From the downstream point of view, overlapping means that it has to start problem-solving before the problem is well defined; goals fluctuate while the group tries to achieve the goals. The downstream group has to learn to live comfortably with this ambiguity. First of all, the downstream group has to develop skill in forecasting the final form of the upstream output using the "clues" available at each stage. Close communication and cross-participation between upstream and downstream is the key for development of such skills. In die development, for example, forecasting the magnitude of the engineering changes for each stage is the key to deciding when to start die design, when to start machining, and so on.

Making Trade-offs:  Based on its forecast, the downstream group has to make a flying start. There are always risks associated with this. Downstream needs therefore to know how to make trade-offs between the risks of change and the benefits of an early start. For example, die designers make the cutting margin of dies as thin as possible, based on their assessment of the possible magnitude of die design changes. This reduces costs and time for subsequent machining. However, if the cutting margin is too thin, one may not be able to absorb the engineering changes, resulting in higher rework cost. Knowing how to make trade-offs is a crucial factor in die design.

Flexibility: Forecasts are important, but one cannot fully depend on the forecast. The downstream group thus needs flexibility to cope with unexpected changes. Developing skills of quick diagnosis and quick remedy are very important here. In die making, for example, unexpected engineering changes in the upstream are inevitable. The question is, then, how to minimize the negative results of such changes. Part of this involves techniques such as build-up welding or clever use of cutting margins. But part of it involves short set ups and rapid "changeovers" in the production process.

## (2)    Upstream Conditions

Early Feedback: Upstream people, on the other hand, have to forecast the consequences of their own output to the downstream areas and take them into account up-front. Early feedback from downstream, as well as early involvement of downstream in upstream stages, is of particular importance. For example, body and styling engineers need to get information on the manufacturability and costs of their designs by involving die engineers at the early development stages, such as concept generation and product planning. These efforts will reduce subsequent surprises on both sides, reducing uncertainties and facilitating overlapping.

Reducing Unnecessary Changes: Upstream should also make efforts to reduce unnecessary engineering changes. This does not mean that they should eliminate changes altogether. Certain engineering changes to improve competitiveness are desirable for the long-term survival of the product. Meaningless changes due to careless design mistakes and miscommunication, however, should be reduced. Also, engineering changes due to ignorance of downstream requirements and constraints such as, manufacturability and maintainability, have to be minimized. These two types of changes cause downstream disappointment and reduce motivation for a flying start.

## (3)    Upstream-Downstream Integration

Integration Mechanisms: As we have seen, the overlapping approach requires more complicated information processing between upstream and downstream than does the phased approach. More preliminary information is released in small batches. People have to forecast and reforecast what others will do. Small feedback loops are needed to facilitate quick mutual adjustments. All these features imply larger information loads across upstream and downstream functions. This implies that successful overlapping requires mechanisms for effective integration across the organizational units. Our interviews suggest that the Japanese companies use various integration mechanisms to handle the large information work load. We found that direct personal contacts across functions, liaison roles at each unit, cross-functional task forces, cross-functional project teams, and a system of "product manager as integrator" were used extensively in product development in the Japanese companies. However, the mix is significantly different from company to company.

uncertainties, can alter their strategies to provide more manufacturing flexibility.

Our model is normative in the sense that we expect companies which adhere to it to have higher performance than those which do not. For example, the model implies that strategic needs influence manufacturing flexibility and ultimately the selection of compatible programmable automation. Alternatively, computerized technology may become an end in itself. The emphasis is on making it larger, increasing its degree of automation, and implementing it faster. Purchased technology influences the kinds and degrees of flexibility which in turn constrain strategic objectives in directions not compatible with the environment. This lack of compatibility will reduce performance.

## 2.1. Fleshing Out the Model

As a further step in model construction we have identified six critical environmental uncertainties and linked each with a strategic objective and a type of manufacturing flexibility. In Table 1, the first four sets are market oriented because uncertainty originates in the nature of the demand for products. The last two sets are process oriented since uncertainty lies in the manufacturing technology and/or its inputs.

### TABLE 1

### LINKS BETWEEN THE MODEL'S KEY CONCEPTS

| Uncertainties | Strategic Objectives | Flexibilities |
|---|---|---|
| Demand for the kinds of products offered | Product Diversity | Mix |
| Length of product life cycles | Product Innovation | Changeover |
| Approximate product characteristics | Customer Requirements | Modification |
| Amount of aggregate product demand | Market Share | Volume |
| Machine downtime | Customer Delivery Times | Routing |
| Process functions or input characteristics | Product Quality | Specification |

Uncertainty as to which products the market will accept produces a strategic need for product diversity. One way to meet this need is to incorporate mix flexibility into the factory. Then the capability of handling a range of products without having to resort to changeovers is built in.

Uncertainty in the length of product life cycles creates a strategic need for product innovation over time. A factory therefore requires changeover flexibility, the ability to substitute new products for those currently in the mix.

When a firm introduces a new product or modifies a standardized design, uncertainty exists as to which product attributes customers desire. The associated objective of meeting customer requirements can be attained through modification flexibility. Then the potential exists for implementing minor design changes in a given product.

Uncertainty in the level of demand for a company's products impedes the objective of increasing or maintaining marketing share. A factory with volume flexibility can adjust production upwards or downwards within a large range. Then unexpected surges in demand can be met by increasing production.

Uncertainty in the form of machine breakdowns hampers the strategic need to meet delivery times specified by customers. A factory with rerouting flexibility allows alteration of the sequence of processes through which the developing product moves so that uncontrollable delays will not halt production.

Uncertainties in the functioning of the manufacturing technology or in the composition and dimensions of inputs hamper realizing a product quality objective. Incorporating specification flexibility into a factory contributes to reducing defects because human and mechanical adjustments exist to cope with unexpected variations.

## 2.2. International Comparisons

The model explores manufacturing flexibility in a given society. How can it be adapted for making international comparisons? We need to show which parts are likely to differ for companies with the same task environments in contrasting societies. Then we need to determine which variables may account for these differences. In so doing we will be identifying research problems that require intensive study. To date, the few comparative studies on topics related to the model have tended to be exploratory and qualitative in nature.

Culture, the pattern of norms and roles embedded in a society's paramount values [11], may account for a significant portion of net national differences once task environment effects have been considered. Because it is such an ambiguous concept its use as an explanatory variable has often been implicit. Net differences in organizational characteristics are frequently just assumed to be cultural in nature. Instead theory building based on specific cultural factors is needed [4]. Theory building, however, must deal with the possibility that culture influences qualitative organizational factors more so than quantitative ones. For example, it may influence the content of and inter-relationships among roles more than the number of different roles [4].

Moving from right to left in Figure 1 we would expect to find net national differences in the characteristics of programmable automation on the shop floor. These differences may be in hardware and software characteristics such as size (number of machines), degree of integration, degree of automation, and complexity. However, workforce characteristics such as work organization, skills and training are most likely to be affected, with culture being a significant explanatory variable.

Sorge et al. [14] studied twelve West German and British firms using CNC equipment. They focused on who does parts programming as an indicator of the type of work organization. Given the task environment (in terms of factory size and batch size) they found that a specific cultural factor, a nation's system of education and training, was influential. British companies exhibited a greater degree of job specialization brought about by an educational and training system which separates technical and operating apprenticeships. Programming was more likely to be done by planners and production engineers than operators. In Germany less job specialization exists due in part to a national training system in which those who first achieve operating status can then aspire to technical positions. Consequently, operators are more likely to share in programming tasks.

There may be national differences in the kinds and/or amounts of manufacturing flexibility existing in similar situations. One possible reason is differences in the mix of methods used to obtain flexibility. American companies, for example, may rely on programmable automation, while Japanese and Swedish firms may depend upon the talents and motivation of employees. Second, differences may exist in the way a particular method is used. Jaikumar [10] surveyed flexible manufacturing systems in Japan and the United States which made similar products and had similar technical characteristics. He discovered that average mix flexibility in terms of the number of parts produced was ninety-three in Japan and ten in the United States. Average changeover flexibility in terms of the number of new parts introduced per year was twenty-two in Japan and only one in the United States. Jaikumar attributed these large gaps to the ways in which the systems were managed, knowledge readily transferable to other societies.

At the strategic level net national differences may exist in the emphasis placed on adapting to and regulating uncertainties. The extent to which culture is an explanation is not well understood. Japanese companies excel in neutralizing uncertainties, especially those which are process-oriented, thus eliminating some need for flexibility [9],[12]. The Just-in-Time system depends upon uncertainty regulation in order to freeze production schedules, to have parts arrive on time, and to produce high quality items. Japanese flexible manufacturing systems have high utilization rates because they are designed to eliminate anticipated contingencies [10].

Simultaneously Japanese firms are proficient in adapting to uncertainties which occur unexpectedly or as the result of removing in-process inventories. If something goes wrong the whole manufacturing operation is quickly notified and works together to solve it [9]. This flexibility is achieved through automated monitoring devices, multiskilled workers, and the authority for workers to stop the line.

Compared to the Japanese, American operations managers spend less time regulating uncertainties and more time adapting to unanticipated crises. U.S. factories may therefore have more sophisticated methods for attaining flexibility. This approach's danger is that flexibility may be used as a crutch. It is tempting to avoid searching out the root causes of technical problems, to eschew rigorously adhering to standards, and to be overly tolerant of mistakes, when adjustments can be made to the resulting crises. American firms' experience with in-process inventories, a major source of flexibility, is a case in point.

International comparisons of the developmental process would be invaluable in helping American and European firms meet the East Asian competitive challenge. First, does the process found by Abernathy [1] to exist for certain U.S. industries apply to the same industries in other countries? Second, how do mature industries in industrialized lands deal with new competitive uncertainties requiring more manufacturing flexibility? Comparisons could be made of the form the revitalization process takes in different countries. It would also be useful to compare the role of inertial forces such as adherence to mass production assumptions or short term orientations in impeding successful accommodations. The aforementioned cultural factor, a nation's education and training system, may help explain the existence of certain inertial forces if recent criticisms of American business schools are valid.

## 3. A PILOT STUDY

Our initial empirical work was a pilot study involving a limited but important part of the conceptual model. We focused on the work organization characteristics of programmable automation, and on the relationship of manufacturing flexibility to the new technology. This was done in the United States and France so that international comparisons could be made. To have some control over task environment effects at a broad level we conducted the study in automobile plants in both countries.

Two American and one French auto company participated. Each was represented by a single plant. Within the plants key steps in manufacturing a car were studied. These included three engine fabrication activities (EF1, EF2, EF3), two engine assembly activities (CA1, CA2) and two body assembly activities (BA1, BA2). Three of the activities were in American plants (EF1, BA1, BA2) and four were in the French plant (EF2, EF3, CA1, CA2).

For each activity we investigated changes in work organization and manufacturing flexibility which accompanied a switch from conventional to programmable technology. The latter was defined as a means of production for which the functions are controlled by computers, microprocessors or programmable controllers (PCs). This meant transfer lines with PCs in the fabrication activities, conveyors and programmable machines controlled by PCs in the engine assembly activities, and conveyors and robots run by PCs in the body assembly areas.

Data were collected using a twenty-four page structured instrument containing questions on specific flexibility, innovation, production process, capacity, work organization and performance characteristics. Each question used a five point scale to inquire whether a particular characteristic had decreased a lot(-2), decreased (-1), not changed (0), increased (+1), or increased a lot(+2). The questionnaire was administered to one knowledgeable person in each activity.

## 3.1. Work Organization Results

Table 2 shows changes in various work organization characteristics for the six manufacturing activities for which data are available. Country effects between the United States and France turned out to be stronger than detailed task effects between fabrication and assembly. The methodology employed for this determination reflected the paucity of data. The observations for each work organization characteristic were arranged in a 2x2 table based on the task variable's two levels and the country variable's two levels. We calculated the difference between the means for the two task levels and then for the two country levels. Comparison of the magnitudes of the two differences for each work organization characteristic indicated that eight country differences were larger than their corresponding task differences, in some instances by large amounts. In one instance the differences were equal (Task Definition) and in another the task difference was larger (Discretion over Work Planning). Further computations which also took into consideration variances yielded the same results.

According to Table 2 there has been little if any change in the original mechanistic work structures in the American plants. Seven of the ten characteristics have average values indicating either no change or a change of less than 0.5 in absolute value. The remaining three are all less than 1.0 in absolute value.

The averages for individual characteristics accurately reflect the situation at the activity level. Direct workers' (operators') average skill level has remained at the same low level while the range of skills has decreased. There has been no change in their qualification levels or in the amount of their training. As an example, no increase has occurred in the low level of operators' inspection activities. The high level of task repetition remains the same; that is, operators still do the same tasks in the same way every day. Neither has there been any change in the high degree to which their work is defined (structured in advance). The average increase in operator planning activities reflects the introduction of quality circles in one activity. The large degree of machine control over work pace has not changed. The time foremen spend on process problems has decreased.

The French plants exhibit a clear move toward more organic work structures. All ten average values are positive with five being 1.0 or

higher. In general they accurately reflect the situation at the activity
level. Operator skills and the range of skills have increased. The same
is true for qualifications and amount of training. This is reflected in
the large increase in the amount of inspection performed. Task
repetition has decreased but there has not been much of a change in task
definition. Discretion over work planning and work pace have increased
but differentially across activities. The time that foremen devote to
problems has increased but only in one plant.

TABLE 2

CHANGES IN WORK ORGANIZATION CHARACTERISTICS (PILOT STUDY)(a)

| Characteristic | American | | | | French | | | |
|---|---|---|---|---|---|---|---|---|
| | EF1 | BA1 | BA2 | AVG | EF2 | CA1 | CA2 | AVG |
| Operators: | | | | | | | | |
| Skill Level | 0 | 0 | 0 | 0 | +2.0 | +1.0 | +1.0 | +1.3 |
| Range of Skills | -0.2 | -1.5 | 0 | -0.6 | +2.0 | +1.0 | +1.0 | +1.3 |
| Qualification Level | 0 | 0 | 0 | 0 | +2.0 | +1.0 | +1.0 | +1.3 |
| Amount of Training | 0 | -0.2 | 0 | -0.1 | +1.0 | +0.5 | +1.0 | +0.8 |
| Amount of Inspection | -1.0 | 0 | 0 | -0.3 | +2.0 | +2.0 | +1.5 | +1.8 |
| Task Repetition | 0 | 0 | 0 | 0 | -1.0 | -1.0 | -1.0 | -1.0 |
| Task Definition | 0 | 0 | 0 | 0 | 0 | -1.0 | 0 | -0.3 |
| Discretion Over Work Planning | 0 | 0 | +2.0 | +0.7 | 0 | 0 | +2.0 | +0.7 |
| Discretion Over Work Pace | 0 | 0 | 0 | 0 | 0 | +1.0 | +2.0 | +1.0 |
| Foremen: | | | | | | | | |
| Time Spent on Process Problems | -1.0 | -0.5 | -1.0 | -0.8 | 0 | 0 | +2.0 | +0.7 |

(a) Data were not available from EF3.

## 3.2. Manufacturing Flexibility Results

Table 3 provides changes in the six manufacturing flexibility dimensions for each of the seven activities. It also reports on global measures. The global change in an activity's flexibility is obtained in the following manner. The four market oriented flexibilities (mix, changeover, modification, and volume) are averaged as are the two process oriented aspects (rerouting and material). Then an average is taken of these two figures. Bright's Scale [3] is used to measure automation levels before and after the introduction of programmable automation. It runs from 1 (lowest) to 17 (highest).

The same analysis used for the work organization data shows that detailed task effects predominate over country effects, although not as clear cut an indication exists. For each type of flexibility we calculated the difference in means for the two task levels and for the two country levels. Disregarding sign, four task differences were larger than, one was equal to, and one slightly smaller than their corresponding country differences. The global task difference was a good deal larger. Additional calculations which also considered variances did not alter the results. Once more, part of the country effect is due to an unavoidable confounding with a detailed task effect. The two French assembly activities are for engines while the two American assembly activities are for bodies.

## TABLE 3

### CHANGES IN FLEXIBILITY AND AUTOMATION (PILOT STUDY)

| Characteristic | Fabrication | | | | Assembly | | | | |
| | EF1 | EF2 | EF3 | AVG | CA1 | CA2 | BA1 | BA2 | AVG |
|---|---|---|---|---|---|---|---|---|---|
| Mix Flexibility | 0 | +1.0 | +2.0 | +1.0 | 0 | +2.0 | +1.0 | +2.0 | +1.3 |
| Changeover Flex.(a) | +0.5 | +0.5 | +0.5 | +0.5 | −1.5 | −1.0 | −1.0 | +1.0 | −0.6 |
| Modification Flex.(a) | +1.0 | +1.8 | +0.5 | +1.1 | −1.0 | −0.5 | +0.5 | +1.5 | +0.1 |
| Volume Flex. | 0 | +1.5 | +1.0 | +0.8 | −2.0 | −1.0 | +0.7 | +1.0 | −0.3 |
| Rerouting Flex. | 0 | 0 | +1.0 | +0.3 | 0 | 0 | −2.0 | −1.0 | −0.8 |
| Material Flex. | 0 | 0 | 0 | 0 | −1.0 | −1.0 | −1.5 | −2.0 | −1.4 |
| Global Flex. | +0.2 | +0.6 | +0.8 | +0.5 | −0.8 | −0.3 | −0.7 | −0.1 | −0.5 |
| Automation Level | 0 | +3.0 | +2.0 | +1.7 | +9.0 | +3.0 | +10.0 | +7.0 | +7.3 |

(a)  The scores of two questionnaire items.

In Table 3, five out of the six flexibility dimensions for engine fabrication increased on average. In general these changes reflect the situation at the activity level. The increases are concentrated in mix, changeover, modification and volume flexibility, all of which are designed to handle market uncertainties. Little or no increase occurred in rerouting and material flexibility which handle process uncertainties.

For assembly, four out of the six flexibility aspects decreased on average. These changes do not always represent what occurs at the individual activity level. Some differences exist between CA1 and CA2 versus BA1 and BA2 perhaps caused by detailed task effects between engine and body assembly. Flexibilities relevant for market uncertainties showed some tendency to decrease on average, mainly due to CA1 and CA2. Changeover flexibility decreased and volume flexibility decreased a little. Modification flexibility basically remained the same. Mix flexibility increased reflecting the processing of a greater number of components. However, subsequent investigation in the American assembly plants revealed that the range of component characteristics decreased (-1.0 in BA1, BA2). Decreases occurred in rerouting and material flexibility, both of which are geared toward process uncertainties. For fabrication the average global change in flexibility is +0.5 which represents a small increase. The average change in automation is +1.7. The original automation levels were 15 in EF1, 11 in EF2, and 11 in EF3. For assembly, the average global change in flexibility is -0.5, a small decrease. The average automation change is +7.3. The original automation levels were 4 in BA1, 4 in BA2, 5 in CA1, and 3 in CA2.

Overall, in fabrication, flexibility increased a little and automation increased, while in assembly, flexibility decreased a little and automation increased. Unfortunately, Bright's Scale is ordinal so one cannot say definitely that the magnitude of the automation level change in fabrication was less than in assembly. However, the large divergence in the average change scores does make it seem reasonable. This divergence reflects a technical change in fabrication in which already automated control systems were refined, but in assembly in which labor intensive processes were essentially replaced by automation.

## 4. MANUFACTURING FLEXIBILITY AND PROGRAMMABLE AUTOMATION IN FRENCH INDUSTRY

The current step in our research is a mail survey of a large sample of French manufacturers who have adopted some form of programmable automation. Difficulties in identifying a population of users made it infeasible to select a random sample. Consequently, the results of the subsequent statistical tests must be interpreted with caution. Over 800 alumni of the Ecole Nationale Superieure des Arts et Metiers identified as holding manufacturing, production, methods, works management, industrial manufacturing or director positions, were chosen for the sample. They received an abbreviated version of the pilot study's questionnaire, which asked them to concentrate on one example of computerized automation in their firms based on its importance or

representativeness.    Responses were received from 163 companies of which
107 had experience with the new technology.

We have conducted some preliminary analyses of the data from the eighty-
one firms which use programmable automation in fabrication.    It is not
possible to determine how representative this sample's characteristics
are of the population of French fabrication activities which have
programmable automation.    To our knowledge no comparable population
figures exist.

Most companies were in the small to medium size range with 23% having
less than 200 employees, 40% between 200 and 1,000 employees, 25% between
1,000 and 5,000 people, 7% greater than 5,000 with 5% unclassified.    The
companies' products include industrial equipment and components (22%),
electricity and electronics (12%), consumer durables and nondurables
(23%), miscellaneous mechanical (27%), other (7%), and unclassified (9%).
The production systems included 20% open job shops, 40% closed job shops,
23% mass production, 14% continuous process, with 3% unclassified.

The technology consists of NC and CNC machines (48%), flexible manufacturing systems or cells (7%), transfer lines controlled by programmable
controllers(17%), miscellaneous equipment including robots (20%) and unclassified equipment (7%). Most companies purchased their technology
recently (therefore our results should not be considered definitive).
Fifty-four percent of the equipment had been in place for one year or
less, 35% for between one and five years, 7% for greater than five years
with 4% unclassified.

In general the large sample confirms the pilot study's finding that
French work organization become more organic when computerized automation
is introduced. Table 4 indicates the average changes in the five characteristics of the work organization for which data were collected.    Direct
workers, indirect workers and factory managers were queried.

### TABLE 4

### AVERAGE CHANGES IN WORK ORGANIZATION CHARACTERISTICS (LARGE SAMPLE)

| Characteristic | Direct Workers | Indirect Workers | Factory Management |
|---|---|---|---|
| Skill Level | 0.87** | 0.88** | 1.02** |
| Range of Skill | 0.86** | 0.87** | 1.10 |
| Task Repetiton | -0.40** | -0.34** | -0.43** |
| Task Definition | 0.56 | 0.40 | 0.48 |
| Discretion Over Work Planning | 0.16* | 0.07 | -- |

*Significant at the 0.05 level
**Significant at the 0.01 level

We tested the hypothesis that there would be no average change in the organic direction for any of these characteristics due to introduction of programmable automation.

One tailed t-tests were conducted indicated that the average changes in these for characteristic direct workers are in the organic direction and compatible with the pilot study's findings, with one exception: skill level has gone up (+0.87), range of skills has increased (+0.86), task repetition has decreased (-0.40), and discretion over work planning has increased (+0.16). The only discordant note concerns task definition which has moved in a more mechanistic direction contrary to the pilot study's findings.

The results for the indirect workers and the factory managers are essentially the same as for direct workers. For both groups skill level, range of skills and task repetition exhibited average changes in the organic direction which were significant beyond the 0.01 level. Task definition, however, became more mechanistic. For indirect workers discretion over work planning changed in the organic direction but the magnitude is not significant at the 0.05 level. Data were not collected on this characteristic for factory managers.

TABLE 5

**PROPORTIONS OF FIRMS WITH INDICATED CHANGES
IN MANUFACTURING FLEXIBILITY DIMENSIONS**

| | Scale Score | | | | | | |
|---|---|---|---|---|---|---|---|
| Flexible Dimension | Large Decrease -2 | Decrease -1 | No Change 0 | Increase +1 | Large Increase +2 | Average Change | Propor. <0 |
| Mix | 0.03 | 0.05 | 0.29 | 0.25 | 0.39 | 0.93** | 0.37 |
| Changeover | 0.06 | 0.29 | 0.39 | 0.19 | 0.06 | -0.10 | 0.75 |
| Modification | 0.04 | 0.11 | 0.31 | 0.23 | 0.31 | 0.66** | 0.46 |
| Volume | 0.00 | 0.04 | 0.27 | 0.41 | 0.29 | 0.95** | 0.30 |
| Routing | 0.20 | 0.37 | 0.23 | 0.14 | 0.06 | -0.51 | 0.80 |
| Material | 0.14 | 0.29 | 0.44 | 0.10 | 0.04 | -0.39 | 0.86 |
| Market (Average of Mix, Changeover, Modification,& Volume) | | | | | | 0.61** | 0.14 |
| Process (Average of Routing & Material) | | | | | | -0.44 | 0.79 |
| Global (Average of all dimensions) | | | | | | 0.08 | 0.47 |

**Significant at the 0.01 level

The large sample also substantiates the pilot study's finding that programmable automation will have both increasing and decreasing effects on flexibility. Table 5 shows for each dimension the proportion of companies having the indicated scale score, the average change, and the proportion of firms which stayed the same or decreased. It also has three combined measures: a company's market flexibility is the average of proportion of firms which stayed the same or decreased. It also has three combined measures: a company's market flexibility is the average of its scores on the first four individual dimensions. Its process flexibility is the average of its scores on the remaining two aspects. Global flexibility, the average of a company's market and process scores, represents our aggregate measure. For each, the average change and the proportion of firms with values less than or equal to zero are indicated.

Our hypothesis, that the average change in a particular flexibility measure would exhibit no increase, was tested using a one-tailed t test. Among the individual aspects, there were average increases in mix (+0.93), modification(+0.66) and volume (+0.95) flexibility which were significant beyond the 0.01 level. The first aspect, however, was defined in terms of number of items rather than the range of item characteristics. The pilot study suggested that the latter operationalization might decrease in a large sample. The hypothesis could not be rejected for the following flexibilities: changeover (-0.10), routing (-0.51), and material (-0.39). It is also instructive to examine the proportion of firms for which a given aspect decreased or stayed the same. It ranged from a healthy minority of 0.30 for volume flexibility to an overwhelming majority of 0.86 for material flexibility.

For the combined measures, market flexibility exhibited the only significant average increase (0.61). The overwhelming majority of firms reported some improvement (proportion 0.86 = 1 - 0.14). Process flexibility decreased (-0.44) with the overwhelming majority of firms registering a fall or no change. Global flexibility, our aggregate measure, hardly changed with about half the firms showing decreases or no change.

TABLE 6

AVERAGE CHANGES IN FLEXIBILITY AS A FUNCTION
OF ORIGINAL AUTOMATION LEVEL

| Characteristics | Original Automation Level (OAL) | | | | | |
|---|---|---|---|---|---|---|
| | 1 | 2 | 3 | 4 | 5 | 6 |
| Market Flexibility | 0.69 | 0.52 | 0.58 | 0.81 | -- | -- |
| Process Flexibility | -0.91 | -0.22 | -0.06 | 0 | -- | -- |
| Global Flexibility | -0.11 | 0.15 | 0.26 | 0.41 | -- | -- |
| Sample Size(a) | 27 | 36 | 9 | 4 | 0 | 0 |

(a) Five observations were unclassified

We began to seek explanations for these results by analyzing the impact
of the automation level of the conventional process which was replaced
(OAL=original automation level). We used simplified version of Bright's
Scale to measure automation. The seventeen levels were collapsed into
five (based on Bright's general categories) and we added a sixth level
reflecting the type of automation which has been recently developed. The
scale, therefore, runs from 1 (manual) to 6 (capable of recognizing environmental changes and adapting to them.)

The pilot study suggests that average change in flexibility dimensions
are generally negative at low OAL's and increase to become positive at
higher OAL's. The strength of this tendency varies for the different
flexibility measure. (See Table 6) The data in Table 6 must be
considered with caution as few observations exist at OAL=3,4 and none at
OAL=5,6.

The pattern for market flexibility does not conform very well to expectations. It has no negative values and the value for OAL=1 is out of line.
There is, however, a steady increase from OAL=2 onwards. The pattern for
process flexibility is closer to expectations with negative values at low
OAL's which steadily increase to zero at OAL=4 (and presumably positive
values beyond). The global measure displays our anticipated effect but
not in a striking manner. Its values steadily increase from a very small
negative figure at OAL=1 to a small positive value at OAL=4. As before,
the magnitudes are surprisingly low.

To provide some statistical support for these results we utilized regression analysis with each combined flexibility measure as dependent
variable and OAL as independent variable. We tested the hypothesis that
the slope of the regression line is less than or equal to zero using a
one-tailed t test. Rejection supports our contentions since it implies a
positive relationship between the variables. Parameters were estimated
using the seventy-six observations at the firm level. For market
flexibility the slope's value of -0.02 was not significant at the 0.05
level. However, the values for process flexibility (0.39) and for the
global measure (0.18) were significant beyond the 0.01 level. Caution is
advised in interpreting these results because OAL is an ordinal scale,
but we can take some comfort in the high significance levels.

We would also like to say that an inverse relationship exists between the
magnitude of the change in automation level and the original automation
level as suggested by the pilot study. Unfortunately, we don't have data
to properly test this hypothesis. There is no guarantee that large
changes in automation level as measured by Bright's Scale are greater in
magnitude than small changes. It was clear, however, that the observed
changes in automation were overwhelmingly positive given the OAL level.
Of the seventy-six observations, seventy-two were increases, four represented no change, and zero were decreases.

On the tenuous assumption that changes in Bright's Scale categories are
associated with magnitude changes, some statistical tests were made. The
average change on the scale was 2.85 at OAL=1, 1.86 at OAL=2, 1.33 at
OAL=3, and 1.00 at OAL=4. Regression analysis of the change (dependent

variable) versus OAL (independent variable) yielded a negative slope significant well beyond the 0.01 level. The analysis corrected for possible
spurious correlation caused by the dependent variable being a
mathematical function of the independent variable. We also formed a 2x2
contingency table by dividing each of the two variables into high and low
categories. Using the chi-square test the hypothesis of independence was
rejected well beyond the 0.01 level.

Considered together the results for the changes in global flexibility and
automation level as a function of OAL parallel those for the pilot study
given our data's limitations.


## 5. CONCLUSIONS


The findings concerning work organization contribute to a growing amount
of research that has observed net national differences (e.g. [14]).
However, our small amount of comparative data makes the results tentative
and discussion of cultural or other explanations speculative. Automobile
firms in the United States and France have made different work organization decisions in conjunction with the adoption of programmable automation. The American activities remained mechanistic undoubtedly
reflecting the traditional belief that workers are a source of
uncertainty as opposed to a resource. The French auto activities became
more organic apparently reflecting the review that new complex expensive
technology requires direct workers to have higher skills, qualifications,
and training, less task repetition, and more discretion. On average the
French manufacturing activities from the mail survey also became more
organic with the exception of an increase in task definition. Further
investigation is needed to see if this pattern repeats at the individual
activity level. Manufacturing flexibility comparisons between Japan and
the U.S. made by Jaikumar [10] exhibited strong country differences. Our
results for France and the U.S. were affected more by task factors. It
appears that flexibility does not necessarily increase when programmable
automation is introduced. For example, almost half of the firms in the
mail survey experienced a decrease in global flexibility. Whether gains
or losses occur depends upon the characteristics of the conventional
process which is replaced. The average change in global flexibility is
negative at low original automation levels and increases to become
positive at high OAL's. These average changes given OAL are rather small
in magnitude.

Our findings have consequences for understanding developmental trends in
U.S. and French manufacturing. When programmable automation is adopted
by a factory with a labor intensive manufacturing process, flexibility
will decrease somewhat and the automation level will increase. In our
opinion the magnitude of the latter's increase will be large. This type
of plant not originally advanced in its evolution will continue to change
according to the developmental curve. In particular for auto assembly
plants the habitual sacrifice of innovation for efficiency is continuing.
Given recent evidence that market preferences have changed and that
product innovation is proliferating in the auto industry [2], assembly
may become too rigid.

If computerized automation is adopted by a factory with traditional
automation, flexibility and automation level will increase. In our
opinion the magnitude of the latter's increase will be small. This kind
of factory, originally in an advanced state of evolution, will undergo a
revitalization. Renewal, however, is not along the lines of Abernathy,
Clark, and Kantrow's [2] dematurity theory which predicts backward movement along the developmental curve. Since innovation and efficiency are
simultaneously fostered the curve shifts upward. Auto fabrication is an
example. This is in line with the auto industry's needs to meet technologically superior products and cost pressures at the same time.

Programmable automation in the two countries seems to do a better job of
increasing market oriented as opposed to process oriented flexibilities.
In view of increased efforts to control process uncertainties by getting
things right the first time one can argue that this is not a problem.
Available evidence, however, indicates that the Japanese who are masters
of uncertainty regulation also concentrate on developing process
flexibilities. In our view this should also be a priority in Western
factories.

We have just begun to scratch the surface of a topic which is
increasingly important for operations managers. In the future there is a
need for continued theory development on how specific cultural factors
affect the model. Ultimately, a different variation of the model for
each industrialized society studied is possible. Second, we have not yet
investigated the extent to which the pattern of results for manufacturing
flexibility is due to programmable automation's technical limitations
versus managerial decisions affecting the technology's design and operation. Jaikumar [10] believed the latter factor was the most important.
Third, it would be useful to have a flexibility scale which uses
objective as opposed to perceptual data to measure levels rather than
changes. Finally, we need to extend our empirical studies to include
other aspects of the model such as uncertainties, strategies,
developmental trends, and sources of flexibility other than programmable
automation. This would provide a comprehensive picture of the role of
manufacturing flexibility in the modern factory.

## ACKNOWLEDGEMENT

The authors appreciate the statistical advice of Der-Ann Hsu and E.
Soofi, the computational work of Douglas Grief, and the financial support
of the French Foundation for Business Education (FNEGE).

## REFERENCES

[1] ABERNATHY, W.J., The Productivity Dilemma: Roadblock to Innovation
in the Automobile Industry The Johns Hopkins University Press,
Baltimore, 1978.

[2] ABERNATHY, W.J., K.B. CLARK, and A.M. KANTROW, Industrial Renaissance: Producing a Competitive Future for America, Basic Books, New York, 1983.

[3] BRIGHT, J.C.,"Automation and Management", Division of Research, Graduate School of Business Administration, Harvard University, Boston, 1958.

[4] CHILD, J.,"Culture, Contingency, and Capitalism in the Cross National Study of Organizations", in: B. Staw and L.L. Cummings, (eds.), Research in Organizational Behavior, 1980.

[5] CHILD, J.,"Organizational Structure, Environment, and Performance: The Role of Strategic Choice", Sociology, Vol. 6, 1972, 1-22.

[6] GERWIN, D. and J.C. TARONDEAU, "Consequences of Programmable Automation for French and American Automobile Factories: An International Case Study", in: Lev, B. (ed.), Production Management: Methods and Studies, Elsevier, North-Holland, Amsterdam 1986, 85-98.

[7] GERWIN,D. and J.C. TARONDEAU, "La Flexibilité dans les Processus de Production: Le Cas de L'Automobile", Revue Française de Gestion, No. 46, June-July-August, 1984, 37-46

[8] GERWIN, D. and J.C. TARONDEAU, "Case Studies of Computer Integrated Manufacturing Systems: A View of Uncertainty and Innovation Processes", Journal of Operations Management, 2 (February, 1982) 87-99.

[9] HAYES, R.H.,"Why Japanese Factories Work", Harvard Business Review, July-August, 1981, 57-66.

[10] JAIKUMAR, R.,"Postindustrial Manufacturing", Harvard Business Review, November-December, 1986, 69-76.

[11] LAMMERS, C.J. and D.J. HICKSON, "Are Organizations Culture Bound?" in: Lammers, C.J. and Hickson, D.J., (eds.), Organizations Alike and Unlike, Routledge and Kegan Paul, London, 1979, 402-419.

[12] SCHONBERGER, R.C., Japanese Manufacturing Techniques, The Free Press, New York, 1982.

[13] SKINNER, W., Manufacturing: The Formidable Competitive Weapon, John Wiley, New York, 1985.

[14] SORGE, A., G. HARTMENN, M. WARNER, and I. NICHOLAS, Microelectronics and Manpower in Manufacturing, Gower Press, Aldershot, U.K., 1983.

[15] SWAMIDASS, P.M. and W.T. NEWELL, "Manufacturing Strategy, Environmental Uncertainty and Performance: A Path Analytic Model" Management Science, 33, 4 (April, 1987) 509-524.

MANAGING INTERNATIONAL MANUFACTURING
K. Ferdows (Editor)
© Elsevier Science Publishers B.V. (North-Holland), 1989


INTERNATIONAL MANUFACTURING STRATEGIES
A COMPARATIVE ANALYSIS


Aleda ROTH,
Boston University


Arnoud DE MEYER,
INSEAD


Akio AMANO,
Waseda University


## 1. INTRODUCTION


The rapid emergence of new manufacturing capabilities, including dramatic advances in manufacturing technologies and organizational infrastructures, is having a significant impact upon worldwide competition. Consideration of this new industrial frontier warrants assessment of how manufacturing strategies vary internationally. While it is evident that functional strategies should be developed in the context of the business unit strategy, there is little empirical evidence illustrating how manufacturing strategies become operational for the competitive advantage (St. John 1986). Much of the current research in manufacturing strategy relies upon in-depth case studies and the "intuitive guidance" of experienced individuals; however, a much broader empirical perspective is necessary to augment previous research and to lay the foundation for understanding how manufacturing strategy is systematically pursued for the competitive advantage.

The purpose of this research, extending the work of Miller and Roth (1986 and 1987), Nakane (1986), Roth (1987), De Meyer, Nakane, Miller and Ferdows (1987), and De Meyer and Ferdows (1987) is to use statistical tools to explain how manufacturing resources are orchestrated to build competitive strength in each of three different regions of the world: North America, Western Europe and Japan. As in these works, we use the data collected in a collaborative research program of the "Manufacturing Futures Project," a collaborative research program of Boston University, INSEAD and Waseda University. In this study, manufacturing strategies are characterised by the sets of action programs. That is, the study starts from a set of action programmes as they are pursued by manufacturers in the three regions. Through regression analyses, we illustrate how each key action program is specifically linked with competitive priorities of flexibility, quality, delivery and price within each region.

The significance of the research is threefold. First, by focusing upon the strategic impact of operations, systematic ways in which manufacturing executives around the world are emphasizing process, facilities, capacity, vertical integration, and infrastructure decisions are exposed. Do the manufacturing programs have direct bearing upon the policies that manufacturers adopt for competition? Skinner's (1978) seminal work suggested they should. If this is the case, then the key action programs to improve manufacturing effectiveness should correlate with one or more competitive priorities. In this study, differing from the previous research in this area, we test this with statistical tools.

Second, the study contributes to the development of operational definition of manufacturing strategy. For each world region, the portfolios of action programs which have been shown to correspond with each competitive priority provides a useful point of comparison.

Finally, this explanatory research serves as a benchmark for further research on international manufacturing strategy. By suggesting the ways in which the paradigms differ from region to region, the study will stimulate future research on effective or ineffective strategies.

This analysis is intended to be exploratory and descriptive in the sense that it attempts to explain how choices in manufacturing are made in different world regions; it is not prescriptive. Our research focuses upon the relationships between individual manufacturing programs which are being emphasised by the business unit and their association with the competitive priorities of the business unit. The research does not cover the overall importance of priorities and programs as they are ranked by senior executives. This is the subject of other related work (Miller and Roth (1986), De Meyer and Ferdows (1986), and Nakane (1986)).

## 2. METHODOLOGY

### 2.1 Sample

The empirical results examined here are obtained from the 1986 North American Manufacturing Futures Survey (Miller and Roth 1986), the European Manufacturing Futures Survey (De Meyer and Ferdows 1986), and the Manufacturing Futures Survey in Japan (Nakane 1986). Since 1983, research teams at Boston University (Boston, U.S.A.), INSEAD (Fontainebleau, France), and Waseda University (Tokyo, Japan) have been carrying out yearly surveys of large manufacturers. The mailing lists contain the names of the largest manufacturers in North America, Europe and Japan.

In 1986, about 1000 executives in large manufacturing firms in North America, 1500 in Europe and 600 in Japan received the surveys. Of these, 188 completed surveys were returned by the North American executives; 172, by the Europeans [1]; and 168, by the Japanese. The data is derived from a convenience sample. No attempt is thus made to generalise beyond the population covered in the survey.

The unit of analysis in this study is a manufacturing business unit (MBU). An MBU is either a division, a plant or an entire company depending upon how the company is organised. In a decentralized, highly diversified firm with a divisional organization, the MBU is most likely a division. On the other hand, the plant or entire company are more appropriate MBUs for large, single-product, functionally organized firms. The common underlying thread spanning the MBUs is that each represents the level in the organization where manufacturing strategies are made for the business unit's products and markets. In other words, it is the level in the organization where manufacturing strategy is determined.

The samples in each global region represent a wide range of industries based upon two digit Standard Industrial Codes (SIC):machinery/ intermediary goods, electronics, consumer nondurables, and industrial and basic industries. The relative proportion of survey respondents in four broad industrial types (machinery/intermediary goods, electronics, consumer nondurables and industrial and basic industries) is summarized in Table 1.


**INDUSTRY PROFILES**

| INDUSTRY | NORTH AMERICA Percent | EUROPE Percent | JAPAN Percent |
|---|---|---|---|
| Machinery/intermediary goods | 30 | 23 | 31 |
| Electronics | 25 | 23 | 30 |
| Consumer nondurables | 09 | 12 | 05 |
| Industrial and Basic | 32 | 42 | 33 |

Source:  De Meyer, Nakane, Miller and Ferdows (1987)


**TABLE 1**


The 1986 respondents in the North American, European and Japanese firms participating in the study report average sales revenues of $1028 million, $689 million, and $1037 million, respectively (in U.S. dollars). Due to wide fluctuations in the dollar, yen and European currencies, the average sales figures for each global region are difficult to compare precisely. They do, however, reflect the relatively large size of firms participating in the study. Total manufacturing costs as a percent of sales were 65.1 percent for the Europeans, 60.1 percent for the North Americans,and 72.3 percent for the Japanese. This can be an indication of the importance of manufacturing in the companies in the sample.

## 2.2. Measures

The Manufacturing Futures Project survey instrument contains more than 100 questions; however, for purposes of comparing global manufacturing strategies, eight questions on competitive priorities of the business unit and 36 questions profiling key action programs and tools for organizational effectiveness are used.

Tables 2a and 2b depict the key action programmes and the competitive priority variables used in this research.

### KEY ACTION PROGRAMS AND ACTIVITIES

---

### VARIABLE DESCRIPTIONS (MNEMONIC LABEL)

Giving workers a broader task range (BROAD JOBS)
Giving workers more planning responsibilities (WORKER PLANNING)
Changing labor management relationships (LABOR/MGT RELATIONS)
Direct labor motivation (DL MOTIVATION)
Manufacturing reorganization (REORGANIZATION)
Worker safety
Quality circles
Automating jobs (DL AUTOMATION)
Supervisor training
Improved maintenance (MAINTENANCE)
Zero Defects
Production/inventory control systems (PPIC)
Lead time reduction (REDUCE LEAD TIMES)
Purchasing management  (PURCHASING MGT)
Vendor quality
Computer aided manufacturing (CAM)
Computer aided design (CAD)
Reducing set up times (REDUCE SET UPS)
Value analysis/product redesign (VALUE ANALYSIS)
Group technology
Reducing size of manufacturing workforce (REDUCE WORKFORCE)
Capacity expansion (EXPANSION)
Reducing the size of the manufacturing units (REDUCE MFG UNITS)
Plant relocation (RELOCATION)
Developing new processes for old products (NEW PROC/OLD PROD)
Developing new processes for new products (NEW PROC/NEW PROD)
Narrowing product lines/standardizing (STANDARDIZING)
Developing a manufacturing strategy (STRATEGY PLANNING)
Integrating manufacturing information systems (MFG INFO SYSTEMS)
Integrating information systems across functions (LATERAL INFO SYSTEMS)
Reconditioning physical plants (RECONDITIONING)
Introducing robots (ROBOTS)
Flexible manufacturing systems (FMS)
Closing plants
Statistical Quality Control of Process (SPC)
Statistical Quality Control of Product (SQC)

---

TABLE 2a

## MBU'S COMPETITIVE PRIORITIES

---

VARIABLE DESCRIPTIONS (MNEMONIC LABEL)

Ability to offer low prices (PRICE)
Ability to make rapid volume changes (VOLUME FLEXIBILITY)
Ability to offer consistent quality (CONFORMANCE)
Ability to provide high performance products (PERFORMANCE)
Ability to provide after sales service (SERVICE)
Ability to make rapid design changes/introduce new products
(PRODUCT FLEXIBILITY)
Ability to provide dependable delivery promises (DEPENDABILITY)
Ability to provide fast deliveries (SPEED)

---

**TABLE 2b**

In order to tap the conceptual domain of an intended manufacturing strategy as represented by the current set of action programs, 36 questions on activities, tool or programs to improve the effectiveness of operations were presented to the respondents (Table 2a). Manufacturing executives were asked to indicate the degree of emphasis the business unit places (or has definite plans to place over the next two years) on each key action program. Responses were obtained on a 5 point Likert-like scale ranging from "1" representing "no emphasis" to "5", "critical emphasis".

The conceptual domain of the MBU's competitive priorities is measured on the basis of the executives' responses to each of eight competitive abilities (Table 2b). For each of the eight competitive abilities, respondents rated the question as it pertained to the MBU's competitive success over the ensuing five years. Again, responses were coded on a 5 point Likert-like scale, from "no effect" to "very critical to success".

A certain degree of multi-colinearity could be expected among the eight competitive priorities. The intention to emphasize Conformance or Performance as a competitive priority can indeed be expected to be correlated. Theoretically, (Skinner 1978) existence of only four factors-- quality, delivery, flexibility and cost efficiency--could be predicted.

Principal component analyses were performed to check the existence of such theoretically derived factors.[2]

The analysis of both the European and the North American data confirmed the theoretically predicted factors (Table 3). The Japanese date, however, did not. Only three factors could be identified which could be labelled as "response flexibility", "quality" and "cost efficiency". For the Japanese, the distinction between flexibility and dependability of the delivery is blurred. For them, the flexibility becomes a more

## COMPETITIVE PRIORITIES

| EUROPE/NORTH AMERICA | | JAPAN | |
| --- | --- | --- | --- |
| Factor label variables | Defining variables | Factor label | Defining |
| 1. Flexibility | Product flexibility Volume flexibility | 1. Response flexibility | Speed dependability flexibility Product flexibility |
| 2. Quality | Conformance Performance Service | 2. Qualities | Conformance Performance Product flexibility |
| 3. Delivery | Dependability Speed | 3. Cost efficiency/ Economies of scale | Price Volume (negative) |
| 4. Cost efficiency | Price | | |

## TABLE 3

encompassing concept of response to customer requirements, whatever that may entail-- speed and service of delivery, change in design specifications, or changes in production volume. The second factor is almost identical to the European/North American factor of quality. Notice, however, that the Japanese quality factor includes product flexibility. The third factor is similar to the European/North American cost efficiency factor. It explicitly recognises the inverse relationship between volume flexibility and low prices. Low prices are explicitly correlated with a better and more stable capacity utilization.

Though differences exist between the Japanese and the North American/European data--and to a very minor extent also between the European and North American result--they do not seem to be strong enough to reject the theoretical constructs of competitive priorities in manufacturing. As a consequence, four new indices were constructed based on the North American/European de facto definitions. Since the samples cannot be called representative for manufacturing, neither in Europe, North America or Japan, it would be presumptuous to construct the indices on the basis of the weights of the variables composing the factors derived from the principal components analysis.

Rather than constructing a highly questionable weighted average of the variables, we opted to compute the four indices representing the competitive factors by averaging the ratings of the variables of which they are composed. For example, the "Quality" sale is computed for each MBU by averaging the rating for conformance, performance and service. The "Delivery" scale is computed by averaging the MBU's mean degree of emphasis on product flexibility and volume. Cost efficiency is defined as the emphasis on price. We recognise the arbitrariness of this procedure, but any other combination would be equally arbitrary, and would falsely suggest that we know what are the respective weights of, for example, conformance, performance and service to define the complex category of quality.

It is, of course, difficult to compare a large set of action factors across three regions. It seemed thus logical to try to reduce these 36 factors through a principal component analysis to a limited set of components. However, attempts to locate a reasonable set of comparable factors over the 36 key action program variables across North America, Europe and Japan was not successful. The manner in which the global regions typically "bundle" their strategic action portfolios are quite different (Roth (1987), De Meyer and Ferdows (1987)) [3]. Thus, we based our analysis on the <u>individual</u> action programs (depicted in Table 2a) and not upon the differentiation among "clusters" (factors) of related programs. It is precisely the differences in the bundling of action programs which in fact we finally studied.

The analysis was done in two stages due to a) the high degree of multicolinearity among the 36 action programs, b) our inability to define common constructs (through factor analysis) across global regions whereby the program data could be reduced into independent factors, and c) the ease of applying a standard, uniform treatment to the data for comparison purposes. In Stage I, for each region, candidate sets of specific action programs which are significantly correlated with each competitive priority are identified. In Stage II, we test the hypotheses that within each region the candidate set of action programs, taken as a whole, are good predictors of the respective competitive priority index.

Accordingly, in Stage I, for each region, a series of 36 multiple regression analyses were performed using the competitive priority indices as the predictor variable set. (See Appendix A). Each action program was treated separately in order to study the impact of quality, delivery, flexibility and price on that variable. In essence, the regression analyses capture the relative associations between the set of competitive priorities deemed essential for the firm's competitive advantage and the relative degree of emphasis that manufacturing executives place upon the individual action programs.[4]

These regressions are used to screen out a reasonable set of action plans which seem to be associated by the respondents with their choice of a particular competitive priority. Since it is our goal here to explore the set of potential action plans which can eventually be associated with a priority, we have chosen to use a high value of alpha (significance

level of .20 or less). We insist that we have chosen this high level  of
alpha  for exploratory reasons.  It is our aim to find the largest set of
action programmes which can be associated with a   particular  competitive
priority,   not   the minimal set.  Since we are aware of the fact that the
reader might disagree with this choice,  we   have   represented   the  significance  level corresponding to each regression coefficient in Appendix
A.

In  Stage  II,  the  portfolio of action programs which are statistically
linked with each competitive capability were used as predictor  variables
in   another  set of multiple regression analyses.  The purpose of running
the additional regressions was to assess the total amount of variance  as
measured by the coefficient of determination in each competitive priority
which can be explained by its  linearly  associated  strategy  portfolio,
taken  as  a  set.  In other words, if a portfolio of action programs accounts for a significant amount of the known variability of the priority,
we  will have  some  evidence that firms in a particular region are systematically using a certain set of manufacturing programs  for  achieving
that competitive advantage.

This procedure circumvents the need to test individual regression coefficients  in  Stage II since a) only programs shown to be associated with a
competitive priority are contained in the respective feasible sets and b)
we only wish to determine the total variance explained.  The existence of
multicolinearity between the  individual  action  programs  only  impacts
tests  on regression coefficients but not the total variance explained by
the model.

Separate  sets of the regression analyses using the particular portfolios
of manufacturing programs derived in Stage I were performed for  each  of
the   four   theoretically   constructed   indices  for  the  competitive
priorities.  The Stage II  analysis  is  only  available  for  the  North
American and European data, and we will use the results consequently only
to explore differences between these two regions.


## 3.  RESULTS


Stage I summary regional profiles of the multiple regression analyses  of
each  key  action program on quality, delivery, flexibility and price are
presented in Appendix A.  Each independent  and  dependent  variable  is
rated  on  the  questionnaire  on  a  scale  from 1 to 5; therefore, each
regression coefficient reflects the relative order of magnitude that each
independent competitive priority index plays in predicting the particular
degree of emphasis upon the action programs.

The  individual  regressions  obtained from Stage I (Appendix A) are summarized in a rather nontraditional manner in figures 1 to 4.   A  primary
purpose  of  the analysis is to explore which sets of action programs may
be typical  of  each  competitive  priority  over  the  three  geographic
regions.    Therefore, rather than discuss each action program separately
in terms of its associated set of competitive priorities, we chose to  do
the  inverse--i.e.  discuss  each  competitive capability in terms of its

associated set of action programs, which reflected the Stage II analysis.

The next four sections describe the action program portfolios relating to quality, flexibility, delivery and price.  In order to facilitate the interpretation of the results, these programs have been grouped into major decision categories predicated upon their theoretical associations (Wheelwright 1978).  The category "vertical control" was preferred over "vertical integration" since the action programs in this category related more towards achieving influence or power over the value chain rather than to obtaining ownership.  The inclusion of the specific action programs in each category was based upon the professional judgment of the authors and augmented by empirically derived factors (Roth 1987, De Meyer and Ferdows 1987).  The grouping of action programs, however, has no bearing upon the analytical results; it merely serves to ease interpretation by structuring the results in a well known framework.


## 3.1 Competing through Quality

The manufacturing strategy portfolios of the Europeans, Japanese, and the North American executives vary when quality is the desired competitive capability (Figure 1).  The North American and Japanese portfolios of key action programs are sparse in contrast to the Europeans, and generally reflect that less systematic variation may be explained by quality objectives in the first two regions. We have used the regression coefficients obtained in the Stage I regression to rank the action programmes in terms of their contribution to support a particular competitive priority.  The two leading programs in the North American and European portfolios are investments in computer aided design (CAD) and computer aided manufacturing (CAM). These programs are aimed at improving operations through manufacturing engineering (CAM) and design engineering (CAD).  CAD/CAM links are the first step in the automation of physical manufacturing. The use of CAD/CAM is generally associated with a number of manufacturing improvements, one of which corresponds to significant reductions in scrap and rework levels.  That both European and North American manufacturers view CAD/CAM as a significant part of their manufacturing strategy for developing quality is anticipated from the popular literature.  CAM capabilities may be perceived as a critical success factor permeating international boundaries since it arises in the Japanese strategy as well.  For the Japanese, the quality strategy variables having the largest regression coefficients are programs for zero defects, new processes for new products, and vendor quality.

Areas of overlap among the international strategic portfolios pertaining to the quality advantage are very limited.  All three global regions include only value analysis in their quality portfolios; therefore, an analysis of the product appears to be a more universal component of a quality strategy.  The European and American manufacturing executives are likely to plan activities which are associated with materials flow management (or just-in-time systems) such as programs aimed at reducing manufacturing lead times, reducing set up times and/or group technology.

## Competing Through Quality: Global Strategic Action Portfolios[1]

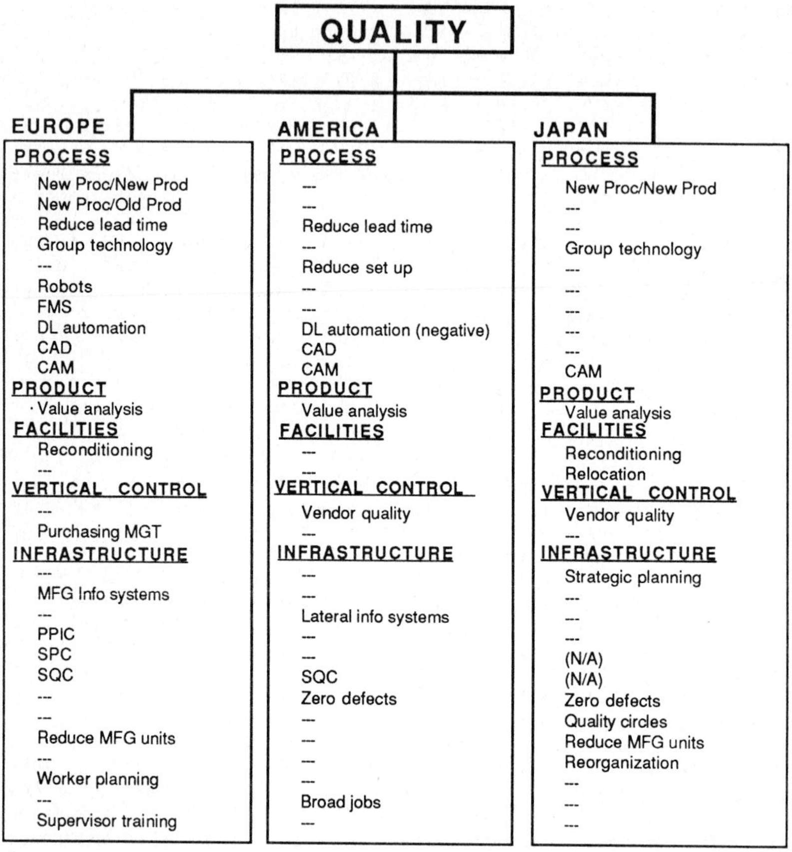

| QUALITY | | |
|---|---|---|

| EUROPE | AMERICA | JAPAN |
|---|---|---|
| **PROCESS** | **PROCESS** | **PROCESS** |
| New Proc/New Prod | --- | New Proc/New Prod |
| New Proc/Old Prod | --- | --- |
| Reduce lead time | Reduce lead time | --- |
| Group technology | --- | Group technology |
| --- | Reduce set up | --- |
| Robots | --- | --- |
| FMS | --- | --- |
| DL automation | DL automation (negative) | --- |
| CAD | CAD | --- |
| CAM | CAM | CAM |
| **PRODUCT** | **PRODUCT** | **PRODUCT** |
| · Value analysis | Value analysis | Value analysis |
| **FACILITIES** | **FACILITIES** | **FACILITIES** |
| Reconditioning | --- | Reconditioning |
| --- | | Relocation |
| **VERTICAL CONTROL** | **VERTICAL CONTROL** | **VERTICAL CONTROL** |
| --- | Vendor quality | Vendor quality |
| Purchasing MGT | --- | --- |
| **INFRASTRUCTURE** | **INFRASTRUCTURE** | **INFRASTRUCTURE** |
| --- | --- | Strategic planning |
| MFG Info systems | | --- |
| --- | Lateral info systems | --- |
| PPIC | --- | --- |
| SPC | --- | (N/A) |
| SQC | SQC | (N/A) |
| --- | Zero defects | Zero defects |
| | --- | Quality circles |
| Reduce MFG units | --- | Reduce MFG units |
| --- | --- | Reorganization |
| Worker planning | --- | --- |
| --- | Broad jobs | --- |
| Supervisor training | --- | --- |

[1]Strategic Action Portfolio Variables Abstracted from Appendix A.

*(N/A) Data not availible*

### FIGURE 1

The Japanese manufacturers pursuing quality goals overlap on group technology programs. The Europeans portray an affinity towards developing
new processes for old products and investing in automation which sub-
stitutes for direct labor. The latter is exemplified by technology
programs employing robots and flexible manufacturing systems. In contrast, the North American sample results depict a negative association
between automating jobs and quality priorities. Automation per se is not
part of the Japanese quality portfolio.

Quality objectives drive reconditioning, a facilities management decision, in both the European and Japanese data sets. The American executives do not perceive reconditioning to be part of their quality activities. Vertical control activities show up significantly in all
regions. Vendor quality is seen in the Japanese and American quality
strategy; and purchasing management appears in the European portfolio.
This could indicate an attitudinal difference towards vendors. North
American and Japanese respondents are emphasizing more collaborative
arrangement with vendors whereas the Europeans still focus upon contractual agreements. This corroborated by other data of the questionnaire
(De Meyer, et al, 1987).

With respect to infrastructural decisions, the inclusion of human
resource management activities coincide with the European and American
portfolios but not with the Japanese. Including workers in the planning
process and supervisor training are significantly associated with quality
competitive capabilities in the European sample; however, the North
American manufacturers rely more upon giving workers a broader range of
jobs. Infrastructure policies on information systems fail to show a
correspondence with quality goals in any systematic fashion across global
regions. Manufacturing information systems and production, planning and
inventory control (PPIC) emerge in the European group; lateral information systems, in the American region; and strategic planning, in Japan.

Quality goals are correlated with reducing the size of the manufacturing
unit in the European and Japanese groups. The Japanese are likely to
mention reorganization of facilities. Statistical product and process
control are associated with quality goals in Europe; however, the North
American manufacturers place statistically significant weight upon
statistical product control and zero defects. Unfortunately, the
Japanese data set does not include questions on statistical process and
product control which would have been expected to be included among the
top Japanese quality programs.

The Stage II regression of the constructed index for the quality priority
with significant action plans indicates that the strategic portfolios
defined in Stage I analysis are significantly aligned with their quality
objectives. Let us remind the reader that in this Stage II analysis, we
use the action programs mentioned in figure 1 to predict the score for
the constructed index for the competitive priority. The European
portfolio of action programs results in a multiple correlation of .64
with the quality index; the corresponding R-square statistic indicates
that over 40 percent of the variability in the quality index is explained
by the limited set of action programs. The explanatory power of the
European strategic portfolio of action programs is remarkably high. This
finding strongly suggests that those European manufacturers who have
chosen to emphasize quality as a competitive priority have developed a
coherent strategy. One that is primarily based upon the drastic upgrading of the technological structure and upon simultaneous improvements of
the manufacturing infrastructure as well.

On the other hand, the explanatory power of the American strategic
portfolio is somewhat less with only 18 percent of the variance in
quality explained. While Miller and Roth (1986) reported that quality
was a central theme of American manufacturing, these data suggest that

many American manufacturers may have been pursuing quality objectives in ways that are not measured in the survey or through nonmanufacturing areas. Alternatively, since so many American manufacturers report quality objectives, there is less variation in the data to link programs with quality. For example, in the American sample, about 70 percent of the respondents have a quality index between 4 and 5, whereas only 55 percent of the European executives had a similar span on the quality index. Even so, specific programs for quality management in North America are not strongly associated with quality priorities in identifiable ways, but rather, as reported in the following sections they are aligned more strongly with flexibility and price.

## 3.2 Competing through Flexibility

Developing flexible manufacturing capabilities may be one of the most difficult goals to achieve. They are also considered to be the next competitive battle in global manufacturing. North American and European manufacturers are gearing up to make major inroads on their flexibility capabilities (Figure 2). Both are planning sweeping restructuring in their operations; however, the European manufacturers, in contrast to their North American counterparts, may be more intense in their efforts (as determined by the relative magnitudes of the regression coefficients of flexibility on the action programs) and are more systematic in their coverage of strategic operations decision areas. Both of these factors may give the Europeans a competitive advantage in closing the flexibility gap. Unexpectedly, the Japanese flexibility portfolio does not appear to be as full, consisting of only three action programs which are systematically linked to flexibility. This result may be an artifact of the Western view of flexibility. It reflects the relative difficulty in conducting comparative analyses when the underlying paradigms may differ. Recall that in the factor analysis of the competitive priorities, for the Japanese delivery and service was an integral part of flexibility; therefore, this finding should be cautiously interpreted.

Improvements in materials flow capabilities are linked to flexibility goals globally. In particular, programs to reduce manufacturing lead times and set up times are in each region's portfolio. Group technology is specifically mentioned by both the Europeans and the Americans. Other technological programs pertaining to the development of new processes for both new products and to the introduction of robots and flexible manufacturing systems are important parts of the European strategy(5). Introducing robots are not an important element in the North American flexibility strategy; however, both new processes for new products and flexible manufacturing systems are tagged in the American sample. the importance of CAM and value analysis as action programmes in a flexibility portfolio is demonstrated by their presence in both the North American and European strategies. The Europeans seeking a flexibility advantage showed a proclivity towards CAD and programs to narrow the product lines.

The Europeans are strongly emphasizing vertical integration activities in

conjunction with their flexibility goals. Here vendor management activities accentuated by purchasing management and vendor quality are
manifest. Vendor quality is also observed in the American portfolio.

Besides planned production process changes, many infrastructural changes
are correlated with flexibility in the European region in contrast to

## Competing Through Flexibility: Global Strategic Action Portfolios[1]

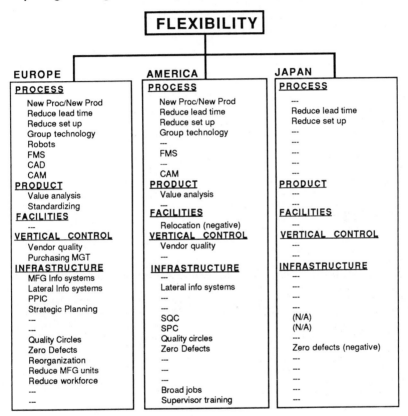

| EUROPE | AMERICA | JAPAN |
|---|---|---|
| **PROCESS** | **PROCESS** | **PROCESS** |
| New Proc/New Prod | New Proc/New Prod | --- |
| Reduce lead time | Reduce lead time | Reduce lead time |
| Reduce set up | Reduce set up | Reduce set up |
| Group technology | Group technology | --- |
| Robots | --- | --- |
| FMS | FMS | --- |
| CAD | --- | --- |
| CAM | CAM | --- |
| **PRODUCT** | **PRODUCT** | **PRODUCT** |
| Value analysis | Value analysis | --- |
| Standardizing | --- | --- |
| **FACILITIES** | **FACILITIES** | **FACILITIES** |
| --- | Relocation (negative) | --- |
| **VERTICAL CONTROL** | **VERTICAL CONTROL** | **VERTICAL CONTROL** |
| Vendor quality | Vendor quality | --- |
| Purchasing MGT | --- | --- |
| **INFRASTRUCTURE** | **INFRASTRUCTURE** | **INFRASTRUCTURE** |
| MFG Info systems | --- | --- |
| Lateral Info systems | Lateral info systems | --- |
| PPIC | --- | --- |
| Strategic Planning | --- | --- |
| --- | SQC | (N/A) |
| --- | SPC | (N/A) |
| Quality Circles | Quality circles | --- |
| Zero Defects | Zero Defects | Zero defects (negative) |
| Reorganization | --- | --- |
| Reduce MFG units | --- | --- |
| Reduce workforce | Broad jobs | --- |
| --- | Supervisor training | --- |

[1] **Strategic Action Portfolio Variables Abstracted from Appendix A**

*(N/A) Data not availible*

**FIGURE 2**

relationships. These are the only five key action programs which are
systematically emphasized by the North American manufacturers desiring
delivery capabilities. A Stage II regression of the delivery index on
these five action programs produces a statistically significant but weak

Competing Through Delivery: Global Strategic Action Portfolios[1]

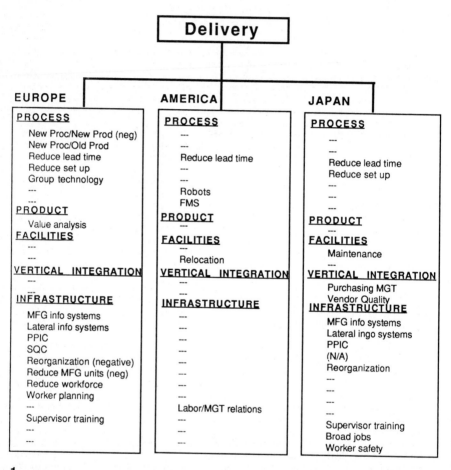

1
## Strategic Action Portfolio Variables Abstracted from Appendix A

*(N/A) Data not available*

FIGURE 3

R-square (8 percent). In other words, only 8 percent of the variation in the delivery index is explained by these five action program variables. It is plausible that time based competition has not yet been perceived as a threat or that American manufacturers are not gearing up in ways that are captured in the survey as are their allies. Alternatively, while the Americans may have become aware of the need to compete on timely delivery, they have not yet been able to put together a coherent set of policies to realize this objective. This is clearly an area for follow-up investigation.

In contrast, both the Europeans and Japanese are systematically planning more structural and infrastructural action portfolios corresponding to delivery objectives. Material flow management programs including group technology and other activities to reduce manufacturing lead times and reduce setups dominate the European delivery theme. The Japanese also are working on reducing manufacturing cycle times through lead time and set up reduction programs. Additionally, the Europeans are considering new process related activities for delivery. Developing new processes for old products is positively related to delivery but new processes for new products has a negative relationship. In other words, the Europeans appear to be upgrading their processes to increase the differentiation of their existing products through an emphasis on better delivery.

The inverse association between delivery and developing new processes for new products is partially explained by the fact that the Europeans are wrestling with delays in new product introduction. In pursuit of time based competition, they will use existing products rather than new products that inherently pose enough problems of their own. Value analysis and statistical product control techniques to investigate and improve the quality and reliability from the perspective of function and price, serve to support the European delivery model.

Vertical control is evident in the Japanese delivery strategy. The Japanese data suggest that both purchasing management and vendor quality are significant for delivery in Japan. Facility maintenance is correlated with delivery in Japan.

Infrastructure plays a key role in Japan and Europe where information based activities comprised of manufacturing information systems, lateral information systems and production/inventory control systems are correlated with delivery goals. Other infrastructural delivery based programs are predicated on human resource policies and organizational structure. Giving workers broader jobs, supervisor training, and worker safety are corollaries of the Japanese delivery theme, as is reorganization. Concomitantly, the Europeans stress other infrastructural programs including statistical product quality control (SQC), worker planning, supervisor training and streamlining their operations through reduced workforce. Reducing the size of the manufacturing units and reorganization are negatively related to delivery. The latter association again suggest that the reduction of the workforce is not necessarily a symptom of the overall shrinkage of the European activities, but rather a means to lower the impact of one of the elements which is perceived to be a major source of inflexibility.

The Stage II analysis reveals that the European delivery portfolio products about 24 percent of the overall variability in delivery. The R-square is three times greater than the proportion of the total delivery variance explained in the American sample. This finding provides some evidence that Europeans may have stronger delivery portfolios, as assessed by the variables in this study, than the Americans in that they are attacking their delivery goals in a more systematic manner.


## 3.4 Competing through Price

Price competition manufacturing strategies are generally terse in terms of the number of related action programs in all three regions (Figure 4). Furthermore, Stage I analysis indicates that there is little commonality among the three regions with respect to developing price (low cost) capabilities. In Europe and North America, robots are included in the process strategy. North America adds other direct labor automation programs for the price advantage. Japanese strategy, on the other hand, is characterized by reducing manufacturing lead times and CAD, the only two process oriented programs in their portfolio. Both Japan and Europe include standardization as a major product decision variable corresponding to low price capabilities. Value analysis is related to price in the Japanese products strategy. Facilities decisions to close plants are incorporated in the American price portfolio; relocation, in the Japanese.

What is readily apparent from the data is that infrastructure decisions, while markedly different regionally, are important components of the price strategy. The Europeans focus on reorganization but not on quality management (zero defects and statistical product control). By contrast, the American price strategy embellishes a number of infrastructural improvement programs such as quality management (statistical product and process control and quality circles), human resource programs (broad jobs and labor/MGT relations) and reducing levels of the workforce; and the Japanese, on human resource programs (direct labor motivation and worker safety). Unlike North America, the Japanese strategy exhibits an inverse relationship between emphasis on low price and expanding the role of the workers through job enlargement. In other words, the Japanese employ job specialization in accomplishing low price capabilities.

Restructuring for low price in American manufacturing may be characterized by squeezing facilities and direct labor as evidenced by the decisions to close plants and to substitute automation for labor. Even placing emphasis upon workers through quality circles and job enlargement drives the burden for low cost capabilities toward labor economies. That the American manufacturing strategy portfolio contains statistical process and product control most likely reflects the common prescription that "quality is free" (Crosby 1979). By contract, the Japanese price strategy is to focus upon enhancing the productivity of labor by process and product improvements which are supported by infrastructural changes. Their price strategy is one that lends itself to revitalization and renewal of the manufacturing function.

## Competing Through Price: Global Strategic Action Portfolios[1]

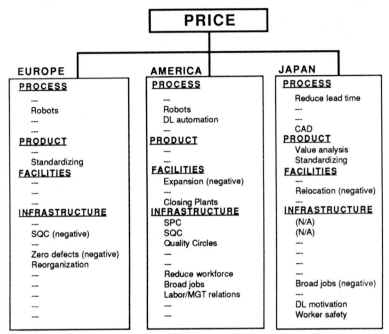

| EUROPE | AMERICA | JAPAN |
|---|---|---|
| **PROCESS** | **PROCESS** | **PROCESS** |
| --- | --- | Reduce lead time |
| Robots | Robots | --- |
| --- | DL automation | --- |
| --- | --- | CAD |
| **PRODUCT** | **PRODUCT** | **PRODUCT** |
| --- | --- | Value analysis |
| Standardizing | --- | Standardizing |
| **FACILITIES** | **FACILITIES** | **FACILITIES** |
| --- | Expansion (negative) | --- |
| --- | --- | Relocation (negative) |
| --- | Closing Plants | --- |
| **INFRASTRUCTURE** | **INFRASTRUCTURE** | **INFRASTRUCTURE** |
| --- | SPC | (N/A) |
| SQC (negative) | SQC | (N/A) |
| --- | Quality Circles | --- |
| Zero defects (negative) | --- | --- |
| Reorganization | --- | --- |
| --- | Reduce workforce | --- |
| --- | Broad jobs | Broad jobs (negative) |
| --- | Labor/MGT relations | --- |
| --- | --- | DL motivation |
| --- | --- | Worker safety |

[1]**Strategic Action Portfolio Variables
Abstracted from Appendix A**

*(N/A) Data not availible*

**FIGURE 4**

In terms of the variance in price explained by the strategic manufacturing portfolios in Stage II analysis, the Europeans and Americans are similar (12 percent and 13 percent, respectively). There are many other factors, which are not taken into account by the observed manufacturing strategies corresponding to developing low price capabilities. Is it possible that manufacturers hope to be able to offer low prices through cost reduction programs in other areas of the firm rather than in manufacturing? Or beyond that if the ability to offer low price is associated with mature products, then the manufacturing strategies for these products, over and above those which tweak the current system, may be negligible. For example, a do nothing strategy is not captured in the survey. In the North American sample, these data in particular may reflect the hollowing of the factory since so little revitalization or renewal appears in the action portfolio.

## 4. CONCLUSIONS

We have shown how the portfolios of key action programs vary across each geographic region based upon the constructed indices for the competitive priorities of quality, flexibility, price and delivery.

The first conclusion can be summarised as follows: to pursue similar competitive priorities--the North America, Japanese and European respondents to the 1986 Manufacturing Futures Survey used different portfolios of action programmes. With flexibility as the competitive priority of the manufacturing business unit, the European portfolio of action programs is more extensive both in terms of structure and infrastructural components. In terms of structural decisions, for the Europeans, technology is given a major role in developing flexible manufacturing capabilities. The emphasis upon technology is accompanied by vertical control, product design changes, streamlining operations and developing strong information systems throughout. On the other hand, the Japanese are clearly more focused in their approach to flexibility than either the Europeans or the Americans; however, the fact that flexibility, quality and delivery is an integral part for the Japanese may very well yield a stronger portfolio when delivery and flexibility or quality and flexibility are taken as a priority set. The American strategy is in between the Europeans and the Japanese. They place more emphasis upon infrastructure than upon structural components of manufacturing strategy. Notably, in each global region, kernel components of a flexibility based manufacturing strategy are programs to reduce manufacturing lead times and reduce set ups.

Quality priorities, like flexibility, depict the Europeans as having a broad mix of strategic action plans and the Japanese having a more focused set. The American strategy is a hybrid. The elements of global manufacturing strategy decision variables vary widely. Investment in process technology is a dominant quality theme of the Europeans. The infrastructural activities of the European portfolio spans information systems, quality management, organization and human resources. While the strategic variables are more focused, the Japanese do appear to attach higher value to facilities decisions than their industrial counterparts. Two programs, CAM and value analysis, are contained in the quality portfolios of each global region.

The delivery portfolio of the Japanese has the broadest mix of strategic decision variables; it covers process, facilities, vertical control and infrastructure. Vertical control through supplier management appears to be the major manufacturing strategy component for which the Japanese have an edge. Like the Japanese, the European delivery portfolio is rich in the number of programs; however, the Europeans are more likely to invest in process technology than either the Americans or the Japanese. Both the Europeans and Japanese show strength in their emphasis upon infrastructure. The American delivery portfolio is weak in terms of the mix and depth of its strategic action portfolio. For the Americans, technology is the avenue which is perceived to be consistent with delivery. Why infrastructure changes are not explained by American delivery priorities remains an enigma. The sole variable which spans delivery priorities globally is reduced manufacturing lead time.

Capabilities for competing on price are predicated upon facilities and infrastructure decisions globally; however, the details of the action portfolios of each region are divergent. The Japanese appear to take a process and product strategy whereas the Americans focus upon infrastructure and consolidation for low price capabilities. The Europeans are somewhat in the middle with respect to programs associated with price. Notably absent from the price portfolio of each region is attention to vertical control activities.

The second conclusion follows from the analysis of the variances in the data for the North American and European action profiles. The lower R-square in the Stage II analyses suggest that the average European respondent is slightly more focused in pursuing a particular competitive priority. That is their action plans are designed more in function of chosen priorities.

We should not forget that our research is highly exploratory at this stage. The most valuable contribution of exploratory research is the formation of avenues for further research. We see four of those avenues.

First, we have grouped our strategic action data into categories based upon theoretical constructs of strategic manufacturing decision variables. This was a worthwhile first endeavor so that some semblance of order could be imposed upon the data; however, this research is only a rudimentary start at defining global strategies. But the data seem to suggest that the Japanese model of competitive priorities is somewhat different from their Western counterparts. Whether different constructs of competitive priorities exist in time has to be tested--if diverse constructs exist, manufacturers seeking to transfer ideas and technology across international boundaries, must be wary less they fail to understand the underlying paradigms peculiar to the region of origin--.

Second, from such an analysis, we can hypothesize that the Japanese strategy portfolios will be different when the Japanese priority constructs are used as predictor variables. In particular, the relationships between the Japanese competitive priority constructs and their action portfolios should be studied in future research.

Third, why do the Europeans generally show a wider array of programs for three of the four priorities than Americans? Moreover, for those action programs which are included in both the Americans and European portfolios, why are the Europeans more intense (the regression coefficients generally greater) than Americans? Can we hypothesize that the Europeans are generally more cautious and slow in adopting new programs in manufacturing but that once they have chosen to act upon a particular strategy, that they will take a whole series of systematic steps towards a coordinated strategy? And what is the payoff for this degree of consistency?

In contrast, American firms have been accused of not giving manufacturing the necessary clout in the strategic planning process and for their reliance on "quick" fixes to manufacturing ailments. Does the relatively low percent of variance in the competitive priorities explained by the American portfolios support this assertion that the American manufacturers are not orienting their programs towards a manufacturing mission?

Or is it that the American manufacturing policies are more unique to a particular firm than across firms? Does the high emphasis on robots and FMS without correspondingly high commitment to infrastructure and other key manufacturing decisions portend trouble for American manufacturers seeking time based competition as an essential strategic force? Or is it that a large group of American manufacturers have an unshakeable belief in technology and they hope that all the other elements of manufacturing will follow automatically from the investments in technology?

Fourth, the data lend support to the observation made by Hayes (1981) that the "Japanese have achieved their current level of manufacturing excellence mostly by doing simple things well and slowly improving them all the time." Does the appearance of "focus" and the strategically oriented alignments of facilities, vertical control and infrastructure in the Japanese portfolios provide further evidence that the Japanese are continuing to make long term commitments in the things they did well in the past? Why don't the Japanese appear to be as technologically oriented as the Europeans?

Despite the limitations, the results of this initial exploratory investigation on international manufacturing strategies are quite promising and could have important managerial implications. We have described how action programs are systematically linked with stated competitive priorities of senior manufacturing executives worldwide. Development of manufacturing strategy can be improved through the construction of operational yardsticks which heretofore have been unavailable. This paper is a first step in this direction.

## FOOTNOTES

[1] Represented in the European sample are companies from all EEC countries, except Greece, Luxembourg and Portugal but complemented by Austria, Finland, Norway, Sweden, and Switzerland.

[2] The input to the pricipal component analysis was the inter item Pearson correlation coefficient matrices with unities in the diagnols. A Varimax rotation was applied to the initial factors. To determine the number of factors to be selected, the eigen value-one criterion and seree test were used. Factors were named on the basis of variables which have a factor loading of .40 or more.

[3] Besides the reported European and American factor analyses, the Japanese key action program data were subjected to factor analysis (unpublished data). The Japanese data exhibited again some distinctly different bundling of action programmes.

[4] Alternatively, the candidate set of action programs which are correlated with each action program could have been obtained through bivariate correlation analysis. Choosing regression, gives the association between the dependent variable and each independent variable taking into account the influence of the other competitive programs.

# BIBLIOGRAPHY

ABEGGLAN, J.C. and STALK Jr., G., Kaisha, the Japanese Corporation, Basic Books, Inc., New York 1985.

ABERNATHY, W.J., CLARK, K.B. and KANTROW, A.M., "The New Industrial Competition", Harvard Business Review, September-October, 1981.

CROSBY, P.B., Quality is Free, McGraw Hill, New York, 1979.

DE MEYER A. and FERDOWS K., "Managerial Focal Points in Manufacturing Strategy", International Journal of Production Research, 1987, Vol. 25, No. 11.

DE MEYER A., NAKANE, J., MILLER J.G., FERDOWS F., "Flexibility, the Next Competitive Battle", Boston University School of Management, Manufacturing Roundtable Series, February 1987. INSEAD Working Paper No. 87. (To appear in Strategic Management Journal in 1988).

HAYES, R., "Why Japanese Factories Work", Harvard Business Review, July-August, 1981.

HAYES, R.H. and WHEELWRIGHT S.C., Restoring our Competitive Edge - Competing through Manufacturing , J. Wiley and Sons, New York, 1984.

HEUTE, L. and ROTH A., "Linking Manufacturing Capabilities with SBU Startegic Directions", Proceedings of the 1987 Annual Meeting of the Decision Science Institute, Boston MA, November 1987.

HILL, T.J., Manufacturing Strategy - The Strategic Management of the Manufacturing Function, MacMillan Education, London 1984.

MILLER, J.G. and ROTH, A., "Report on the 1986 North American Manufacturing Futures Survey", Boston University School of Management, Manufacturing Roundtable Research Report Series, June 1986.

MILLER, J.G., and ROTH, A., "Manufacturing Strategies: Executive Summary of the 1987 North American Manufacturing Futures Survey", Boston University School of Management, Manufacturing Roundtable Research Report Series, July 1987.

MILLER, J.G., NAKANE, J. and VOLLMANN T., "The 1983 Global Mnaufacturing Futures Survey", Boston University School of Management, Manufacturing Roundtable Research Report Series, April 1983.

MILLER, J.G. and VOLLMANN, T., "The 1984 Manufacturing Futures Project Summary of the North American Survey Responses, Time Series Analyses, and Analysis by Insdustry Groupings", Boston University School of Management, Manufacturing Roundtable Research Report Series, May 1984.

MILLER, J.G., "The 1983 Manufacturing Futures Project", Boston University School of Management, Manufacturing Roundtable Research Report Series, 1983.

NAKANE, J., "Manufacturing Futures Survey in Japan:  A Comparative Survey 1983-1986", System Science Institute, Waseda University, Tokyo, May 1986.

OHMAE, K., The Mind of the Strategist,  The  Art  of  Japanese  Business, McGraw Hill, 1982.

PORTER, M., Competitive  Advantage:   Creating  and  Sustaining  Superior Performance, Free Press, New York, 1985.

ROTH A. and MILLER J.G., "1987 Manufacturing  Futures  Factbook",  Boston University  School  of  Management,  Manufacturing  Roundtable  Research Series, 1987.

ROTH,  A.,  "Differentiated  Manufacturing Strategies for the Competitive Advantage:  An Empirical  Investigation",  Boston  University  School  of Management,  Manufacturing  Roundtable  Research  Report Series, February 1987.

SKINNER, W., Manufacturing  in  the Corporate Strategy, John Wiley, New York, 1978.

SKINNER W., Manufacturing:  the Formidable Competitive Weapon, New York, 1985.

ST. JOHN C., "Operations Strategy:  A Review and Bibliography",Operations Management Review, Vol.4, No.4, 1986.

WHEELWRIGHT, S.C. and R. HAYES, "Competing  Through  Manufacturing", Harvard Business Review, Vol. 63, 1985.

WHEELWRIGHT,  S.C.,  "Reflecting  Corporate  Strategy  in  Manufacturing Decisions", Business Horizons, Vol. 21, 1978.

APPENDIX A

## OLS Regression Results of Key Action Plans on Competitive Priorities

| Dependent Variables | Independent Variables Regression Coefficients | | | | | | |
|---|---|---|---|---|---|---|---|
| Key Action Plans | FLEXIBILITY B(P) | PRICE B (P) | DELIVERY B (P) | QUALITY B (P) | Intercept | Multiple R | R Square (P) |
| **BROAD JOBS** | | | | | | | |
| North America | .16 (.16) | .21(.02) | | .20 (.13) | 0.77 | 0.25 | .06 (.02) |
| Europe | | | | | 1.89 | 0.19 | .03 (.31) |
| Japan | | -.22 (.15) | .22 (.05) | | 3.58 | 0.25 | .06 (.08) |
| **WORKER PLANNING** | | | | | | | |
| North America | | | | | 2.08 | 0.11 | .01 (.72) |
| Europe | | | .18 (.18) | .32 (.01) | 0.59 | 0.32 | .10 (.00) |
| Japan | | | | | 2.21 | 0.15 | .02 (.56) |
| **LABOR/MGT RELATIONS** | | | | | | | |
| North America | | .28 (.01) | .22 (.14) | | 1.50 | 0.23 | .05 (.05) |
| Europe | | | | | 3.34 | 0.05 | .00 (.99) |
| Japan | | | | | 2.47 | 0.16 | .03 (.48) |
| **DL MOTIVATION** | | | | | | | |
| North America | | | | | 2.00 | 0.17 | .03 (.28) |
| Europe | | | | | 3.19 | 0.20 | .04 (.21) |
| Japan | | .32 (.03) | | | 1.50 | 0.28 | .08 (.03) |
| **REORGANIZATION** | | | | | | | |
| North America | | | | | 1.93 | 0.12 | .02 (.61) |
| Europe | .39 (.00) | .22 (.02) | -.15 (.20) | | 2.31 | 0.36 | .13 (.00) |
| Japan | | | .24 (.02) | .22 (.07) | 2.21 | 0.32 | .10 (.01) |
| **WORKER SAFETY** | | | | | | | |
| North America | | | | | 3.69 | 0.13 | .02 (.58) |
| Europe | | | | | 2.43 | 0.16 | .03 (.46) |
| Japan | | .25 (.10) | .20 (.07) | | 1.95 | 0.29 | .09 (.02) |
| **QUALITY CIRCLES** | | | | | | | |
| North America | .21(.09) | .19 (.06) | | | 0.57 | 0.21 | .05 (.08) |
| Europe | .28 (.06) | | | | 0.97 | 0.24 | .06 (.08) |
| Japan | | | | .28 (.02) | 1.93 | 0.30 | .09 (.02) |
| **DL AUTOMATION** | | | | | | | |
| North America | | .19 (.06) | | -.20(.16) | 1.62 | 0.21 | .05 (.09) |
| Europe | | | | .39(.00) | 1.48 | 0.32 | .10 (.01) |
| Japan | | | | | 2.74 | 0.20 | .04(.28) |
| **SUPERVISOR TRAINING** | | | | | | | |
| North America | .22 (.03) | | | | 2.63 | 0.19 | .04 (.17) |
| Europe | | | .21(.04) | .17 (.09) | 2.20 | 0.32 | .10 (.01) |
| Japan | | | .18 (.06) | | 2.15 | 0.24 | .06 (.11) |
| **MAINTENANCE** | | | | | | | |
| North America | | | | | 2.61 | 0.13 | .02 (.54) |
| Europe | | | | | 2.64 | 0.17 | .03 (.42) |
| Japan | | | .21(.05) | | 2.38 | 0.23 | .05 (.15) |

| | | | | | | | |
|---|---|---|---|---|---|---|---|
| **ZERO DEFECTS** | | | | | | | |
| North America | .23 (.08) | | | .34 (.03) | 1.48 | 0.25 | .06 (.03) |
| Europe | .55 (.00) | -.25 (.04) | | | 1.80 | 0.42 | .17 (.00) |
| Japan | -.28 (.12) | | | .53 (.00) | 0.73 | 0.34 | .12 (.00) |
| **PPIC** | | | | | | | |
| North America | | | | | 3.11 | 0.14 | .02 (.46) |
| Europe | .29 (.00) | | .27 (.01) | .13 (.20) | 1.34 | 0.46 | .21 (.00) |
| Japan | | | .39 (.00) | | 2.19 | 0.40 | .16 (.00) |
| **REDUCE LEAD TIME** | | | | | | | |
| North America | .38 (.00) | | .20 (.17) | .25 (.07) | 0.48 | 0.35 | .13 (.00) |
| Europe | .46 (.00) | | .30 (.02) | .27 (.02) | -0.75 | 0.53 | .28 (.00) |
| Japan | .18 (.18) | .19 (.17) | .21(.04) | | 0.85 | 0.37 | .14 (.00) |
| **PURCHASING MGT** | | | | | | | |
| North America | | | | | 2.09 | 0.15 | .02 (.39) |
| Europe | .20 (.06) | | | .25 (.02) | 1.88 | 0.33 | .11 (.00) |
| Japan | | | .39 (.00) | | 0.76 | 0.46 | .21 (.00) |
| **VENDOR QUALITY** | | | | | | | |
| North America | .16 (.16) | | | .31(.02) | 1.74 | 0.24 | .06 (.03) |
| Europe | .23 (.05) | | | | 2.18 | 0.23 | .05 (.11) |
| Japan | | | .13 (.20) | .41(.00) | 1.14 | 0.39 | .15 (.00) |
| **CAM** | | | | | | | |
| North America | .21 (.10) | | | .43 (.00) | -0.14 | 0.32 | .10 (.00) |
| Europe | .23 (.10) | | | .70 (.00) | -1.10 | 0.48 | .23 (.00) |
| Japan | | | | .27 (.11) | 0.82 | 0.24 | .06 (.10) |
| **CAD** | | | | | | | |
| North America | | | | .51 (.00) | 0.66 | 0.29 | .08 (.00) |
| Europe | .44 (.00) | | | .50 (.00) | 0.01 | 0.45 | .20 (.00) |
| Japan | | | .26 (.20) | | 0.84 | 0.23 | .05 (.12) |
| **REDUCE SET-UP** | | | | | | | |
| North America | .25 (.05) | | | .20 (.17) | 1.05 | 0.23 | .05 (.04) |
| Europe | .65 (.00) | | .25 (.09) | | -0.34 | 0.51 | .26 (.00) |
| Japan | .20 (.17) | | .18 (.10) | | 2.54 | 0.24 | .06 (.10) |
| **VALUE ANALYSIS** | | | | | | | |
| North America | .17 (.15) | | | .21 (.12) | 1.74 | 0.19 | .04 (.15) |
| Europe | .27 (.04) | | .27 (.06) | .22 (.11) | 0.49 | 0.39 | .15 (.00) |
| Japan | | | .22 (.18) | .30 (.03) | 0.84 | 0.29 | .08 (.02) |
| **GROUP TECHNOLOGY** | | | | | | | |
| North America | .22 (.09) | | | | 0.83 | 0.21 | .04 (.15) |
| Europe | .33 (.02) | | .21 (.14) | .38 (.01) | -0.29 | 0.45 | .20 (.00) |
| Japan | | | | .31 (.02) | 1.72 | 0.23 | .05 (.14) |
| **REDUCE WORKFORCE** | | | | | | | |
| North America | | .31 (.01) | | | 2.03 | 0.23 | .05 (.04) |
| Europe | .23 (.13) | | | .25 (.11) | 2.15 | 0.21 | .05 (.17) |
| Japan | | | | | 2.73 | 0.11 | .01 (.82) |
| **EXPANSION** | | | | | | | |
| North America | | -.25 (.01) | | | 2.92 | 0.19 | .04 (.17) |
| Europe | | | | | 2.37 | 0.18 | .03 (.34) |
| Japan | | | | | 2.66 | 0.17 | 03.(42) |

| | | | | | | |
|---|---|---|---|---|---|---|
| **REDUCING MFG UNITS** | | | | | | |
| North America | | | | 1.09 | 0.13 | .02 (.57) |
| Europe | .29 (.03) | | -.29 (.04) | .32 (.02) | 0.73 | 0.31 | .09 (.01) |
| Japan | | | | .34 (.02) | 0.73 | 0.29 | .09 (.02) |
| **PLANT RELOCATION** | | | | | | |
| North America | -.26 (.04) | | .26 (.09) | | 1.56 | 0.19 | .03 (.19) |
| Europe | | | | | 1.86 | 0.14 | .02 (.60) |
| Japan | | -.34 (.02) | | .19 (.13) | 2.31 | 0.25 | .06 (.09) |
| **NEW PROC/OLD PROD** | | | | | | |
| North America | | | | | 2.59 | 0.14 | .02 (.48) |
| Europe | | | .25 (.10) | .39 (.01) | 0.78 | 0.32 | .10 (.01) |
| Japan | | | | | 3.11 | 0.17 | .03 (.46) |
| **NEW PROC/NEW PROD** | | | | | | |
| North America | .55 (.00) | | | | 0.54 | 0.40 | .16 (.00) |
| Europe | .48 (.00) | | -.23 (.09) | .36 (.01) | 1.44 | 0.41 | .17 (.00) |
| Japan | | | | .46 (.00) | 0.82 | 0.37 | .14 (.00) |
| **STANDARDIZING** | | | | | | |
| North America | | | | | 1.69 | 0.18 | .03 (.21) |
| Europe | .36 (.01) | .19 (.09) | | | 0.73 | 0.30 | .09 (.01) |
| Japan | | .22 (.20) | | | 0.54 | 0.24 | .06 (09) |
| **STRATEGIC PLANNING** | | | | | | |
| North America | | | | | 1.59 | 0.17 | .03 (.26) |
| Europe | .20 (.09) | | | | 1.77 | 0.24 | .06 (.08) |
| Japan | | | | .16 (.20) | 1.72 | 0.22 | .05 (.18) |
| **MFG INFO SYSYTEMS** | | | | | | |
| North America | | | | | 2.02 | 0.19 | .03 (.18) |
| Europe | .27 (.01) | | .20 (.06) | .20 (.05) | 1.21 | 0.44 | .19 (.00) |
| Japan | | | .34 (.00) | | 3.32 | 0.26 | .07(.05) |
| **LATERAL INFO SYSTEMS** | | | | | | |
| North America | .15 (.20) | | | .17 (.20) | 2.08 | 0.18 | .03 (.20) |
| Europe | .17 (.12) | | .33 (.01) | | 1.39 | 0.36 | .13 (.00) |
| Japan | | | .33 (.02) | | 2.34 | 0.24 | .06 (.09) |
| **RECONDITIONING** | | | | | | |
| North America | | | | | 2.10 | 0.14 | .02 (.50) |
| Europe | | | .23 (.08) | | 1.12 | 0.23 | .05 (.12) |
| Japan | | | .19 (.08) | | 1.28 | 0.28 | .08 (.03) |
| **ROBOTS** | | | | | | |
| North America | | .19 (.06) | .24 (.10) | | -0.09 | 0.23 | .05 (.05) |
| Europe | .63 (.00) | .21 (.10) | | .44 (.00) | -1.80 | 0.50 | .25 (.00) |
| Japan | | | | | 1.21 | 0.19 | .04 (.31) |
| **FMS** | | | | | | |
| North America | .45 (.00) | | .31 (.05) | | -0.77 | 0.37 | .14 (.00) |
| Europe | .55 (.00) | | | .31(.02) | -0.67 | 0.48 | .23 (.00) |
| Japan | | | | | 1.8 | 0.25 | .06(.08) |
| **CLOSING PLANTS** | | | | | | |
| North America | | | .25 (.03) | | -0.02 | 0.20 | .04 (.14) |
| Europe | | | | | 1.16 | 0.16 | .03 (.47) |
| Japan | | | | | 1.25 | 0.17 | .03 (.47) |
| **PROCESS SPC** | | | | | | |
| North America | .44 (.00) | .31 (.00) | | | 0.35 | 0.36 | .13 (.00) |
| Europe | | | | .22 (.10) | 2.10 | 0.25 | .06 (.07) |
| Japan* | | | | | | | |
| **PRODUCT SPC** | | | | | | |
| North America | .38 (.00) | .19 (.08) | | .29 (.05) | 0.26 | 0.32 | .10 (.00) |
| Europe | .14 (.12) | -.14 (.20) | .19 (.15) | .23 (.07) | 1.69 | 0.33 | .11 (.00) |
| Japan* | | | | | | | |

*Statistical process and product control programs are not available in the Japanese data set.

PART THREE


MANUFACTURING AND GLOBAL COMPETITION

MANAGING INTERNATIONAL MANUFACTURING
K. Ferdows (Editor)
© Elsevier Science Publishers B.V. (North-Holland), 1989                215


LEARNING, PRODUCTIVITY, AND U.S.-JAPAN INDUSTRIAL "COMPETITIVENESS"


Marvin B. LIEBERMAN

Stanford University


1. INTRODUCTION


In global manufacturing industries such as autos and electronics, American
firms that were once dominant have now been overtaken by Japanese
producers.   In  this  chapter  I  assess  this  international  shift   in
manufacturing  competitiveness.   I  argue that the ascendancy of Japanese
manufacturers has been limited to a specific class of industries where the
Japanese  have  achieved  more  rapid  rates  of  learning and process improvement.  The comparatively slow diffusion of manufacturing methods from
Japan  to  the  US  has enabled this competitive advantage to be sustained
over time.

My  general  framework  for  comparing  US  and Japanese manufacturing industries is derived from economic models of  competition  in  environments
where  learning  is  important [1].  These models reveal that competition
depends on three key parameters: (1) the learning curve "slope" or  learning  rate, (2) the time horizon or discount rate used in making investment
decisions, and (3) the rate at which information acquired through learning
diffuses  among  firms.  These parameters define the equilibrium number of
producers  and  the  behavior of prices and profits.  More importantly, when
the   parameters  differ  among  firms,  they  determine  which  producers
ultimately dominate the market, and which may fail to survive.

In  this  chapter  I  present evidence that in certain types of industries
Japanese  firms  have  maintained  faster  learning  rates,  longer   time
horizons,  or  lower  rates  of information leakage than US firms.  Within
each country, of course, firms are not homogeneous.  But there do seem  to
be important international differences in behaviour and performance.  As a
specific example, I  compare  the  productivity  records  of  six  US  and
Japanese auto companies over the 1950-85 period.

The organization of the chapter is as follows:

Section  2  documents  the  inter-industry pattern of Japanese productivity
growth and exports.

Section  3 considers policies such as "just-in-time" scheduling and an emphasis on shop floor decision-making that appear to accelerate the  learning process in many Japanese companies.

Section 4 examines factors that might lead Japanese firms to pursue longer investment time horizons than their US competitors. These include differences in cost of capital, capital budgeting, and managerial incentives.

Section 5 considers why US and Japanese firms may differ in their average rates of technological absorption and leakage. This is followed by a concluding section and a discussion of managerial implications.


## 1. RELATIVE PRODUCTIVITY GROWTH AND EXPORT SHARES

Do Japanese manufacturing firms have faster rates of learning and productivity growth than their US counterparts? And if so, does this hold true

### Japanese and U.S. Manufacturing Labor Productivity Indexes by Sector, 1960-85

| Year | All Mfg | Ferrous Metals | Machinery | Ceramics | Chemicals | Petroleum Products | Paper &Pulp | Textiles |
|---|---|---|---|---|---|---|---|---|
| Japan: | | | | | | | | |
| 1960 | 100.0 | 100.0 | 100.0 | 100.0 | 100.0 | 100.0 | 100.0 | 100.0 |
| 1965 | 148.9 | 163.0 | 154.9 | 146.4 | 185.6 | 196.0 | 141.9 | 141.9 |
| 1970 | 280.8 | 367.8 | 334.1 | 247.9 | 409.5 | 416.5 | 270.0 | 227.2 |
| 1975 | 378.7 | 498.8 | 483.2 | 308.0 | 545.4 | 466.4 | 360.8 | 295.9 |
| 1980 | 590.8 | 727.7 | 908.9 | 462.6 | 859.6 | 492.9 | 545.5 | 389.1 |
| 1985 | 732.0 | 830.3 | 1310.6 | 523.2 | 1114.9 | 496.8 | 690.6 | 448.6 |
| US: | | | | | | | | |
| 1960 | 100. | 100.[a] | 100.[b] | 100.[c] | 100.[d] | 100.[e] | 100.[f] | 100.[g] |
| 1985 | 206. | 194. | 205. | 186. | 416. | 227. | 242. | 290. |
| Ratio[h]: Japan/US | 4.3 | 6.4 | 2.8 | 2.7 | 2.2 | 2.9 | | 1.5 |

[a.] Steel (SIC 331) only.
[b.] Average for construction machinery and equipment (SIC 3531), machine tools (SIC 3541, 3542), major household appliances (SIC 363) and motor vehicles and equipment (SIC 371).
[c.] Structural clay products (SIC 325).
[d.] Synthetic fibers (SIC 2873, 2824).
[e.] Petroleum refining (SIC 2911).
[f.] Paper, paperboard and pulp mills (SIC 2611, 2621, 2631, 2661).
[g.] Average for yarn mills (SIC 2281) and hosiery (SIC 2251, 2252).
[h.] Japan index for 1985 divided by U.S. index for 1985.

Sources
Japanese data are from Economic Statistics Annual, Research and Statistics Department, Bank of Japan, March 1987 and previous years.

U.S. data are from Productivity Measures for Selected Industries, 1958-85, U.S. Department of Labor, March 1987; and Statistical Abstract of the United States.

TABLE 1

in a broad range of manufacturing industries, or is it limited to certain types of products?

Over the period from 1960 to 1985, manufacturing labor productivity grew in Japan at an average rate of 8.3% per year, compared with 2.9% in the US. But Japanese productivity growth was not distributed evenly across manufacturing industries. Japanese productivity growth has been disproportionately concentrated in industries producing high-volume products where a large number of interdependent processing steps must be coordinated (Abegglen and Stalk, 1985).[2] Industries with these characteristics include autos, consumer electronics, cameras, watches, and copying equipment. In other industries, the absolute level of Japanese productivity, and the rate of productivity growth, have been comparable to that observed for US firms. This has been true, for example, in capital-intensive process industries such as paper and chemicals, and in relatively simple assembly industries such as textiles and clothing.[3]

Table 1 documents this pattern of differential productivity growth. The table reports labor productivity indexes for several manufacturing sectors in Japan over the period from 1960 to 1985. The index numbers show that productivity grew most rapidly in the machinery manufacturing sector, where the potential for economies of coordination across processing steps tends to be greatest.

Direct comparison with productivity growth in the US is hampered by the lack of compatible industry and sector definitions for the two countries. But the US data in Table 1, which approximate the Japanese categories, reveal that while Japan had more rapid productivity growth in all categories, the Japan/US differential was greatest in the machinery sector. Thus, Japanese productivity growth in the machinery sector stands out from other sectors in Japan as well as from the comparable sector in the US.

Over the long term, no country can sustain a net export surplus across the majority of its industries; exchange rates and price levels adjust to restore rough trade balance.[4] A uniform percentage productivity increase in all industries within a given country raises domestic living standards but does not enhance the country's "competitiveness" in world markets. However, shifts in productivity among domestic industries do affect comparative advantage and hence the international competitiveness in domestic firms.[5] Japan's pattern of relative productivity growth appears to have influenced its comparative advantage in international trade. Table 2 gives the Japanese share of US imports by product category, as well as the industry distribution of total Japanese exports. In 1985 Japan accounted for more than a third of US imports of office machinery, telecommunication and sound apparatus, (primarily consumer electronics), watches and clocks, and automobiles. All of these categories consist largely of high-volume products requiring the coordination of numerous interdependent manufacturing steps.

What might account for the more rapid productivity growth of Japanese firms in these industries? I argue that it stems primarily from two factors: (1) the just-in-time approach to coordinating production flows, and (2) the human resource management policies of Japanese firms. Typically, in multi-stage manufacturing industries there are substantial opportunities for reducing coordination and transaction costs between processing steps. Long-term reductions in average total cost reflect the sum of

*M.B. Lieberman*

many accumulated improvements; major "breakthrough" innovations are un-
common, since individual process innovations are unlikely to affect more
than a few related steps. In such industries, competitive advantage is
gained through persistence and consistency in seeking a multitude of small
process improvements.

### JAPAN'S SHARE OF U.S. IMPORTS, AND DISTRIBUTION OF JAPANESE EXPORTS, BY PRODUCT CATEGORY

| Product Category | U.S. Imports in 1985 (billions of U.S. $) | Percent of U.S. Imports from Japan | Distribution of Japanese Exports (to all countries, 1982) |
|---|---|---|---|
| Telecomunication and Sound Apparatus | $18.6 | 60.5% | 13.6% |
| Office Machinery and Automatic Data Processing Machines | 11.6 | 48.7 | 2.3 |
| Transport Equipment | 58.4 | 40.4 | 20.5 |
| Watches, Clocks and Parts | 1.4 | 35.1 | 1.0 |
| Iron, Steel & Ferrous Metal Products | 10.3 | 29.8 | 11.4 |
| Professional, Scientific, and Controlling Instruments and Electrical Machinery and Parts | 20.9 | 27.2 | 3.6 |
| Heavy Industrial Machinery & Parts | 27.4 | 25.4 | 17.4 |
| Non-Ferrous Metal Products | 13.6 | 15.5 | 3.5 |
| Leather, Wood and Other Products | 45.4 | 12.1 | 15.6 |
| Chemicals | 14.5 | 9.7 | 4.6 |
| Textiles and Clothing | 21.2 | 7.3 | 2.9 |
| Aircraft and Parts | 3.6 | 3.7 | 0.5 |
| Agricultural Products | 23.0 | 2.1 | 1.1 |
| Crude Materials | 64.3 | 0.3 | 1.1 |
| Commodities and Articles not Classified | 11.1 | 6.7 | 1.1 |
| Total | $34.5 | 19.9% | 100% |

Sources
OECD Economic Surveys 1984/1985: August 1985.
NIPPON a charted survey of JAPAN 1984/85.
Highlights of U.S. Exports and Import Trade: December 1985.

### TABLE 2

## 3. ACCELERATED LEARNING IN JAPANESE FIRMS

At the firm or plant level, productivity growth can arise from many
sources. These sources may be external to the firm, as in the case of
process technology obtained through license or capital equipment purchased
from suppliers. But in many industries, the most important productivity
improvements come from the problem solving efforts of the workforce---
including managers, engineers, and production workers. I broadly define
"learning" as the component of productivity growth derived from these
internal problem solving efforts and activities. To be sure, this
internal/external distinction is often difficult to draw precisely. For
example, a considerable amount of internal problem solving effort may be
required to assimilate technology purchased from outside. But the
distinction is nevertheless an important one, since a firm's competitive
edge comes largely from its superiority at internal problem solving. This

is because within a given industry, all producers can normally gain access
to external sources of process technology on roughly equal terms.

Various types of activities may contribute to learning. A few examples
are:
  - improvement by individual employees at well-defined tasks;
  - improvements attained through group activity (e.g., quality
    circles);
  - formal suggestions submitted by individuals and groups;
  - equipment and tooling enhancements by plant engineering staff;
  - formal and informal interaction between the firm's employees
and key outsiders, such as equipment suppliers and customers.

These activities may yield improvements in plant organization, product
design, work methods, equipment, and worker skill. In general, the
learning process encompasses a wide range of activities and can shape the
operations in numerous ways.

The data in Table 1 imply that Japanese producers have maintained rapid
"learning" in the machinery sector, where production characteristically
requires the coordination of many sequential manufacturing steps. Japanese
firms have focused their problem solving efforts on ways to reduce the
cost of executing and coordinating these interdependent activities. There
are a number of reasons why Japanese producers have excelled at this; I
limit my discussion to two types of policies that have facilitated the
learning process:

  (1) just-in-time scheduling, and
  (2) policies pertaining to the management of human resources.

## 3.1 "Just-in-time" Production Philosophy

The two primary components of a "just-in-time" program are: (1) reduction
of work-in-process inventories between manufacturing steps, and (2)
reduction of machine set-up times at each step. These actions link
production steps more closely together and make the process more continuous. Reduced inventory holding costs are the most obvious benefit,
but the gains typically go much deeper. Reduction of work-in-process inventories exposes defects in the manufacturing process forces managers and
workers to eliminate sources of variability. In short, the "just-in-time"
approach provides a specific set of targets and a discipline to ensure
continued learning and process improvement.[6]

The "just-in-time" production philosophy is normally applied in conjunction with stringent quality control procedures. Originally developed in
the US, these procedures have been applied more uniformly and systematically by Japanese firms. By tracing quality defects and rooting them out,
the entire production flow can often be streamlined. The ultimate impact
of these techniques is to reduce transaction costs within the firm and
between the firm and its suppliers. Inventory costs, scheduling and
procurement costs, and rework and repair costs can often be cut dramatically. Thus, transaction costs, which show up largely in the form of
manufacturing overhead, are substantially reduced (Miller and Vollmann,
1985). By one estimate, two-thirds of the labor productivity of Japanese
competitors results from more productive utilization of overhead functions

(Abegglen and Stalk, 1985). Such overhead savings are especially critical in the electronics and machinery industries, where overhead costs account for more than half of total value added (Miller and Vollmann, 1985).

## 3.2  Human Resource Policies

A second set of characteristics that contributes to more rapid learning in Japanese companies relates to their internal organization and human resource management policies. In Japanese firms, workers' jobs are seldom specified in detail, and workers are frequently rotated among various jobs and operating levels of the firm. Teamwork across functional areas is strongly encouraged---one important link is between engineers engaged in the design of new products, and those developing the manufacturing processes to be used on the factory floor (Clark and Fujimoto, 1988). By comparison, the emphasis in many American firms is on efficiency attained through job specialization and hierarchical control (Aoki, 1986; Imai, Nonaka and Takeuchi, 1985).

One system of organization is not necessarily better than another; their relative merits depend on the product and process technologies being used, and the types of information flows that best facilitate productivity improvement (Aoki, 1986). The American system of hierarchical control should be most effective in industries where primary innovations are developed at a high level within the firm (e.g., an R&D laboratory) or come from outside sources and can be easily transferred to the production floor. The Japanese approach should prove more effective in industries where process improvements require interdepartmental coordination and numerous small modifications on the factory floor that are not visible at higher levels in the managerial hierarchy. In short, the Japanese approach may be more efficient where factory-level learning-by-doing is important, whereas the American system may be more effective for developing and implementing "breakthrough" product innovations that can be manufactured via standard production processes.

Koike (1984) documents the extent of job rotation in Japan, as compared with US practices. Rotation gives Japanese workers a broader set of problem solving skills and the ability to cope with unexpected contingencies on the shop floor. The lifetime employment system and seniority wages in Japan gives workers incentive to make suggestions for process improvement. This compares with greater specialization in the US as workers move up a "job ladder". The shorter job tenure and higher interfirm mobility of US workers reduces incentives for investment in firm-specific problem solving skills. Interfirm mobility may also increase the rate of organizational "forgetting", as worker-embodied learning exits from the firm.

The extent of grass-roots problem solving in Japanese companies is emplified by statistics on the number of suggestions submitted by employees. In 1983, company employees made 1.7 million specific suggestions at Toyota, and 2.8 million suggestions at Mazda (Toyota Motor Corporation, 1984; Mazda Motor Corporation, 1984). In the case of Mazda this represents more than 100 suggestions per employee per year, of which more than 70% were "accepted" by the company. The mere fact that firms collect detailed statistics on employee suggestions and display them prominently in company reports attests to the priority placed on low-level problem solving.

The Japanese emphasis on grass-roots problem solving and improvement through just-in-time coordination is particularly well suited for complex, high-volume fabrication and assembly industries. The auto industry is perhaps the best example of an industry with such characteristics. Below, I consider historical evidence on rates of learning and productivity growth for Japanese and American automobile producers.

### 3.3 Comparative productivity growth of US and Japanese Automobile Manufacturers

Numerous recent studies have documented an absolute productivity advantage of Japanese firms in automobile manufacturing (Harbour, 1981; National Academy of Engineering, 1982; Abernathy, Clark and Kantrow, 1983; Flynn, 1983; Branstad, 1984; Cusumano, 1985; Aizcorbe, Winston and Friedlaender, 1987). In the early 1980s the cost differential was typically estimated at approximately $2000 per car, attributed primarily to differences in productivity, rather than wage effects. Shifts in exchange rates have since narrowed this cost gap, at least temporarily.

The gap between US and Japanese productivity in the auto industry did not come about overnight. The current differential reflects a long process of incremental productivity improvement by Japanese automakers. Cusumano (1985) documents the process by which Toyota and Nissan transferred automotive technology from the West, and added indigenous improvements that enabled them to surpass the Western productivity level. Interestingly, Toyota and Nissan pursued different approaches to technology transfer and innovation (Toyota is less automated), but the end result has been high productivity for both firms relative to US levels.

Figures 1, 2, and 3 present data on productivity growth for three Japanese automakers (Toyota, Nissan and Mazda) and the three major US producers from the early 1950s through 1985.[7] The figures show that the Japanese experienced significantly faster growth in labor producti-vity, which was not simply the result of substituting capital for labor.

Figure 1 plots labor productivity for each of the six companies, measured as vehicles per employee per year. I have adjusted these figures for differences in the extent of vertical integration, [8] but not for dif-ferences in vehicle complexity, capacity utilization, or hours worked.[9] On average over the 1950-85 period, labor productivity grew at 7.2% per year in Japan, compared with 2.1% in the US.[10] Allowing for differences in average vehicle value between the US and Japan, it appears that Toyota and Nissan's labor productivity began to surpass the US level during the late 1960s, and is now significantly higher. Much of the initial post-war growth in Japanese productivity stemmed from acquisition of foreign technology and attainment of basic scale economies. However, productivity increases recorded since the 1960s largely reflect a more rapid rate of indigenous "learning". Figure 1 also documents the extraordinary increase in labor productivity achieved by Mazda after 1975, when the firm's operations were reorganized to incorporate key elements of the Toyota production system (Harvard Business School, 1982; Pascale and Rholen, 1983). Mazda's adoption of just-in-time manufacturing and increased

reliance on decentralized problem solving had  dramatic  effects.  Mazda's
labor  productivity  during  the 1960s and early 1970s was barely on a par
with US producers; currently, it nearly equals that of Toyota.

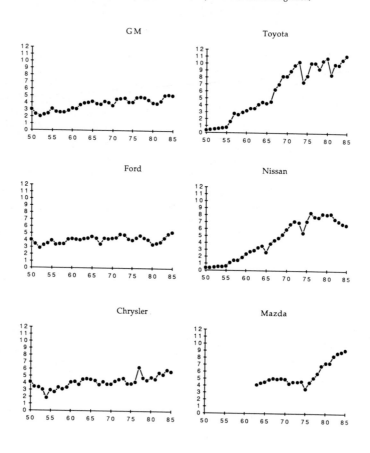

Labor Productivity of US and Japanese Automakers
(Vehicles per Employee, Per Year, Adjusted for Vertical Integration)

FIGURE 1

Figure 2 plots capital stock per vehicle produced.(11)  Capital  stock  is
defined  as  net  property,  plant  and equipment, as obtained from annual
reports of each firm . Since the 1960s, capital investment per vehicle has
been  falling for Toyota and Mazda, and roughly constant for Nissan. Thus,
Japanese capital intensity was not  increasing  over  time,  as  might  be
expected  if  firms  were  simply  substituting  capital for labor in the
production process.  In general, the Japanese level of capital  investment
per  vehicle  appears  comparable  to  that  of US producers.  The American

firms, and to some extent the Japanese, show a sharp increase in investment in the early 1980s, which reflects retooling activity.

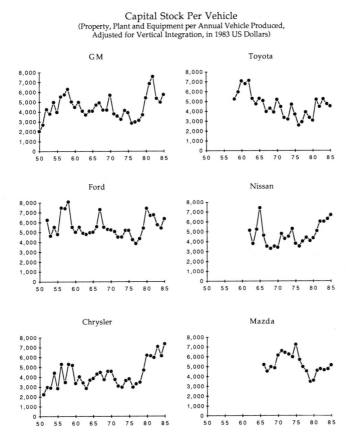

Capital Stock Per Vehicle
(Property, Plant and Equipment per Annual Vehicle Produced,
Adjusted for Vertical Integration, in 1983 US Dollars)

**FIGURE 2**

Figure 3 plots capital stock per employee. This ratio increased gradually over time at Toyota and Nissan; all firms show considerable increases after 1980. For Toyota and Nissan, the pattern of constant or falling capital stock per vehicle (Figure 2), combined with increasing capital stock per worker (Figure 3), implies an increase in the span of control of individual workers, as sequential machine operations were more closely linked. Thus, closer coupling of production steps led to a gradual decline in required labor input per car, while capital input remained roughly constant.

Capital Stock Per Worker
(Property, Plant and Equipment per Employee, in 1983 US Dollars)

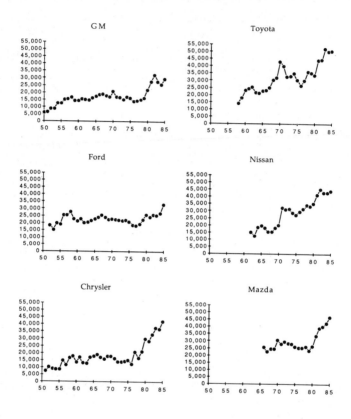

**FIGURE 3**

## 4. DIFFERENCES IN TIME HORIZON BETWEEN US AND JAPANESE FIRMS

It is sometimes alleged that US firms focus on the short run whereas Japanese firms take a long term view. With a longer time horizon, Japanese firms would invest in productivity improvement projects that would appear unattractive to US competitors. A longer time horizon might also lead Japanese firms to adopt more aggressive pricing strategies, potentially inducing exit by US firms.

Why might Japanese firms adopt a longer time horizon in their investment decisions? Possible reasons include: (1) Japanese firms enjoy a lower cost of capital, so future returns are discounted at a lower rate, (2) capital budgeting procedures in the US are biased against long term benefits, which are more fully considered in Japan, and (3) lifetime employment for Japanese managers gives them greater incentives to adopt a long time horizon in decision making. I consider these three arguments in turn.


## 4.1 Cost of Capital Differences Between the US and Japan


The question of whether Japanese firms enjoy a capital cost advantage over US producers is a topic of continuing debate (e.g., Chase Financial Policy, 1980; Hatsopoulos, 1983; US Department of Commerce, 1983; Baldwin, 1986; Flaherty and Itami, 1984; Ando and Auerbach, 1985, 1987). A detailed summary of this debate is well beyond the scope of this chapter, but I survey some of the major arguments.

Factors that might give Japanese firms a lower average cost of capital include differences in national tax policy, government policies relating to international financial flows or bankruptcy laws, and differences in financial institutions and corporate structure. Japanese firms might enjoy a lower cost of capital if these factors reduce the after-tax cost of debt or equity or if they reduce risk, thereby enabling Japanese firms to make greater use of debt financing.[12]

One capital cost factor that can be unequivocally rejected is differences in national tax policy (Ando and Auerbach, 1985; Baldwin, 1986). US and Japanese tax laws are similar; if anything, the US tax code has been relatively more generous toward business investment. A second reason why the cost of debt or equity might be lower in Japan is that barriers to international capital flow prevent the equalization of returns across countries. Japanese governmental and institutional barriers to international capital flows have been significant in the past but have now largely eroded (Baldwin, 1986). The high personal savings rate in Japan, coupled with barriers to capital outflows, might enable Japanese corporations to tap a large pool of domestic funds at low cost. However, there is evidence that over the 1960–1980 period real market returns to debt and equity were actually higher in Japan than in the US (Baldwin, 1986). Thus, it does not appear that lenders required lower rates of return for comparable types of investment instruments in Japan.

Most studies that find a Japanese capital cost advantage attribute it primarily to the ability of Japanese firms to maintain higher financial leverage (e.g., Chase Financial Policy, 1980; Hatsopolous, 1983; US Department of Commerce, 1983; Flaherty and Itami, 1984). Two questions are raised by such assertions: (1) Do Japanese firms really maintain the extraordinary debt ratios frequently cited; and (2) If so, what enables these firms to maintain significantly higher leverage than US producers in the same industry?

Several recent studies have concluded that the difference in financial leverage between US and Japanese firms is largely illusory (Kester, 1986; Michel and Shaked, 1985). Japanese accounting practices tend to understate the magnitude of equity investment in the firm. There has, moreover, been a general move in Japan toward greater equity financing in recent years (Flaherty and Itami, 1984).

The ability of Japanese firms to maintain high leverage stems primarily from the structure of financial institutions in Japan, which may have the effect of reducing risk (Wright and Suzuki, 1985; Flaherty and Itami, 1984; Ouchi, 1984; Baldwin, 1986). In Japan (and also in many European countries) banks lie at the center of groups of interrelated companies and hold a mix of financial instruments in these companies, including short term debt, long term debt and equity. Banks are often indirectly involved in management of the firm, and in situations of financial distress can reorganize the firm without invoking the long and costly legal proceedings necessary under US bankruptcy laws. Also, close ties between bank and firm in Japan may circumvent information imperfections in the outside capital market and eliminate the monitoring costs required to protect creditors in the US. These factors could, in combination, give Japanese firms lower capital costs, which would promote a longer time horizon in investment decisions.

## 4.2 Differences in Capital Budgeting Processes

Even if Japanese and US firms have the same cost of capital, they may differ in the way they allocate this capital to investment projects. Comparative evidence on capital budgeting procedures in the US and Japan reveal some differences in approach that might bias American firms towards an unreasonably short time horizon (Hodder, 1986; Hodder and Riggs, 1985; Hayes and Garvin, 1982).

Hodder (1986) provides the only detailed comparison of US and Japanese capital budgeting practices. While he argues that Japanese and US procedures are more similar than is commonly believed, two major differences do stand out. The first is the apparent misuse of risk-adjusted discount rates in the US, and improper adjustment for inflation. American firms often assess risky projects using discount rates of up to 30%, as compared with a standard figure of 10% used by Japanese companies.[13]

The second major difference is that Japanese firms typically engage in more extensive discussion of project assumptions, focusing on possible scenarios and management responses. A wide range of managerial staff participate in these discussions. Factors that are difficult to quantify, such as improved quality and enhanced competitive position, are brought out and often incorporated in the formal analysis. In the end, this ability to identify and analyze critical input assumptions is probably more important than the fact that the numerical processing methods used in Japan are less sophisticated than those applied by most American firms. Indeed, it has been argued that American firms often emphasize financial technique at the expense of economic and strategic substance (Hayes and Garvin, 1982).

## 4.3 Differences in Managerial Time Horizon

Aside from these differences in capital budgeting procedures, it is possible that individual managers are more inclined to take a short term view in American companies. One common argument is that the greater interfirm mobility of managers in the US tends to distort managerial incentives.

In the US, managers frequently move from firm to firm or from division to division within a given firm. This makes it difficult to trace long term consequences back to the original decision maker. Also, a manager's financial compensation is often linked to the short-term operating performance of the business unit with which he or she is currently involved. In this context, managers may be inclined to emphasize projects that have high immediate returns, but low or even negative long term consequences.

In Japanese firms, by contrast, most managers stay with a single firm for their entire career. Final promotion decisions, which are the capstone of the executive's career and carry great prestige and financial consequences, are based on an assessment of the executive's entire, career-long record. Japanese firms are better able to track the long term outcomes of executive actions and use this information in final promotion decisions. Thus, Japanese managers may face greater incentives to take a long term view in decision making.

A related point is that Japanese managers tend to emphasize long term growth objectives more strongly than purely financial returns. Given the commitment of Japanese firms to lifetime employment in an environment with rapid increases in labor productivity, it is essential that managers seek out new growth opportunities to ensure continued survival of the firm. Survey evidence shows that Japanese and US managers differ strongly in their relative weighting of growth versus profitability objectives (Kagono, et al., 1984).

## 5. INTERFIRM AND INTERNATIONAL DIFFUSION OF PROCESS TECHNOLOGY

Economic models of competition underscore the importance of technology diffusion. Diffusion reduces the disparity in firms' relative costs and can influence the average rate of productivity growth within a given industry.[14] Moreover, firms that are able to absorb innovations from outside while preventing leakage of internally-developed improvements can gain cost advantages over their competitors. This logic can be extended to the national level; for example, Japan would naturally tend to gain comparative advantage in a given industry if Japanese firms collectively absorb technology from abroad more readily than foreign firms absorb technology from Japan. What are the specific channels by which technology diffuses among competing firms? A wide range of diffusion channels have been identified (Mansfield, 1982, 1985; Rodgers, 1982; Von Hippel, 1987). These include: interfirm mobility of employees; "reverse engineering" of competitor's products; patent licensing; dissemination of capital-goods innovations through equipment suppliers; informal communication among technical personnel; and technology exchange programs established by national governments and industry associations.

There is large research literature on interfirm and international diffusion of "discrete" process innovations, e.g., numerically-controlled machine tools, basic oxygen furnaces, float glass.[15] This literature relates diffusion speed to measurable characteristics such as expected profitablility, firm size, etc. There is also a literature on "technology transfer" from technologically-advanced countries to less-developed nations (e.g., Stobaugh and Wells, 1984). The latter type of diffusion

has largely taken place through multi-national corporations or explicit
licensing agreements between individual firms. However, there has been
very little research on the diffusion of process technology among directly
competing firms. The sole study deriving quantitative measures of such
diffusion is Mansfield (1985), who shows that most information on new
processes leaks to competitors within one to two years. There is also
some rough evidence from learning curve studies that on average, less than
20% of industrial learning is kept proprietary (Boston Consulting Group,
1978; Lieberman, 1982).

Here I argue that an important distinction should be made between the
"discrete" innovations typically considered in the research literature,
and what might be termed "manufacturing systems" innovations. By
"manufacturing systems" innovations I mean the collection of many small
improvements in capital equipment, work methods and managerial practices
that in combination often yield major productivity gains. It is often
difficult to pin down precisely the nature of these innovations. Partly
for this reason, they tend to diffuse more slowly than discrete process
innovations. To the extent that the Japanese have focused on such
"systems" innovations, while the US has emphasized more basic research and
"breakthough-type" developments, technology would diffuse more slowly from
Japan to the US than vice versa.


## 5.1  Impediments to Diffusion of "Manufacturing Systems" Innovations


As discussed in section 2, Japanese productivity growth has been highest
in industries where numerous production steps must be coordinated. The
key to productivity improvement in such industries is the ability to make
continued small improvements distributed throughout the production
process. Typically, these improvements are embodied in many pieces of
capital equipment [16] and in the form of specific skills acquired by
production workers, process engineers, and mangerial personnel.[17] This
myriad of small improvements is inherently more difficult to transfer than
innovations that are embodied in product designs or patents or a few key
pieces of machinery.

This distributed process learning is not, of course, impossible to transfer internationally. Japanese firms have generally met with considerable
success in establishing US clones of their Japan-based plants (e.g.,
Business Week, 1986). The productivity of these plants has usually ap-
proached, and sometimes surpassed, the level of comparable plants in
Japan. The NUMMI plant in Fremont, California (a joint venture of GM and
Toyota) is a close copy of Toyota's Takaoka plant in Japan. NUMMI's labor
productivity and quality are currently near Takaoka levels, roughly 50%
higher than those prevailing at other GM plants (Krafcik, 1986). Other
Japanese auto plants in the US, such as the Nissan plant in Tennessee, are
reputed to be less efficient. Nevertheless, all of these plants have been
run under close supervision of the Japanese parent company; transfer of
technology to US automakers has thus far been comparatively limited.
Successful transfer of "manufacturing systems" technology normally
requires substantial person-to-person contact. For example, NUMMI's
successful start-up was dependent upon the early presence of about one
hundred Toyota managerial and engineering personnel, and the fact that
over two hundred American production team leaders and managers were sent

to Japan for training at Toyota's Takaoka facility. Diffusion to other GM plants should eventually occur as GM employees, managers, and parts suppliers gain increased experience with the Toyota approach. But this is unlikely to be a rapid process, given the massive size of GM's operations.[18]

The manufacturing systems innovations of Japanese firms appear to diffuse more rapidly within Japan than across the Pacific Ocean. For example, the just-in-time system pioneered by Toyota was adopted by many Japanese companies during the 1970s. According to Henderson (1986), Japanese firms that adopted programs to convert to the Toyota production system were able to achieve about 80% of the system in two years, even though it took Toyota twenty years of development. Perhaps the most dramatic case is Mazda, whose production system was quickly modified after the firm went technically bankrupt in 1974. Mazda's subsequent productivity growth, as illustrated in Figure 1, attests to the results.

Diffusion within Japan is facilitated by the existence of numerous technical associations and professional societies that provide channels for information exchange. Japan lacks the intellectual property tradition of the West, and reciprocity-based information trading is common practice among Japanese employees.[19] Cultural homogeneity and common values may also promote rapid diffusion in Japan. However, one factor that retards diffusion is the practice of lifetime employment.

International differences in culture, language, or institutional structure can help keep technological improvements impacted within the country where they were first developed. In the case of the US and Japan, information has historically flowed more easily from the US to Japan than vice versa. This reflects the more open nature of US institutions, but also the fact that Japanese firms have made relatively greater investment in information acquision channels. There is an important asymmetry even at the basic level of language acquisition---few Americans learn Japanese, but many Japanese study English.[20]

## 6. CONCLUSION AND MANAGERIAL IMPLICATIONS

In recent years, Japan has gained global comparative advantage in manufacturing industries that require the coordination of numerous interdependent processing steps. Such industries include autos, consumer electronics, cameras and office equipment. In other industries that lack this coordination requirement, Japanese firms have failed to develop major cost advantages or attain large global market shares.

The key to Japanese productivity has been the ability to efficiently manage the linkage between process steps, gradually transforming the manufacturing process to be more like a continuous flow. The just-in-time and human resource management policies of Japanese firms have facilitated this transformation. Once achieved, Japanese productivity advantages have been sustained by the slow diffusion of "manufacturing systems" innovations from Japan to the US and other countries. There is some evidence that Japanese firms have also benefited from a longer time-horizon in investment decisions, as promoted by low-cost capital, more effective capital budgeting, or less myopic managerial incentives.  These factors  may  well  have  enhanced  the  average  rate  of  manufacturing productivity growth; however, they would not  have  favored  the  specific industries  where  productivity  growth  has  been greatest in Japan.  For example, a Japanese capital cost advantage would  favor  capital-intensive industries such as  pulp  and  paper,  petroleum refining, chemicals and steel.  With the exception  of  steel,  Japanese  exports  have  not  been concentrated  in  these  industries.  Thus, it seems unlikely that capital cost and time horizon differences have played a primary  role  in  shaping the international "competitiveness" of Japanese firms.

Japanese  companies  have  demonstrated  that  effective  management  and continuous   improvement  of  manufacturing  operations  can  yield  major competitive  advantages.  Indeed,  Japanese  producers  have  been  most successful  in  those  industries  where superior manufacturing management provides the greatest  competitive  leverage  (as  opposed  to  advantages gained  from  low  labor  or  materials  costs, or patentable technology). While the impact of just-in-time and human resource policies as  practiced by  Japanese  firms  is  now widely appreciated, foreign competitors often fail to adopt comparable policies or  implement  them  effectively.   The diffusion  of  "manufacturing  systems"  innovations  is impeded by their inherent complexity, and by the  limited  extent  to  which  they  can  be codified.   As   a   result,   manufacturing  systems  innovations  yield competitive advantages that are  more  sustainable  than  those  derived  from many other sources, such as new product designs or innovative advertising.

At  the  firm  level,  manufacturing  managers  need  to  stimulate  the organizational   learning   process   and   influence   the  diffusion  of technological knowledge.  Manufacturing  technology  diffuses  across  two sets  of  firm  boundaries:  external  and  internal.  External boundaries separate the firm from other  firms;  internal  boundaries  separate  the firm's own operating units or plants.  These boundaries imply the need for two sets of diffusion policies: (1) policies for managing the transfer  of process  technology  between  the firm and the outside environment, and (2) policies for managing such transfers within the firm itself.

Firms differ greatly in their objectives for external technology transfer. Following World War II, for instance, Nissan and Toyota made  dramatically different  choices  regarding  technology inflow: Nissan actively imported technology from abroad, while Toyota pursued a much more  autonomous  path (Cusumano,  1985).   Firms  that  have  achieved technical leadership have clear incentives to restrict technology outflow.   However,  firms  often maintain  a  more  open stance, and reciprocity in technology exchange can sometimes provide for mutual gains.   Von  Hippel  (1986)  documents  the occurence  of  such  exchanges  among  all  but one of the firms in the US minimill sector; these practices seem  to  have  accelerated  the  average productivity  growth  of  the minimill producers relative to the integrated steel companies.  Similarly, the recent Sematech joint  venture  among  US semiconductor  producers  provides  for  exchange of manufacturing process technology, which may accelerate the average rate of  productivity  growth in  the US relative to Japan.  Managers must also choose among the specific mechanisms available for external technology transfer.   Direct  licensing is  most  feasible  when  process technology is well-defined and discrete. Capital goods suppliers often serve as important  conduits  for  technology flows,  both  within  and  among  countries.  Links can  sometimes  be established with potentially competing firms through  international  joint ventures (e.g., NUMMI), equity ownership (e.g., Ford's 25% ownership of Mazda), or voluntary R&D joint ventures (e.g., Sematech). Direct investment abroad can also provide a means to more effectively tap into technology. Texas Instruments, for example, has capitalized on its operating presence in both Japan and the US to set up twin semiconductor plants that draw upon the "best of both worlds" in terms of capital equipment and manufacturing approaches. Internal transfer raises a different set of issues: new manufacturing techniques, whether developed internally or acquired from outside, must be disseminated throughout the firm and adapted where necessary to local conditions. This requires policies for interplant communications, personnel rotation, and so forth. At NUMMI, for instance, Toyota trained a core staff of middle managers, most of whom have returned to Japan, plus a group of about fifty lower level managers and engineers who serve as the main conduit for training production workers at Toyota's new plants in North America. GM has rotated its NUMMI managers to other GM facilities in an effort (largely unsuccessful so far) to transfer key elements of the Toyota production system. Ford has established an internal television network to promote interplant communication and a common company knowledge base. All three companies have invested considerable resources in these and other efforts to disseminate the accumulated learning of successful plants. Indeed, the effective internal transfer of manufacturing systems knowledge is one of the greatest managerial challenges faced by large companies with decentralized plant operations.

## ACKNOWLEDGEMENTS

I thank Masahiko Aoki, Ana Aizcorbe, Carliss Baldwin, Michael Cusumano, Kasra Ferdows, Michael Harrison, Jeffrey Miller, Nathan Rosenberg, Henry Rowen, Robert Staiger, Steven Wheelwright and numerous others for helpful comments and discussions. Mahendre Gupta, Choon-Geol Moon and Robert Sartain provided excellent research assistance. The National Bureau of Economic Research and the Strategic Management Program at Stanford Business School provided financial support.

## FOOTNOTES

[1] This analytical framework is discussed in greater detail in Lieberman (1987). The relevant economics literature includes Spence(1981), Fudenberg and Tirole (1983), Ghemawat and Spence (1985),and Ross (1986).

[2] A processing "step" brings together two or more materials (as in assembly) or transforms material in some way (e.g., machining or casting).

[3] One interpretation is that Japanese firms have been most successful in industries that have traditionally been organized as batch or disconnected flow processes; the Japanese have streamlined these processes to operate more like continuous flow. Japanese

productivity gains have been smaller in industries producing simple
products (e.g., clothing) where the potential coordination economies
are small, or in industries where most producers have already
achieved continous flow operation (e.g., petroleum refining and
petrochemicals). However, the Japanese have had considerable success
in some industries that are sometimes thought of as continous flow---
in steel, for example they have gained economies through pursuit of
continous casting and other innovations that link sequential
processing stages more closely together.

[4]   There is, however, great contention among economists regarding the
      exact nature and speed of this adjustment process.

[5]   I define "competitiveness" in terms of comparative advantage, rather
      than a nation's ability to maintain a large trade surplus or a high
      (or low) exchange rate. The latter are sometimes thought of as
      measures of "competitiveness" but are indefensible as such. For
      example, a trade surpluss may be an indicator of domestic industrial
      weakness, as in the case of many Latin American countries that are
      currently forced to run large export surplusses to pay off their
      international debts. Similarly, the declining "competitiveness" of
      US industries has remained an issue of political concern for over a
      decade, despite large shifts in the value of the dollar.

[6]   Although the "just-in-time" approach is in many respects a generic
      process innovation, arising from the experiments of Toyota and other
      Japanese companies, the fact that this innovation arose in Japan is
      probably not an accident. High land prices in Japan make it costly
      to hold inventories; thus, it is not surprising that firms search or
      ways to reduce inventory levels. The emphasis on close coordination
      between stages may have a cultural basis: given one of the highest
      population densities in the world, the Japanese have developed a
      remarkably intricate social structure to coordinate human interaction
      (Nakane, 1970). Moreover, the large supply (and comparatively low
      wages) of engineering personnel in Japan makes it economical for
      Japanese firms to allocate greater engineering staff to process
      improvement efforts (Office of Technology Assessment, 1983, p.306;
      Okimoto, et. al., 1984, p.30).

[7]   Appendix A gives a summary of the underlying data.

[8]   For each firm, I adjusted for vertical integration by multiplying the
      total number of vehicles produced by the ratio of value added to
      sales. Thus, each firm is credited with the proportion of its total
      vehicle output attributable to in-house operations. If this
      adjustment is not made, the vehicles per employee figures appear much
      larger than the values shown in Figure 1.

[9]   Each of these adjustments would reduce the apparent productivity of
      the Japanese firms.

[10]  The graphs suggest a recent decline in labor productivity for Toyota
      and Nissan, but this is largely the consequence of failure to adjust
      for the increasing price and complexity of Japanese vehicles in
      recent years.

[11] The values in Figure 2 are estimates of the total fixed capital stock (including capital held by suppliers) per annual vehicle produced. I converted the Japanese figures from yen to US dollars using a purchasing power parity exchange rate, and adjusted all figures for inflation. To correct for differences in vertical integration, I multiplied each firm's capital stock by the ratio of sales to value added. The captial stock per vehicle figures have not been adjusted for shifts in capacity utilization; this leads to considerable year-to-year fluctuation and some overstatement of true values, particularly for US producers.

[12] A firm's cost of capital equals the weighted average of its cost of debt and equity, with each source weighted in proportion to its share of the firm's total capitalization. The direct cost of debt is generally lower than that of equity, due to the tax deductibility of interest payments. If risk could be ignored, increases in the firm's ratio of debt to equity would reduce its weighted average cost of capital. However, increased financial leverage raises the probability of bankruptcy and the risk premium that must be paid to equity holders. This means that beyond a certain point, increases in leverage cause the firm's weighted average capital cost to rise.

[13] It is sometimes alleged that Japanese government policies reduce the level of uncertainty and risk associated with new technologies. If Japanese policies do, in fact, reduce such risk, then Japanese firms may be justified in using a lower hurdle rate to evaluate risky investment projects.

[14] Diffusion can have both positive and negative efficiency effects: more rapid diffusion of technology increases the efficiency of all producers at any point in time, but it also dulls each firm's private incentive to pursue continuing improvements.

[15] See, for example, Davies (1979) and Nasbeth and Ray (1974).

[16] Diffusion of these small equipment innovations is retarded by the fact that Japanese firms typically build much of their production equipment in-house, or make in-house modifications to equipment purchased outside (Hayes and Wheelwright, 1984, p. 368; Schonberger, 1982; Weinstein, et al, 1984, p.63). In electronics, for example, Toshiba makes 50% of its own equipment and Hitachi an even larger proportion (Weinstein, et al, 1984, p.63).

[17] Cost reduction also extends backward to suppliers; by dealing with a limited set of suppliers (often on an exclusive basis), and encouraging them to make efficiency improvements, Japanese firms capture many of the benefits of supplier learning (Asanuma, 1985).

[18] GM has been able to give only a handful of managers extensive training in the NUMMI plant, although many have had superficial exposure through plant tours. Considering GM's total employment of over 700,000 and the need for person-to-person contact, it seems unlikely that diffusion will occur quickly. Transfer of the NUMMI system may also be impeded by resistance from local unions and an established workforce.

[19] For a discussion of such information trading in a non-technological context, see Yoshino and Lifson (1986).

[20] There are a number of explanations for this asymmetry, but in large measure it reflects the relatively greater benefits to be obtained through learning an international language.

Output, Employment, Capital Stock and Vertical Integration of U.S. and Japanese Automakers, 1950-1985.

| Year | Vehicle Production | Employment | Net Property Plant & Equipment[1] | Value Added Sales | Year | Vehicle Production | Employment | Net Property Plant & Equipment[1] | Value Added Sales |
|---|---|---|---|---|---|---|---|---|---|
| | General Motors | | | | | Toyota | | | |
| 1950 | 3,992,298 | 495,627 | 3,037 | .38 | 1950 | 11,706 | 5,887 | NA | .22[2] |
| 1955 | 5,030,994 | 624,011 | 7,721 | .39 | 1955 | 22,145 | 5,772 | NA | .22[2] |
| 1960 | 4,660,996 | 595,151 | 8,570 | .41 | 1960 | 149,694 | 10,091 | 233 | .22[2] |
| 1965 | 7,278,131 | 734,594 | 12,756 | .43 | 1965 | 480,897 | 24,758 | 564 | .22[2] |
| 1970 | 5,308,000 | 696,000 | 14,459 | .48 | 1970 | 1,592,888 | 41,720 | 1,792 | .22 |
| 1975 | 6,629,000 | 681,000 | 11,063 | .43 | 1975 | 2,463,623 | 49,090 | 1,500 | .17 |
| 1980 | 7,101,000 | 746,000 | 16,542 | .43[2] | 1980 | 3,254,942 | 53,060 | 1,797 | .18 |
| 1985 | 9,305,000 | 811,000 | 24,096 | .45 | 1985 | 3,685,511 | 61,665 | 3,126 | .19 |
| | Ford | | | | | Nissan | | | |
| 1950 | 2,314,656 | 201,182 | 2,302 | .35 | 1950 | 12,458 | 6,599 | NA | .20[2] |
| 1955 | 3,322,309 | 269,059 | 5,161 | .32 | 1955 | 22,826 | 6,690 | NA | .20[2] |
| 1960 | 3,153,792 | 266,027 | 5,692 | .36 | 1960 | 129,893 | 11,008 | NA | .20[2] |
| 1965 | 4,595,357 | 364,487 | 8,345 | .36 | 1965 | 352,514 | 26,422 | 519 | .20 |
| 1970 | 4,861,570 | 431,727 | 9,777 | .38 | 1970 | 1,421,142 | 46,986 | 949 | .20 |
| 1975 | 4,690,095 | 416,120 | 8,706 | .36 | 1975 | 2,111,957 | 51,654 | 1,415 | .18 |
| 1980 | 4,426,151 | 432,987 | 11,114 | .34[2] | 1980 | 2,648,674 | 56,540 | 2,008 | .17 |
| 1985 | 5,634,348 | 369,314 | 12,141 | .34[2] | 1985 | 2,427,679 | 57,612 | 2,545 | .16 |
| | Chrysler | | | | | Mazda | | | |
| 1950 | 1,313,239 | 117,405 | 643 | .37 | 1950 | NA | NA | NA | NA |
| 1955 | 1,579,000 | 176,356 | 1,503 | .33 | 1955 | NA | NA | NA | NA |
| 1960 | 1,183,311 | 105,410 | 1,452 | .37 | 1960 | NA | NA | NA | NA |
| 1965 | 2,077,000 | 166,773 | 2,948 | .37 | 1965 | 274,406 | 18,796 | NA | .31 |
| 1970 | 2,434,398 | 228,332 | 4,076 | .37 | 1970 | 429,847 | 26,507 | 815 | .31 |
| 1975 | 2,475,597 | 217,594 | 3,302 | .35 | 1975 | 642,614 | 33,266 | 867 | .19 |
| 1980 | 1,224,923 | 92,596 | 2,793 | .37 | 1980 | 1,121,016 | 27,283 | 722 | .18 |
| 1985 | 2,157,373 | 107,850 | 4,535 | .29 | 1985 | 1,320,167 | 27,609 | 1,288 | .19 |

[1] In millions of 1983 dollars. Implicit price deflators for gross private domestic investment were used to adjust for inflation. The yen to dollar conversion is based on a 1975 purchasing power parity rate for capital formation of 299 yen per dollar, as reported in I. Kravis, A. Heston and R. Summers, World Product and Income: International Comparisons of Real Gross Product, Baltimore, John Hopkins University Press, 1982.

[2] Estimated figure.

All data are from company annual reports. The data cover the consolidated domestic operations of each firm, except in the case of Ford and Chrysler where international operations are included. The Japanese data exclude operations of non-consolidated subsidiaries within each company's supplier group. Non-automotive operations account for less than ten percent of total sales for all six firms.

## APPENDIX A

## REFERENCES

ABEGGLAN, J.C. and G.STALK,Jr., "Kaisha, The Japanese Corporation", New York,Basic Books, Inc.,1985.

ABERNATHY, W.J., K.CLARK, and A.M. KANTROW.,"Industrial Renaissance", Basic Books, New York,1983.

AIZCORBE, A., C.WINSTON, and A.FRIEDLAENDER. "Cost Competitiveness of the U.S. Automobile Industry." In C.Winston, Blind Intersection: Policy and the Automotive Industry, Brookings Institution, Washington, 1987.

ANDO, A. and A. AUERBACH, "The Corporate Cost of Capital in Japan and the U.S.: A Comparison", Working Paper 1762, National Bureau of Economic Research, March 1987.

ANDO, A. and A. AUERBACH, "The Cost of Capital in the U.S. and Japan: A Comparison", Working Paper, National Bureau of Economic Research, March 1987.

AOKI, M.. "Horizontal vs. Vertical Information Structure of the Firm: An Approach to U.S. - Japan Comparison of Industrial Organization", American Economic Review, Vol.76, December 1986, 971-983.

ASANUMA, B., "The Contractual Framework for Parts Supply in the Japanese Automative Industry", Japanese Economic Studies, Vol.13 Summer 1985, 54-78.

BALDWIN, C.Y., "The Capital Factor; Competing for Capital in a Global Environment", In M.Porter, Competition in Global Industries, Harvard Business School Press, Boston, 1986.

BOSTON CONSULTING GROUP, "Cross-Sectional Experience Curves", Boston, M.A.: Technical Report,1978.

BRANSTAD, P.A., "Structural Costs of Complexity in the Automotive Business", Booz-Allen and Hamilton, Inc., paper presented at Fifth World Motor Industry Conference, Geneva, Switzerland, 1984.

BUSINESS WEEK, "Japan, USA." Vol. July 14,1986, 45-55.

CHASE FINANCIAL POLICY, "U.S. and Japanese Semiconductor Industries: A Financial Comparison", Report prepared for Semicoductor Industry Association, 1980.

CLARK, K. and T. FUJIMOTO, "Overlapping Problem Solving in Product Development", In K.Ferdows, ed., Managing International Manufacturing,North Holland, this volume,1988.

CUSUMANO, M.A., "The Japanese Automobile Industry", Cambridge MA: Harvard University Press, 1985.

DAVIES, S., "The Diffusion of Process Innovations", Cambridge University Press, Cambridge 1979.

FLAHERTY, M.T. and H. ITAMI, "Finance." In D.Okimoto, T.Sugano, and F.B.Weinstein, Competitive Edge: The Semiconductor Industry in the U.S. Japan, Stanford, CA: Stanford University Press, 1984.

FLYNN, M.S., "Comparison of U.S.-Japan Production Costs: An Assessment", In R.E. Cole: Automobiles and the Future: Competition, Cooperation, and Change, Ann Arbor, MI: Center for Japanese Studies, The University of Michigan, 1983.

FUDENBERG, D.and J.TIROLE, "Learning by Doing and Market Performance", Bell Journal of Economics, Vol 14, No.2: (Autumn 1983), 522-530.

GHEMAWAT, P. and A.M. SPENCE, "Learning Curve Spillovers and Market Performance", The Quarterly Journal of Economics, Vol.100 (1985), 839-852.

HARBOUR, J.E., "Comparison and Analysis of Automotive Manufacturing Productivity in the Japanese and North Amerrican Automotive Industry for the Manufacture of Subcompact and Compact Cars", Technical Report, Harbour and Associates, Inc., 1981.

HARVARD BUSINESS SCHOOL CASE SERVICES, "Toyo Kogyo Co.LTD.", Boston,MA: Harvard Business School,(1982).

HATSOPOUOS, G.N., "High Cost of Capital: Handicap of American Industry." Study jointly sponsored by the American Business Conference and Thermo Electron Corporation, 1983.

HAYES, R.H. and S.C. WHEELWRIGHT, "Restoring Our Competitive Edge: Competing Through Manufacturing", New York: John Wiley & Sons, 1984.

HENDERSON, B.D.. "The Logic of Kanban", The Journal of Business Strategy, Vol.6 (1986), 6-11.

VON HIPPEL, E.,"Cooperation Between Rivals: Informal Know-How Trading", Working Paper 1759-86, Sloan School of Management, MIT, March 1986.

VON HIPPEL, E., "The Sources of Innovation", Oxford University Press, 1987.

HODDER, J.E., "Evaluation of Manufacturing Investments: A Comparison of U.S. and Japanese Practices", Financial Management, Vol. 15 Spring 1986, 17-23.

HODDER, J.E. and H.E. RIGGS, "Pitfalls in Evaluating Risky Projects", Harvard Business Review, Vol.63 January-February 1985, 128-135.

IMAI.K., I. NONAKA, and H. TAKEUCHI, "Managing the New Product Development Process: How Japanese Companies Learn and Unlearn", In K.B.Clark, R.H.Hayes and C.Lorenz, The Uneasy Alliance, Boston: Harvard Business School Press, 1985.

KAGONO, T. et.al.,"Mechanistic vs. Organic Management Systems: A Comparative Study of Adaptive Patterns of American and Japanese Firms", in K.Sato and Y.Hoshino, The Anatomy of Japanese Business, Armonk, NY: M.E. Sharpe, Inc.,1984.

KESTER, W.C., "Capital and Ownership Structure: A Comparison of United States and Japanese Manufacturing Corporations", Financial Management, Vol.15 Spring 1986, 5-16.

KOIKE, K., "Skill Formation Systems In the U.S. and Japan: A Comparative Study", in Aoki,M., "The Economic Analysis of the Japanese Firm" Amsterdam: North Holland, 1984.

KRAFCIK, J., "Learning form NUMMI", unpublished, Sloan School of Management, MIT, Sept.1986.

LIEBERMAN, M.B., "The Learning Curve, Pricing, and Market Structure in the Chemical Processing Industries", PhD Thesis, Harvard Unversity, 1982.

LIEBERMAN, M.B., " The Learning Curve, Diffusion, and Competitive Strategy", Strategic Management Journal, Vol.8 September-October 1987, 441-452.

MANSFIELD, E.,et al, "How rapidly Does New Industrial Technology Leak Out?", The Journal of Industrial Economics, Vol.34 December 1985, 271-223.

MAZDA MOTOR CORPORATION, "Mazda in Brief", Hiroshimo, Japan, 1984.

MICHEL, A. and I. SHAKED, "Japanese leverage: Myth or Reality?", Financial Analysts Journal,Vol.July/August 1985, 61-67.

MILLER, J.G. and T.E. VOLLMANN, "The Hidden Factory", Harvard Business Review, Vol.63 September/October 1985, 142-150.

NAKANE, J., "Japanese Society", Tokyo: Charles E.Tuttle Co.,1970.

NASBETH, L. and G.F. RAY, "The Diffusion of New Industrial Processes: An International Study", Cambridge University Press, London, 1974.

NATIONAL ACADEMY OF ENGINEERRING, "The Competitive Status of the U.S. Auto Industry", Washington, D.C.,1983.

OFFICE OF THE TECHNOLOGY ASSESSMENT, U.S. CONRESS "International Competitiveness in Electronics", Washington D.C.,1983.

OKIMOTO, D.I., T. SUGANO, and F.B. WEINSTEIN, "Competive Edge: The Semiconductor Industry in the U.S. and Japan", Stanford, CA: Stanford University Press, 1984.

OUCHI, W., "The M-Form Society", Reading, MA: Addison-Wesley Publishing Co., 1984.

PASCALE, R. and T.P. RHOLEN, "The Mazda Turnaround", Journal of Japanese Studies, Vol.9, 1983, 219-263.

ROGERS, E.M., "Information Exchange and Techological Innovation", in Sahal, D., The Transfer and Utilization of Technical Knowledge, Lexington, MA: Lexington Books,1982.

ROSS, D.R., "Learning to Dominate", The Journal of Industrial Economics, Vol.34 June 1986, 337-353.

SCHONBERGER, R.J., "Japanese Manufacturing Techniques: Nine Hidden Lessons in Simplicity", New York: The Free Press, 1982.

SPENCE, A.M., "The Learning Curve and Competition", Bell Journal of Economics, Vol.12 Spring 1981, 49-70.

STOBAUGH, R. and L.T. WELLS,Jr., "Technology Crossing Borders: The Choice, Transfer, and Management of International Technology Flows." Boston, MA: Harvard Business School Press, 1984.

TOKYO MOTOR CORPORATION, "Outline of Tokyo", 1984.

U.S.DEPARTMENT   OF   COMMERCE:   INTERNATIONAL   TRADE   ADMINISTRATION,   "A
Historical Comparison of the Cost of  Financial  Capital  in  France,  the
Federal  Republic  of  Germany, Japan, and the United States", Washington,
1983.

WEINSTEIN, F.B., M. UENOHARA, and J.G. LINVILL, "Technological Resources",
in D.I. Okimoto, T. Sugano, and  F.B.  Weinstein, Competitive  Edge:  The
Semiconductor  Industry  in  the  US  and  Japan,  Stanford,  CA: Stanford
Unviersity Press, 1984.

WRIGHT,  R.W.  and  S. SUZUKI, "Financial Structure and Bankruptcy Risk in
Japanese Companies", Working Paper, 1985.

YOSHINO,  M. and T. LIFSON, "The Japanese Sogo Shosha and the Organization
of Trade", Cambridge, MA: MIT Press, 1986.

MANAGING INTERNATIONAL MANUFACTURING
K. Ferdows (Editor)
© Elsevier Science Publishers B.V. (North-Holland), 1989

# THE "MONEY GAME": NEW PASTIME FOR JAPANESE MANUFACTURERS?

Edward W. DAVIS

University of Virginia

In the face of an appreciating yen and severe economic pressures in recent years, many manufacturing firms in Japan have become involved in new financial activities as a major source of profits. These activities represent a significant change in focus for Japanese manufacturing companies and, along with "hollowing" trends which have become apparent, could hold significant negative implications for the future competitive abilities of these firms.

## INTRODUCTION

Tateho Chemical Industries Ltd. is Japan's largest manufacturer of electrofused magnesia, a material used in furnace linings and refractory raw materials. A mid-sized organization with a workforce of about 300, the company is famous for developing silicon nitride "whiskers", which have a wide range of applications in the aerospace, ceramic, metal and plastic industries, as a reinforcing material. About one-third of its sales are in export markets.

Until September 2, 1987, Tateho had a strong track record in its bottom line performance. For example, during the three years ending March, 1987, the company's net income grew at the average annual compound rate of 24%, one of the highest growth rates among major Japanese corporations. For the year ended March ,1987 the company reported profits of 953 million yen on sales of 6.2 billion yen, a healthy return of 15.3%. Expected sales and profits for the coming year were equally healthy. However, on September 2 the share price of Tateho, listed on Japan's second-largest stock exchange, suddenly began a free-fall. Trading surged to 2.8 million shares, more than 10 times the average daily volume, and the stock price fell the maximum amount allowed by the exchange in one day. On the next day more than 12 million shares of sell orders hit the trading floor as shareholders of the company panicked; no buyers were to be found at any price level, and no shares traded that day. In the midst of this activity, it was revealed that Tateho faced bankruptcy due to losses in the bond futures market. Tateho's chairman announced that the company had lost about $140 million on a position of roughly $714 million in the bond market, with a large amount in futures. The announcement shocked Japanese financial markets, both because of the size of the investment, and because Tateho's net worth was estimated at only $120 million, which meant the firm was technically bankrupt.

How did Tateho get into trouble, and why? Tateho, like other Japanese manufacturing companies, had been heatedly playing the money markets to shore up earnings. Over the past few years, as business conditions deteriorated and the yen appreciated sharply, shrinking export-related profits, Japanese manufacturing firms began to seek out alternatives to their basic business to improve the bottom line. Recently liberalized financial markets in Japan, (in combination with an excess of corporate cash, in many cases) provided an obvious outlet, leading to a boom in corporate financial activity. The practice of "Zaitech" (roughly translated as financial wheeling and dealing), became regarded as a panacea for companies plagued by low export earnings and slow growth.

The historic stock market crash that swept around the globe in October, 1987 produced no cases as extreme as Tateho's, and since that event some Japanese companies reportedly have begun lessening their dependence on Zaitech portfolios. However, a recounting of the evolutionary involvement in Zaitech of Japanese manufacturing firms, makes clear how dramatically the premier manufacturers in the world have changed their behavior in only a few short years.

## ZAITECH: ORIGINS AND BACKGROUND

As Ratcliffe [28] notes, prior to the mid-1980's Japanese corporations were noted for their high debt-to-equity ratios, with heavy reliance on fixed-interest rate borrowing in yen from Japanese banks, with whom they had very close, dependent relationships. Because of financial regulations, there was very limited use of international capital markets. For example, in the early 1970's large Japanese companies raised about 85% of new funds through bank borrowings, almost entirely in yen. But by the mid-80's the share of yen bank borrowings had steadily declined,to about 25%. In contrast, corporate bond issues accounted for only about 5% of funds raised in the early 1970's, but rose to over 20% by the mid-80's. Also, the share of funding from overseas capital markets grew steadily, and by 1985 exceeded Japanese domestic funding for the first time [7].

The Bank of Japan adopted an easy-money policy in 1980, interest rates were liberalized in 1982, and other restrictions on corporate financing eased in early 1984. While the latter of these changes were occurring, a pattern of declining exports due to the appreciating yen, and slowing domestic sales from a slumping economy put manufacturing and trading companies into an increasingly tight profit squeeze, throughout 1985 and 1986. As the Japan Economic Journal noted, [15], the "soaring value of the yen...has struck a blow at Japanese industry. One of ten listed manufacturing firms, 176 in all, suffered operating losses in the 1986 business year ended March 31. One out of eight manufacturing companies operated in the red".

As the squeeze on profits tightened in 1985 and 1986, Japanese manufacturing companies discovered that it was easier to make profits from
financial dealings than from their basic production activities. Fiscally
conservative companies unused to debt, with plenty of cash reserves,
such as Toyota Motor Company (often referred to as "Toyota bank" in
Japan: $6.7 billion in cash and marketable securities in 1986) were able
to earn hundreds of millions in traditionally conservative fashion
through bank deposit interest and other fixed-income investments.
However, companies without much cash also found new ways to make money
through the suddenly-popular Zaitech. For example, it was relatively
simple, but highly profitable, to raise money at rock-bottom rates of 3
- 5% on the Japanese domestic market, and lend it on the international
markets at much higher prevailing rates. Nippon Oil, Japan's largest
petroleum distribution company, raised over $2.8 billion in this fashion
in the past few years at an average interest cost of 3.5%. Income from
such sources generated 79% of Nippon Oil's $140 million pre-tax profit
for the 1986 fiscal year ended March 31,1987.

While such simple interest rate spread-playing has been a favorite
gambit of U.S. and European companies for some time, much more complex -
and higher risk - approaches began to proliferate rapidly among Japanese
companies after the 1984 financial regulation relaxations. Formerly
conservative manufacturing companies began speculating in foreign currency markets, engaging in foreign and domestic stock trades, and
issuing exotic new types of securities on international markets, including exchange rate-swaps, interest rate-swaps, and gold or other
commodity-linked bonds as well as warrant-linked bonds.

A number of manufacturing and trading companies - about 100, by a recent
count [6] - set up their own financial offices abroad to handle these
international transactions. Sharp Corporation even opened its own full-
scale trading room within the company in April, 1986, and made 75% of
its pre-tax profit in the first half of 1986 from Zaitech activities.
Hitachi, Ltd. began investing some of its 5.0 billion dollar hoard in
equity funds and for its 1986 fiscal year (ended March 31, 1987), earned
45% of it pre-tax income from financial activities . Smaller, less well-
known companies were also engaged in financial dealings to dramatically
increase profits. In one such case, Hanway Kogyo, an Osaka-based medium-
sized steel bar producer rang up pre-tax profits of 12.2 billion Yen
with operating profits of only 3.0 billion Yen...... at a time when the
steel industry was in deep recession. And Asahi Kogyo, an air-
conditioner engineering company, chalked up profits worth 1.3 billion
Yen on stock market trading - a figure 60 times larger than its operating profits from mainstream businesses [6].

## THE IMPACT OF ZAITECH

The phenomenon of these large financial profits apparently altered some
of the traditional financial relationships in Japan. For example, in
ostensible disregard of the poor performances from operations, Japanese
manufacturing companies' stock prices consistently hit record high
prices on the Tokyo stock exchange throughout most of 1986. Companies

like Nissan, whose profits from operations were sharply declining or
negative, actually enjoyed record amounts of free liquid assets. In
fact, total Japanese corporate liquidity increased significantly in
1986. A Bank of Japan official noted, "in the past, corporate liquid
assets declined as operating earnings dropped. But this rule does not
apply anymore" [6]. Ironically, supervisors and workers in manufacturing
functions in many of these firms were undergoing severe cost-cutting
programs in response to the higher value of the Yen at the same time
their firm's stock prices were hitting record highs.

Euromoney magazine, in referring to the incongruities of this situation,
commented on the "recent schizoid tone" of Japanese corporate finance,
whereby Japanese CFO's were being "lionized as never before by the
world's bankers and securities houses for their cash and 24-karat credit
ratings, and their companies' stock price highs..... enabling them to
unload a plethora of low-cost, equity-laced financing packages on the
world's investment community.....then they have turned around and reinvested the money in various arbitrage games as part of a fast-growing
Tokyo craze that has come to be known as Zaiteku -making money purely
from financial operations" [8].

The Zaitech craze spread widely, during 1986 and 1987. For example in
June, 1987 the Japan Economic Journal reported "almost all Japanese
manufacturers have been involved in the sophisticated new Zaitech fund
management in an effort to win the game of corporate survival" [20].
Even formerly conservative companies apparently succumbed to the lure.
Olympus Optical company's management, for example, initially resisted
Zaitech on grounds that finance-oriented management "is apt to discourage efforts to produce good-quality products". But in the fiscal
year ended October, 1986 financial profits accounted for almost 40% of
Olympus' pre-tax profits. And Kirin Brewery's management, who were
earlier quoted as saying "we are a manufacturing company, not a finance
company" [6] also began experimenting with overseas investment instruments. Kirin ended its 1986 fiscal year with over 10% of its pre-tax
income from financial activities [9]: not a large figure, but a decided
departure from its past policy of avoiding such non-manufacturing activity.

One result of the Zaitech craze has been that financial managers are
playing a greater role in directing Japanese companies, according to
numerous reports. The Japan Economic Journal, for example, quoted a
director of Mitsubishi as believing that "decision-making of finance is
now the key factor in management, such as portfolio selection, and
mergers and acquisitions, due to lack of business opportunity and keen
competition in manufacturing [20]. But the new role of finance, particularly with respect to the jolting change of philosophy represented
by Zaitech, also has had some observers worried. Corporate treasurers in
Japan have traditionally acted as a restraining force on management
risk-takers; suddenly, as Euromoney noted, "at some companies they are
assuming the role of chief risk-taker. Who is supposed to be acting as a
check on them?" [8].

This lack of checks and balances was also commented upon by Carl Kester
of Harvard, an authority on Japanese economic policy. Kester noted:

"whether an intended result or a mere by-product of changing capital needs, many Japanese manufacturing companies do appear to be escaping the control and discipline imposed by the institutional arrangements accompanying heavy bank borrowing" [23]. In commenting on the dangers inherent in this lack of discipline and control, several months prior to the Tateho scandal, Johsen Takanashi, chief economist of the Mitsubishi Research Institute, cited the experience of a company that raised $15 million for a major capital investment: "while they waited to start the project, they invested in Australian bonds. They lost one third of their money in a couple of months. I am very skeptical about this whole Zaitech boom and people are beginning to recognize there are plenty of pitfalls" [8].

## ZAITECH ACTIVITY IN SPECIFIC COMPANIES

According to The Japan Economic Journal, at least 40 publicly-listed Japanese manufacturing companies had positive pre-tax profits for the 1986 fiscal year solely as a result of financial activities, and about one-third of the firms made some money from their financial dealings [15]. About 50% of these firms made money from such activities during the first-half of 1986, according to an earlier study by the Wako Research Institute [32] (Japanese accounting conventions report financial income as net interest income and dividends plus gains or losses on the sale of investment securities, thus facilitating the identification of such income).

The significance of financial income in the fiscal 1986 results for 20 large, well-known Japanese manufacturing companies is shown in Table 1. For this group, financial income averaged 40% of pre-tax income. These companies were among the "top thirty" manufacturing companies in terms of amount of financial income earned in 1986, according to a report by the equity research department of First Boston Corporation [9]. Financial income equalled or exceeded operating income for about half the top - thirty group, and provided a relatively large percentage of recurring (pre-tax) income for auto and electronics/electric companies, whose earnings have plunged due to the strong yen and other industry pressures since 1985. Recurring income (not shown in Table 1, but can be calculated from the figures given) is pre-tax income before extraordinary items; Japanese investors have traditionally watched recurring income growth for indications of corporate fundamentals while U.S. investors watch net earnings per share. In commenting on these results, the report cautioned investors: "when financial income accounts for one-quarter to one-half of recurring income, keeping your eyes on recurring income alone may miss the real direction of the company's earning power". The report also called attention to arguments in the financial press that the growing contribution of financial income would enable some cash-rich Japanese manufacturing companies to break even at much higher yen/dollar exchange rates, in effect subsidizing their manufacturing activities.

**BANK OF JAPAN STUDIES**

The Bank of Japan, concerned about the changes in corporate financial
practice, issued an October, 1986 study with a tone decidedly critical
of the recent speculative trends [23]. The report noted, among other
things, the "conspicuous characteristic of active short-term transactions of securities aiming at capital gains". For example, turnover
ratios of corporate holdings of domestic government bonds and foreign

**TABLE 1**

**Operating and Financial Income, Japanese Manufacturing Firms
Fiscal Year 1986 ***

| Company | Operating Income | Financial As % of | Fin. Income As % of Pre-Tax Income+ |
|---|---|---|---|
| Toyota | 329.4 | 123.7 | 25 % |
| Hitachi | 84.6 | 39.6 | 45 |
| Nissan Motor | (8.5) | 37.2 | 31 |
| Sharp | 6.9 | 21.4 | 56 |
| Nippon Oil | (1.3) | 15.5 | 79 |
| Nippon Denso | 57.5 | 15.1 | 23 |
| Sony | .8 | 14.9 | 41 |
| Sanyo Electric | (2.8) | 14.8 | 98 |
| Fuji Photo Film | 102.2 | 14.5 | 13 |
| Sumitomo Corp. | 24.4 | 11.8 | 26 |
| Komatsu | 18.8 | 9.1 | 32 |
| Kirin Brewery | 72.1 | 9.0 | 11 |
| Kyocera | 26.9 | 8.2 | 24 |
| Murata Mfg. | 10.2 | 7.6 | 37 |
| Fuji Heavy Ind. | 11.2 | 6.6 | 44 |
| Fujisawa Pharm. | 8.8 | 5.4 | 29 |
| Hitachi Sales | 1.8 | 5.4 | 71 |
| Ricoh | 17.3 | 5.2 | 28 |
| JVC | (4.2) | 5.1 | 39 |

* Year ending March, 1987 for majority of firms shown here. For Toyota,
Sony and Sanyo, FY86 ended in June, October and November, respectively.
All Income figures in billions of yen.

+ Before extra-ordinary items; also called "recurring income" in Japan.
Operating income plus financial income does not necessarily equal pre-
tax income because other non-operating items such as royalty income,
etc. are not included in financial income but affect pre-tax (recurring)
income.

FIGURE 1

# Japanese Manufacturing Companies
## Operating and Non-operating Income as a Percent of Sales

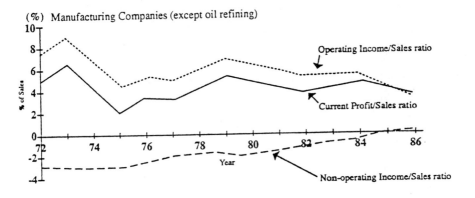

(%) Manufacturing Companies (except oil refining)

Operating Income/Sales ratio

Current Profit/Sales ratio

Year

Non-operating Income/Sales ratio

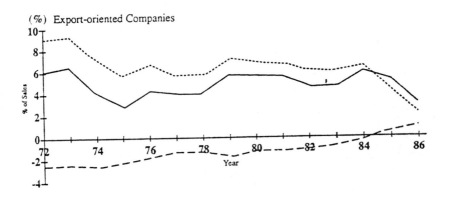

(%) Export-oriented Companies

Year

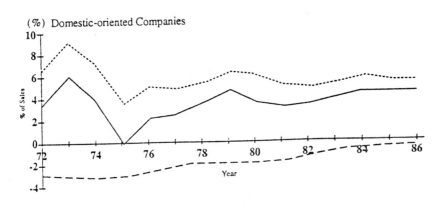

(%) Domestic-oriented Companies

Year

bonds were found to have shown a clear upward trend since 1984, marking
a change in investment behavior from long-term holding for attaining
yields to maturity to the short-term holding of securities aiming at
higher capital gains, with concurrently higher risks. The report concluded that "corporate investments in securities in the current
relaxation period can be termed 'high risk, high return', compared with
past periods of monetary relaxation". The report also warned that firms
were reducing their investment in capital equipment for goods production
in favor of speculative investment in land and financial assets.

In November, 1987 the Bank of Japan produced another study of corporate
financial activities which analyzed the profitability of major firms and
again commented on Zaitech activities through the end of the 1986 fiscal
year (March 31 for most Japanese companies, but in any case prior to the
October market crash) [31]. The report noted that non-operating profit
of Japanese manufacturing companies had become positive for the first
time in 35 years, since the start of the survey in 1951, and attributed
this to profits from financial activities, which compensated for the
"deteriorated operating profit", particularly at export-oriented companies. Figure 1, which is taken from that report, shows the pattern of
operating and non-operating income as a percent of sales over the past
15 years, for all Japanese manufacturing companies as a group, and
separately for the subgroups of export versus domestic-oriented companies. It is interesting that an upward trend in non-operating income
is clear for all three groups, beginning well before the recent period
of increasing liberalization of Japanese financial markets. The level of
non-operating income for the export-oriented group, while about the same
as that of the domestic group for most of the period, has clearly risen
much more steeply in recent years, suggesting a concentration of Zaitech
activity in this category. Also, a gradual decline in operating income
for the export-oriented group is apparent, reflecting the increasingly
competitive environment of these companies.


## ZAITECH AFTER THE CRASH

The Tateho Chemical Company scandal exemplified the worst fears of the
Zaitech skeptics and brought renewed calls for control and a return to
the basics of manufacturing. As one prominent business journal noted
after the affair, "Tateho may have shocked the top management of
Japanese companies into providing tighter controls. The Zaitech scare
.... may encourage companies to concentrate on the area their managers
understand best - the factory floor" [4]. The subsequent October market
crash likewise served to dampen the Zaitech activities of some firms,
according to some media reports. For example, Sanyo Electric, Sony and
several other large firms announced plans to reduce their Zaitech activities, and Hitachi Ltd. increased its plant and equipment investment
in a largely symbolic move away from Zaitech-oriented corporate management. A Tateho Chemical spokesman was also quoted as fervently
announcing, "we have absolutely no ideas about ever engaging in any
Zaitech again" [17].

Judging from other reports, however, the Zaitech passions have apparently not uniformly cooled. For example, the managing director of a manufacturing firm which had been regularly engaging in Zaitech activities prior to the October crash continued to defend the practice afterwards, while criticizing Tateho's extreme position. According to this view, "if a company's securities-related profit is 30% of pre-tax, as it is in our case, then that is the best position. Forty percent raises questions and 50% is dangerous. Tateho's was 90%. Those companies getting 30% from Zaitech are still diversifying and only doing the Zaitech for extra cash" [5]. More recently, in an address to the prestigious Nikkei Business Forum, the president of Nippon Telephone and Telegraph Corporation felt sufficiently concerned about continued focus on Zaitech to warn that "managers of manufacturing companies should not concentrate on money games for financial gains to increase profits" [18]. Latest reports also indicate that despite the October market crash, the outstanding balance of accounts in Japanese money markets on December 31, 1987 was 2.5 times that of the 1985 figure [16]. About two-thirds of the 124-trillion yen increase in the balance came from the Tokyo offshore banking market, and large time deposits with unregulated interest rates soared almost 10-fold from 5 trillion to 47 trillion yen. Against a backdrop of such excess liquidity, warned the Japan Economic Journal, "Tateho is likely to turn out to be the tip of the iceberg" [22].

Zaitech profits have been defended on grounds that they maintain corporate profitability and enhance competitiveness by generating both capital investment and operating funds. As a manager at Hitachi remarked, "Operating profits have been declining, so we are obliged to focus more on cash management" [3]. From a short-term, "money game" point of view the profitability argument obviously makes sense. However, evidence also indicates that Japanese corporations, like their U.S. counterparts over the past two decades, have recently begun cutting back substantially on their capital spending. For example, the Bank of Japan reported that in 1985 only 12% of the total funds raised from money and capital markets by Japanese corporations was reinvested in plant and equipment. The remaining 88% was generally set aside for Zaitech activities [6]. Capital investment declined also in 1986 and recent data on some specific industry groups suggests that plant and equipment investment continued to decline in 1987 as well [14]. Mitsubishi Research's Takahashi has expressed alarm at these recent reductions in capital spending, saying "manufacturing industry has lost the incentive to invest in its real business, and for that reason there is going to be an erosion of the manufacturing competence of this economy" [8].

Zaitech activity has also been defended on the basis that it is essentially no different from the non-manufacturing financially - oriented activities of many Western manufacturing firms, particularly in the USA. There is some truth in this argument, but it is a dubious defense if one agrees with Sony's Akio Morita that overemphasis on the "money game" has reduced the international competitiveness of U.S. manufacturing industries [24]. Moreover, it appears that there are significant differences between Zaitech as it has been practiced recently by Japanese firms, and the financial activities of their Western counterparts.

COMPARATIVE DATA ON U.S. COMPANIES

Figure 2 shows non-operating income for a sample of 175 large U.S. manufacturing companies in 15 industry groups, as reported in [36], plotted against the results for export-oriented Japanese manufacturing companies presented earlier. As can be seen, non-operating income for the U.S. group has been relatively flat compared to the Japanese group. A slight downward trend of the U.S. group in recent years is evident, in contrast to the strong upward trend of the Japanese group, particularly in recent years. Non-operating income for the Japanese group apparently exceeded that of the U.S. group for the first time in 1986. However the relatively small magnitude of the numbers involved, coupled with the possible impact of any differences in reporting between Japanese and U.S. companies cause us to view such a direct comparison with some caution. According to some observers, Japanese accounting methods tend to understate total earnings compared to U.S. accounting standards, but we have not been able to verify this. If true, the level of non-operating income for the Japanese group might well be closer to that of the U.S. group throughout the entire period shown.

Linear regression analysis of a sample of about 100 of the U.S. firms using data for the 1984 – 86 time period failed to show any statistically significant correlation between non-operating income and performance measures such as Return On Assets, Net Income and Cash Flow. Data plots showed a tendency for ROA to vary inversely with the ratio of non-operating income to pre-tax income, but the numerous exceptions and small sample size prevented any definite conclusions in this regard.

FIGURE 2

# Non-Operating Income Comparison
Large U.S. Companies vs. Japanese Export-Oriented Companies

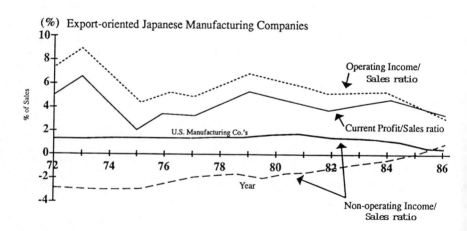

Table 2 gives data on non-operating income for 25 of the U.S. companies over a three-year period, for comparison with the group of 20 similar Japanese companies in Table 1. As can be seen for the U.S. group, the

### TABLE 2

### Representative Non-Operating Income, 1984–86
### Large U. S. Manufacturing Companies

| Company and Non-Operating Income (1986) ($ millions) | | Non-Operating Income As Percent of Income Before Taxes | | |
|---|---|---|---|---|
| | | 1986 | 1985 | 1984 |
| Ford Motor Co. | 14,957 | 29.5% | 37.1% | 32.6% |
| Exxon | 1,319 | 24.6 | 1.1 | 5.1 |
| General Electric | 1,253 | 33.9 | 27.5 | 25.5 |
| IBM | 1,005 | 11.9 | 7.2 | 25.5 |
| Chevron | 886 | 50.9 | 30.8 | 29.4 |
| Chrysler | 564 | 2.4 | 17.8 | 8.0 |
| Boeing | 407 | 39.6 | 33.9 | 42.4 |
| Dow Chemical | 234 | 18.9 | 1233.3 | 62.7 |
| Proctor & Gamble | 163 | 26.4 | 10.8 | 19.2 |
| Eastman Kodak | 129 | 21.6 | -77.6 | 11.8 |
| Digital Equipment | 122 | 7.2 | 13.6 | 14.7 |
| FMC | 103 | 53.5 | 24.5 | 25.9 |
| Rockwell | 91 | 8.6 | 11.8 | 16.0 |
| Eli Lilly | 80 | 9.1 | 10.1 | 9.0 |
| Warner Lambert | 78 | 17.5 | 231.4 | 21.4 |
| Westinghouse | 76 | 9.5 | 30.0 | 34.6 |
| Mead | 54 | 23.8 | 23.7 | 15.9 |
| Bristol Myers | 44 | 4.7 | 13.2 | 7.8 |
| Minnesota Mining | 44 | 3.3 | 4.6 | 4.5 |
| Honeywell | 28 | 70.3 | 11.2 | 14.9 |
| Abbott Labs | 26 | 3.2 | 7.9 | 9.9 |
| Emerson Electric | 7 | 1.0 | -1.2 | 0.1 |
| Goodyear | -135 | -56.7 | 14.1 | 4.4 |
| General Motors | -304 | -20.8 | 28.1 | 31.1 |
| Du Pont | -2,421 | -81.1 | -0.5 | 7.7 |

value of non-operating income in 1986 varied from a high of plus $14.9 billion for Ford Motor Company, to a low of negative $2.4 billion for DuPont.

What is immediately striking about the percent values in Table 2 is their wide range from negative to positive and their variable pattern for individual companies. Omitting the negative values, and the two large positive "exception" values over 100%, non-operating income (which of course includes both financial income and income from other sources) averaged slightly less than 20% of income before taxes for this group. In an attempt to explain the variability and high negative/positive values, as well as the degree of contribution of financial income, a detailed examination was made of data from annual reports, 10-K statements and other sources for 20 of these companies, including most cases where obviously unusual values were apparent over the three-year period (e.g., Chevron, FMC, GM, Goodyear and Honeywell in 1986, and Dow, Kodak and Warner Lambert in 1985). Some of the major findings of this analysis are shown in Table 3.

As Table 3 shows, there were three major factors determining non-operating income for the U.S. companies in the period studied: (1) equity earnings in subsidiary companies, (2) interest and dividends and (3) organizational restructuring actions, including plant rationalizations and business write-offs. The approximate percentage contribution to total non-operating income for the first two factors, for several representative companies in the sample is shown in Table 3. The third factor, provisions for restructuring, business, writeoffs, etc., typically was associated with a large decline in operating income, and produced losses or very low positive values of non-operating income, leading to high positive or negative percent values (e.g., Chevron, FMC, Honeywell, and Dow in the first case and GM, Goodyear, Du Pont and Kodak in the second). In one case (Warner Lambert, 1985), a high positive percent was due to negative values of both operating and non-operating income. All cases in the sample where non-operating income was greater than plus or minus 50% of pre-tax income were found to be primarily due to the third factor above.

Because of U.S. reporting methods, the exact portion of non-operating income attributable to financial activities is often difficult to determine in U.S. companies. A number of the U.S. companies routinely engage in fairly sophisticated financial transactions, primarily to hedge against foreign exchange losses. Such losses (or gains) are usually, but not always, identified separately from interest, dividends and marketable securities earnings, if any. In any event, examination of those cases where non-operating income was more than 25% of pre-tax income (an arbitrary choice) showed that the combined income from such financial transactions was typically less than 15% of total pre-tax income. Boeing, with nearly 100% of non-operating income attributed to dividends and interest for the past three years, was a notable exception. Dow Chemical, in 1985 was another. In the latter case, depressed operating income in 1985 helped produce the maximum percentage observed in this study (1233%). Income from interest and foreign exchange translations amounted to about one-third of that amount, and earnings from equity in subsidiaries about one-half. In 1986 Dow's operating income returned to healthier levels, and income from interest, dividends and foreign exchange transactions fell to a more normal range of 10 - 15% of income before taxes. In all other cases examined where income from identifiable financial transactions and foreign exchange transactions was a relatively high percentage of total income before taxes, it was typically associated more with an unusual drop in operating income rather than any increase in financial income. One such example is General Motors in 1986, where the greatly reduced pre-tax income associated with restructuring write-offs caused income from interest, dividends and marketable securities to be a relatively high 67% of pre-tax income, even though the absolute amount of such financial income was down about 45% from the 1985 figure.

In summary, the non-operating income for these U.S. companies appears typically to be from non-consolidated subsidiaries or from disposal of businesses or special assets. In only a very few cases, such as Boeing, was income from interest and dividends a significant or majority percentage of non-operating income, and in no cases was other reported financial income from such sources as foreign exchange hedging activities or securities investments a major component of non-operating income. For the period examined, the identifiable financial income of the U.S. companies, as a percentage of income before taxes, appears to be about one-third the level of the Japanese companies in Table 1. Thus both the sources and amounts of non-operating income for the U.S. companies appear significantly different from some of their Japanese counterparts.

Regardless of any similarities or differences between Japanese and U.S. financial practice, the pursuit of Zaitech profits appears to be a distinct break with the past competitive strategies of Japanese manufacturing firms. These firms have succeeded, in large part, by pursuing long-term strategies wherein manufacturing superiority has been the primary competitive weapon. Zaitech activities, by their very nature, promote a short-term focus, are financially risky, divert the attention of top management, and decrease the relative importance of manufacturing as a strategic element. By engaging in these activities Japanese manufacturing companies are tending to behave more like U.S. companies than is commonly suspected.

**TABLE 3**

Major Factors Determining Non-Operating Income
of U. S. Manufacturing Companies

| Factor | Examples | Approximate Percentage Of Non-Operating Income, 84-86 |
|---|---|---|
| 1. Income From Equity Earnings In Unconsolidated Subsidiary Companies: | | |
| −with Finance Subsidiaries | Ford Motor Company | 40-60% |
| | Chrysler | 30-60 |
| | General Electric | 35-45 |
| | Dow Chemical (1985) | 55 |
| −without Finance Subsidiaries | Exxon | 75-95 |
| 2. Income From Interest and Dividend | Boeing | 95-100 |
| | IBM | 90-95 |
| | Ford Motor | 30-35 |
| | General Electric | 25-30 |
| | FMC | 15-30 |
| | Chrysler | 10-20 |
| | Dow Chemical (1985) | 35 |
| 3. Restructuring and Rationalization Actions | 1986: Chevron, FMC, Honeywell GM, Goodyear, DuPont | |
| | 1984-85: Dow Chemical, Eastman Kodak, Warner Lambert | |

## CHASING THE CHEAP LABOR DOLLAR AND OTHER "HOLLOWING" TRENDS

The recent behavior of Japanese companies in pursuing short-term profit-making and financial management is only one of several factors which make Japanese manufacturing management appear more, rather than less, similar today to their U.S. competitors. Another is the increasingly geographically-dispersed nature of Japanese manufacturing.

For example, one Japanese management response to the higher-valued yen has been increased shifting of production overseas. An overall indication of this is the significant increase in direct foreign investment by Japanese corporations in 1986, while total investment declined [13]. In particular, there has been a dramatic movement of operations to, and outsourcing from, the "four little dragon" countries of Taiwan, Korea, Hong Kong and Singapore, as well as other low-wage developing countries [2], [33]. One Japanese electric appliance maker rationalizes this in a fashion familiar to U.S. audiences by arguing "at 170 yen to the dollar, labor costs in Japan equal those in the USA and go higher when the yen rises further, so the advantage of producing in the newly industrialized countries in Asia is obvious considering their far lower labor costs" [20]. Additionally, to avoid import barriers and move closer to major markets, Japanese manufacturing operations have recently been established in record numbers in the developed countries, including the USA, and Western Europe. By mid-1987, for example, the number of Japanese majority-owned manufacturing facilities in the USA was double the 1986 figure, for a total of over 564 [12].

This "hollowing" of Japanese manufacturing is similar to what has already been experienced in the USA. It is seen as another element in the "money game" approach to manufacturing in the USA by some observers. For example, Sony Corporation chairman Akio Morita commented critically on this phenomenon in his recently popular biography, Made In Japan [24]:

> "American companies have either shifted output
> to low-wage countries or come to buy parts and
> assembled products from countries like Japan
> that can make quality products at low prices.
> The result is a hollowing of American industry.
> The U.S. is abandoning its status as an in-
> dustrial power".

Mr. Morita's concern might well be directed at Japanese industry today, given the increasing exodus of manufacturing operations from Japan in the past several years as noted above.

Admittedly, Japanese industry still has a long way to go in equaling the U.S. in degree of "hollowing". For example, sales by U.S. foreign manufacturing affiliates have equaled 20% or more of domestic sales since 1980. The comparable figure for Japan is a fraction of this - something on the order of 5% in 1986 [13]. Nonetheless, the offshore movement of manufacturing has caused great concern in some Japanese circles, and appears to be changing the basic structure of Japan's

manufacturing industry. For example, in a 1986 survey of large corporation presidents by the Japan Economic Journal, more than 90% of the
respondents felt that the hollowing of Japanese manufacturing would be a
long-term trend, with significant impact upon Japan's automotive,
electrical, textiles, and metal products industries [19].

## REDUCED COMPETITIVE ADVANTAGE FROM HOLLOWING?

As with the increasing focus on short-term financial gains, we believe
this hollowing trend could significantly affect some of the past competitive advantages which the Japanese have enjoyed. For example, as a
greater percentage of Japanese manufacturing moves offshore and what has
been relatively unique industry infrastructure changes, some of the past
competitive advantages enjoyed by firms in these industries will be
exceedingly difficult to maintain. Differences in manufacturing practice, workforce management, and government regulation due to offshore
location will also play an increasingly important role compared to the
past.

To take one primary industry, for example, Japanese automotive parts
makers usually belong to separate industrial groups, of which the major
automakers, such as Nissan and Toyota, are the key members. The
automakers typically own stock in their suppliers and automaker executives sit on the boards of supplier companies. Relationships between
supplier and automaker tend to be long-term, exclusive and characterized
by trust and loyalty. In essence, the supplier companies are divisions
of the auto companies. Suppliers also share cost information with the
automakers and occasionally with each other, and the companies work
closely together to boost productivity and reduce costs.

One of the many advantages of this situation for the auto companies is
that they need far fewer financial staff personnel than their Western
competitors. The extremely close relationship between supplier and
automaker reduces the need for a large number of accounting people to
exercise controls and checks, as is the case in the U.S. and Europe,
where layers of financial staff are the rule. John Kaplan, controller at
Ford of Europe, cites the advantages of the Japanese approach as an
example which motivated Ford in its 1983 drive to reduce financial staff
head counts in Europe [11].

In contrast to Japan, automotive industry supplier-user relations in
Europe and the USA are still generally characterized by arm's distance,
occasionally almost adversarial, relations. Supplier-based programs such
as just-in-time delivery, long-term contracts and "quality at the
source" can be implemented, but often only at greater effort than in
Japan.

The publicized experiences of Japanese auto, television, copy machine
and other manufacturers in the USA have thus far been almost uniformly
salutory. Some of these plants have achieved levels of quality and
productivity equaling domestic Japanese plants. But these companies have
often imported a majority of the parts in their products (on a value-
added basis) from Japan, or have had their major suppliers set up

operations in this country near their assembly plants, in an attempt to obtain high-quality parts and maintain normal (Japanese) supplier relations. The Japanese manufacturing story in the USA thus far, for autos, TV receivers, copy machines, machine tools and other high value-added products has been primarily a story of assembly only, rather than complete manufacturing businesses. For these and other industries, the difficulty for the Japanese of maintaining a unique competitive advantage in manufacturing will, we believe, increase as more component manufacturing is transferred offshore. In the case of automotive production, at least, the Japanese presence is also motivating domestic manufacturers to higher levels of efficiency and quality, which over time will lessen initial advantages.

The Japanese are impressively resilient in their ability to cope with new competitive pressures, and it would be foolish to underestimate them. They deserve at least a portion of the "omnipotent manufacturing manager" image bestowed upon them overwhelmingly by Western media. But Mckinsey & Company's Kenichi Ohmae, a leading authority on Japanese business, claims that overseas manufacturing companies and facilities acquired by the Japanese often run into serious problems [27]. According to him, about 100 of 107 Japanese overseas business ventures attempted during the past decade, which he studied, failed to be profitable. Kazuo Nukazawa, a leading Japanese economist, says in a recent report that some unconfirmed estimates show more than 80% of Japanese factories in the U. S. as not profitable [34]. A recent survey by the Japan Overseas Enterprises Association reported that the rate of return on U.S. investments by Japanese manufacturing companies is very low by international standards, at a mere 0.2 percent [35]. European manufacturers earned about 6.7 percent on their U.S. investments, while U.S., companies earned 9.4 percent on their investments in Japan. Ohmae is particularly harsh in his assessment of the Japanese ability to develop successful manufacturing business organizations in foreign environments. Among other faults, he criticizes Japanese companies for their tendency to maintain dependent subsidiary operations abroad, instead of developing self-contained businesses with ranking executives. The recent hollowing trends may change this situation, but according to latest reports fewer than 300 of 130,000 senior-level Japanese executives are stationed overseas [21]. All in all, in spite of the many success stories popularized in the press, we doubt that the full story has yet been written.

## SUMMARY CONCLUSIONS

Japanese manufacturing companies are responding to new global pressures on profits much like U.S. manufacturing companies have responded to similar pressures in the past. As operating profits have eroded, a rush to short-term financial profit-making has ensued, possibly diverting management attention from manufacturing priorities. Profits from financial activities have subsidized basic manufacturing activities and in many cases prevented net losses. While the degree of such activities may have been reduced by the October market crash, there are still indications of continued heavy financial involvement. On another, yet related front, there has been increased movement of manufacturing out of Japan

in search of lower labor costs and to be closer to primary markets, such
as the USA. This "hollowing" process will reduce a portion of the unique
advantages that some elements of Japanese industry have enjoyed  in  the
past from a primarily domestic production base, and make it increasingly
harder for them to maintain significant competitive advantages.


## REFERENCES

[1]     Automotive News. "Japanese 'export' supplier pacts". May 4,
        1987.

[2]     Business Week. "Can Japan Keep Its Economy From Hollowing Out?",
        July 13, 1987.

[3]     Business Week. "How Japan Is Beating The Profit Squeeze", May
        11, 1987.

[4]     Business Week. "Japan Writes A New Definition of Zaitech:
        'Investor Beware.'" September 21, 1987.

[5]     Euromoney. "After Tateho, Japanese Scrutiny on Trading Risk."
        Sept./October, 1987.

[6]     Euromoney Corporate Finance Supplement. "Re-tuning Zaitech."
        January, 1987.

[7]     Euromoney Corporate Finance Supplement. "Zaiteku Sends Stocks
        and Tokkin Soaring". January, 1987.

[8]     Fingleton, Eamonn. "Zaiteku Zooms Into The Unknown". Euromoney,
        November, 1986.

[9]     First Boston Equity Research. "Japanese Corporate Earnings:
        Zaitech - A Shot In The Arm To The Bottom Line". July 21, 1987.

[10]    Fortune. "Are Japanese Managers Biased Against Americans?".
        September 1, 1986.

[11]    International Management. "How Ford of Europe Reduced  Its
        Financial Staff Headcount". October, 1985.

[12]    Japan Economic Institute of America. "Japan-U.S. Business
        Report". June, 1987.

[13]    Japan Economic Institute of America. "Offshore Production: Boon
        or Bane for the Japanese Economy?"

[14]    Japan Economic Journal. "Electronics Makers To Cut Plant,
        Equipment Investment." June 6, 1987.

[15]   Japan Economic Journal. "Fund Management: Corporations Zaiteku
       Their Way Around the Rising Yen." September 5, 1987.

[16]   Japan Economic Journal. "Liberalization Draws Horde of Cash Into
       Money Market." March 19, 1988.

[17]   Japan Economic Journal. "Market Crash Crushes Zaitech Strategy."
       October 31, 1987.

[18]   Japan Economic Journal. "NTT Chief: Don't Neglect Technology for
       Money Game." March 19, 1988.

[19]   Japan Economic Journal. "Corporate Heads See Hollowing-out of
       Industry Due to Shift Overseas." June 6, 1987.

[20]   Japan Economic Journal. "Companies Increasingly Turn To
       'Zaitech' To Combat Profit Fall." June 6, 1987.

[21]   Japan Economic Journal. "Sony Deputy President to Head U.S.
       Operation in Globalization Move." July 25, 1987.

[22]   Japan Economic Journal. "Tateho: Just the Beginning ?" September
       19, 1987.

[23]   Kester, W. Carl. "Capital and Ownership Structure: A Comparison
       of United States and Japanese Manufacturing Corporations".
       Financial Management in Japan. Spring, 1986.

[24]   Morita, Akio. Made in Japan. New York: E. P. Dutton. 1986.

[25]   Much, Marilyn. "Global Markets Tempt CFOs". Industry Week,
       March 18, 1987.

[26]   Ohmae, Kenichi. "Japan's Role in the World Economy: A New
       Appraisal". California Management Review, Spring, 1987.

[27]   Ohmae, Kenichi. Triad Power: The Coming Shape of Global
       Competition. New York: The Free Press, 1985.

[28]   Ratcliffe, C. Tait. "Zaitech Funding Cuts Costs". The Banker,
       January, 1987.

[29]   Sundstrom, G. "Study Charts Japanese Invasion of U. S. Parts
       Industry". Automotive News, May 25, 1987.

[30]   The Bank of Japan, Research and Statistics Department. Special
       Paper No. 145, October, 1986.

[31]   The Bank of Japan," Analysis of the Profitability of Major Firms,
       1986". November, 1987

[32]   Wako Research Institute. "One Out of Two Companies in the
       Black". December 24, 1986.

[33]  Wall Street Journal.  "Exodus of Japanese Manufacturers  Abroad".
      September 15, 1986.

[34]  Wall Street Journal.  "Many Foreigners Find  Building  Plants  Is
      Easier Than Making Money in U.S."  July 24, 1987.

[35]  The Japan Economic Journal. "Japanese Investment In  U.S.  Yields
      Painfully Low Returns".  June 6, 1986.

[36]  Standard and Poor's Compustat Services, Inc., Financial Dynamics:
      1987 Industry Composite.

MANAGING INTERNATIONAL MANUFACTURING
K. Ferdows (Editor)
© Elsevier Science Publishers B.V. (North-Holland), 1989

IMPLICATIONS OF CIM FOR INTERNATIONAL MANUFACTURING


Joel D. GOLDHAR

Illinois Institute of Technology


## 1. INTRODUCTION

In both domestic and international firms, traditional factories have been built with mechanical engineering based technologies, industrial engineering organizing concepts, and human brain/paper archive information systems that exhibit economic and operating characteristics that encourage the firm to trade-off innovation in favor of productivity [1]. As a product moves along its life cycle from introduction to maturity, the increase in volume requires a standardization of the product design and a migration from labor intensive to capital intensive production facilities in order to maintain low-cost operations (Figure 1). The strategic cost is in terms of reduced flexibility and slower response time. "Proper" traditional engineering and management practice results in a rigid factory that does its "job" very efficiently but is unable to respond effectively to changes in market demand.

The business strategies that go with this traditional factory are designed to accommodate its constraints and limitations. They include outsourcing, "repositioning" the product, off-shore manufacturing, price competition and imitation/follow-the-leader approaches. These policies will usually result in increased short term efficiencies. They also result in the creation of a product design "umbrella" that invites counterfeiters and clones; and a mature industry with low profits and high exit costs. This situation leads managers to a correct reluctance to invest in new product innovation when doing a good job of process innovation results in a factory that becomes a barrier to the next round of new product development.

The traditional responses to manufacturing challenges - usually a demand to reduce costs and improve quality and yields - have generally been in the form of better industrial engineering and a set of manufacturing policy concepts that include the focussed factory, modular designs, scale economies, outsourcing of low volume and/or complex parts. For multinational companies this has meant the development of networks of focussed factories on a global scale - each one having high scale economies based upon specialization and repetition - and cross shipping of components among countries. The "world car", with its various components built in different factories around the world, is a stereotype example of this strategy.

# PRODUCT vs. PROCESS LIFE CYCLE

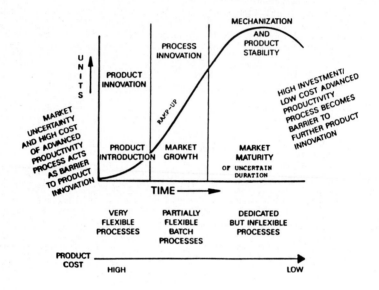

FIGURE 1

The problems inherent in such an approach are the complexity of distribution networks, the scale requirements of traditional technology and the political demands of host nations for greater local content and an upgrading of the complexity of work performed locally. This pattern of a network of specialized plans has worked well to reduce costs by locating greater portions of manufacturing capacity in lower labor cost nations. Its success, however, has been based upon stability of demand and product design and competition based on price. Just as the "good" factory becomes a barrier to innovation; a global network of "good" factories becomes an institutionalized barrier to both innovation and changes in business strategy.

Since 1980 we see evidence of increasingly shorter product life cycles and faster product development cycles, global markets and competition, fragmented markets and sophisticated customers. The traditional factory will not be a satisfactory response to these demands. The recent efforts to apply digital electronic technology to all aspects of design and manufacturing allow us to design a factory that is both responsive and efficient. That can deliver high variety at low cost with short production cycles.

This is the key to computer integrated manufacturing (CIM). It is the use of digital electronics in the form of computers and communications links to create the efficiency of high degrees of integration without rigidities created by mechanical integration. In effect - the Factory of the Future is essentially a computer system with flexible machines and robots as its output devices in place of printers, disc packs, or plotters.


## 2. UNDERSTANDING CIM'S POTENTIALS


To understand the implications of advanced manufacturing technology, two basic ideas require consideration. The first is that the new manufacturing technology is fundamentally different in design, in operation, and in capability from the equipment, process and technology that we are accustomed to in traditional factories. The new technology is smarter, faster, close-coupled, integrated, optimized and flexible. The new factory not only does traditional tasks differently, it can perform tasks not possible in the traditional factory. This means that many of the opportunities that we face, the management styles we need to use, the strategic options that are available to us, and the production decisions that we have to make are going to be contrary to the experience of past successes.

Second, manufacturing is rapidly becoming a science-based activity with high potential for a revolutionary change well beyond what is considered today as the state of the art. The level of scientific and technical knowledge required to understand truly how to design, manage and optimize the kinds of factories we are discussing is well beyond the knowledge of even the most recent college-trained manufacturing engineers. Trends in materials science, control theory, and artificial intelligence combined with the application of computers and communications technology and information science techniques will lead us to the new concept of manufacturing that is orders of magnitudes more powerful than anything in our experience.

The science and technology of manufacturing are becoming much more complex and far more powerful. We are developing a better understanding of the scientific underpinnings of production [2]. This comes from better knowledge of the behavior of solid materials under various process conditions. As an analogy, we might ask why chemical companies have been willing to invest hundreds of millions of dollars in relatively unproven new process technology plants. It is, in my view, because we know enough about the behavior of matter in the fluid state to be able to design and optimize a new process on paper and in the computer, and to build a test-scale pilot before companies make large-scale investments. We do not have many pilot plants for mechanical-based technologies; nor do we have a sense of confidence in our scale-up factors. But we are getting there. We are beginning to learn more about how to simulate factory operations. We are beginning to get better analytical tools. We certainly know more

now about the behavior of materials that we are using in the design of
factory and manufacturing systems. Control theory, artificial intelligence, measurement and sensing capabilities are all advancing at a very
rapid rate.

This new manufacturing will be at its most powerful when the computer and
communications technologies are used with increased scientific understanding of materials and processes to link production processes and
management tasks in that fully integrated, close-coupled, continuous-
flow, still utopian (but not for much longer) factory of the future.
Computer-integrated manufacturing is central to the factory of the future
– a combination of hardware and software and a data base describing the
physical phenomena that allows someone to write a computer program that
models the factory, and communications to provide on-line, moment-by-
moment schedule and performance optimization, and dynamic reallocation of
resources. It is, in a sense, the "perfect information" factory. We are
not quite there yet, but at least now we can set the standard for the future. Mastering these capabilities opens new ways for competition in the
global markets.

## 3.   CHANGING CHARACTERISTICS OF FACTORY

For the old factory, sound operating principles and management techniques
consonant with the old assumptions were developed. Centralization, large
plants, balanced lines, smooth flow, standard product design, low rate of
change, and inventory as a decoupler from the market were all desirable
characteristics of the "good" factory.

The new factory is marked by an entirely different set of desirable
operating characteristics: decentralization, disaggregation, flexibility,
rapid conversion of product lines produced, surge and ramp-up and "turn-
aroundability", responsiveness to innovation, production tied to demand,
multiple functions, and close-coupled systems. These represent sharp
changes both for practitioners of manufacturing engineering and teachers
of manufacturing management. The new factory changes the definition of
productivity to one based on these variables; from a cost focus to a
profitability focus, from "manufacturing" to "service" business.

Other demands to be put on the new factory and included in the definition
of productivity are: minimal downtime for maintenance; maximum product-
family range; the ability to adapt variability in materials and process
conditions; the ability to handle increasingly complex product designs
and technology into the existing systems with minimum disruption and minimum cost. The factory of the future is as likely to be a high-cost factory (capable of dominating the "fashion" market segment through rapid
product design change) as a low-cost price leader.

All of these new operating characteristics and changing criteria for
manufacturing success lead to a set of strategies for maximizing the
value of the factory of the future that are "counterintuitive" to what we
teach in engineering and business schools and also to the things that
worked well in the past. It starts with: <u>invest in flexibility</u> - not

just in the flexibiity of machining or assembly but in the flexibility of the organization as a whole - flexibility in research, engineering, marketing and distribution, and strategic planning.

Once you have that flexible capability you can take control of the market place by deliberately truncating the product life cycle, proliferating the range of products to the extent of customizing them one-by-one, deliberately fragmenting the market into segments so small that they cannot support a traditional economy-of-scale based factory [3].

Furthermore, I would argue for deliberately complicating the product. It goes against everything that we learned and teach in value engineering and reliability engineering and production management. But if the product is simple, it is easy to copy and there are no barriers to entry and no switching costs. What I really mean by "complicate the product" is to gradually embed the uniqueness of the product more and more deeply into the manufacturing process, so that it can't be copied except by making that same kind of investment in flexibility. To add value through service and innovation; capabilities of the process rather than the product, design and technology.

Once you achieve flexibility at low cost, you clearly have to compete broadly across a wide range of market segments and a wide range of products in order to keep that flexible manufacturing system (and that flexible company) busy 24 hours a day, 7 days a week, because you are working with an almost 100 percent fixed-cost manufacturing system. In turn, this will put tremendous burdens for managing variety and flexibility on the marketing and distribution capabilities of the firm.

## 4.  IMPACT ON INTERNATIONAL MANUFACTURING

The exact impacts of CIM on the organization of international manufacturing activities - and international business strategies overall - are hard to forecast at this point. They will depend upon the strategic decisions about the use of technology that each business makes as well as general global economic and political trends. I can only offer a few trends and concepts as hypotheses for further discussion and research.

Certain emerging trends call for major changes in our current thinking about international manufacturing. They are:

1. Increasing political demands for greater, and more complex, local content.

2. Manufacturing process technology that reduces the economic advantages of large scale factories and makes possible a greater variety of low volume manufacturing at a single location at low cost.

3. Increasing fragmentation of markets and more sophisticated customers who have a more localized concept of "value".

4. Increasingly sophisticated local competition.

5. A steady reduction in the percentage of product cost accounted for by direct labor.

6. Increasing globalization of both product and process technologies.

As the economic imperative for specialization and scale disappears, it
will be more difficult to argue against local content courses and to
prevail against sophisticated local competitors who have access to the
same product and process technology.

On the other hand, as these trends develop, more firms will retreat from
global networks of specialized factories and will have to choose between
export from one (or a few) centralized locations or a network of local
facilities that are highly vertically integrated over a broad scope of
products.

In a sense, CIM/FMS technology "levels the playing field" and nearly
eliminates competitive advantage based upon labor costs. The economic
edge will move toward areas with low capital costs and low cost/high
efficiency/high effectiveness knowledge work in product design and
process management. This means that high labor costs locations will no
longer be at a competitive disadvantage but the low labor cost locations
will not be at a disadvantage either – as long as they are able to invest
in the new technology.


## 5. CONCLUSIONS


All of this means that we need a thorough rethinking of corporate policy
for manufacturing. It also suggests that a variety of new answers may
emerge – each one feasible and profitable as a function of the specific
market's competitive dynamics and product technology and customer tastes.
We will see examples of single global scale factories with high levels of
scope economies serving fragmented, but global market segments and in
other situations networks of specialized focus factories contributing to
a single world standard and very likely businesses with a proliferation
of locally integrated factories; all existing together in a complex
global business environment. There is no "standard solution" to the
search for the "best" way to organize manufacturing for the international
market.

CIM technology and the economy of scope it offers will fundamentally
change (reduce) the strategic (economic) imperative for large scale factories and opens up a new range of competitive solutions for both domestic and international businesses. In summary, CIM allows manufacturing
to become a "service business". Thus, international issues in manufacturing will become more closely integrated into the business strategy.
The business strategies suggested for CIM based business will hold for
local or global situations. Only the specific technology, information
flows and organizational structure will need to be fitted to the
specifics of the local competitive situation.

**FOOTNOTES**

[1]   This  point  has  also  been made by C.W. Skinner, "The Productivity
      Paradox, Harvard Business Review, July-August 1986, pp.55-59.

[2]   See  also  J. Goldhar and M. Jelinek, "Plan for Economies of Scope,"
      Harvard Business Review, Nov-Dec 1983, pp.141-148.

[3]   For a rigorous proof of the desirability of market fragmentation and
      product  proliferation  see  Adil  Talaysum,  et  al,   "Uncertainty
      Reduction  Through  Flexible  Manufacturing",  IEEE  Transactions on
      Engineering Management, Vol. EM-34, No. 2, May 1987, p.85.

MANAGING INTERNATIONAL MANUFACTURING
K. Ferdows (Editor)
© Elsevier Science Publishers B.V. (North-Holland), 1989

## INTERNATIONAL COMPARISONS OF APPROACHES TO
## ADAPTATION OF AUTOMATED MANUFACTURING TECHNOLOGIES


Jack BARANSON

Illinois Institute of Technology


## 1. INTRODUCTION

The new generation of automated manufacturing technologies (AMT) have far
reaching implications for the competitive positions and international
structuring of industrial enterprises and national economics. The rate
of introduction of AMT, and the degree of success in managing AMT
Systems, are a function of relative astuteness in managing industrial enterprises and of the national environments in which these enterprises
operate. The introduction of AMT into factory systems is part of the on
going process of adaptation to economic and technological change.
Factory automation holds great promise for giant leaps forward in productivity and in response time to changes in market demands, but it also
poses deep problems of adaptation to change for individuals, enterprise
organizations and societies at large. These implications and some alternative paths to resolving some of the inevitable dilemmas are outlined in
what follows.


## 2. DIMENSIONS OF AUTOMATED MANUFACTURING TECHNOLOGIES (AMT)

The automated manufacturing technologies (AMT) cover a broad spectrum of
production systems, ranging from individual computer-controlled machine
tools and flexible machining centers to completely integrated facilities
under the broad heading of computer-integrated manufacturing (CIM).
Flexible machining centers (FMC) typically consist of an integrated
computer-controlled complex of numerically controlled machine tools,
automated material and tool-handling devices and automated measuring and
testing equipment. FMCs can process any product belonging to certain
specified families of products with a minimum of manual intervention and
short change-over time.

Computer-integrated manufacturing covers a continuum of activities that
includes design, engineering and manufacturing activities (CAD/CAE/CAM).
Computer-aided design and product engineering (CAD/CAE) were originally
developed for the aerospace and automotive industries. Certain versions
of CAD are linked to the production engineering (CAE) of newly designed
components, as well as to the computer-aided manufacturing (CAM) process
itself. The basic components of a CAD/CAE system are a) hardware

(terminals, processors and transmission networks); and b) software to program and process data. CAD/CAE is now used to design electronic and mechanical components for such products as consumer products, computer equipment, automotive and aircraft equipment, and machine tools.

Technical characteristics of CIM factories are derived in large part from continuous-flow processing that is typical of chemical plants. Analogous chemical processing plants, CIM factories are designed to ingest industrial materials, maintain quality control throughout the process, and turn out small-batch quantities of products without any appreciable increase in unit cost. As an added feature, the CIM plant is able to re-design and re-program on an ongoing basis. CIM factories typically use multi-mission tools and reprogrammable robots to produce multiple product outputs. Production management is linked to business decisions (responsive to market demand signals), as well as to procurement, quality control and various accounting bases. Satellite production units are linked to a centrally controlled system through intricate software, complex data systems that monitor and control production.

Successful CIM systems imply an ability to move rapidly and cost-effectively into multiple configurations of components and end-products in response to market changes in demand and production conditions, as well as innate capabilities to shift from high-volume, fixed purpose machinery and equipment or flexible (reprogrammable) manufacturing systems that can quickly and cost-effectively absorb component design changes. CIM systems also depend heavily upon information systems that signal the afore mentioned shifts in market demands and production environments. These information systems need to be structured to transmit change signals rapidly and effectively into CAD/CAM systems. CIM complexes can be designed to produce rapidly and on a continuous-flow basis a broader product mix, with a greater variety of features and near-zero defects with little or no increases in unit costs. More tasks can be performed at a single station using smart (variable purpose) tools. In-factory materials travel shorter paths and work at greater speeds, and production is virtually unmanned and continuous.

CIM technology promises to be especially effective under competitive market conditions in the following product areas:

> products such as machine tools that have to be tailored to individual customer's requirements, preferences or tastes;

> products that require pre-sale consultation with customers to design and adapt what previously had been standardized product;

> products requiring substantial after-sale servicing, training of operations or maintenance of equipment; and

> products where novelty and change are at a premium.

## 3. INTERNATIONAL COMPARISONS OF APPROACHES TO ADOPTATION OF AUTOMATED MANUFACTURING TECHNOLOGIES

### 3.1 Comparison among firms in the advanced economies

There are significant differences among the manufacturing strategies of companies in Japan, North America and Europe [1]. Automated manufacturing strategies in Japan are now focused upon abilities to continue cutting production costs and to respond rapidly to product and process design changes dictated by market conditions. American and European manufacturers, on the other hand, are still playing catch up with Japanese competitors; their emphasis is upon improved quality and delivery performance, and they are preoccupied with upgrading their manufacturing technologies.

One reason why Japanese firms manufacturing CAD/CAM equipment are in a stronger position to cut costs and respond to competitors (relative to U.S. and West European competitors) is because of their strong linkages forward to customer-users and their strong background linkages to their component suppliers [2]. U.S. and European firms have been relying more heavily upon mergers and acquisitions to shore up their competitive manufacturing capabilities; they are also pre-occupied with the cost-profit squeeze that has resulted from rising materials and overhead costs, on the one hand, and an inability to raise prices because of intensive global competition, on the other hand. Global competition is also being driven by dramatically shortened product-life cycles that necessitate expanded efforts to redesign products and adapt process engineering to new designs and new materials.

Another essential feature of Japanese management is that it emphasizes human resource development and management as the essential ingredient of maintaining manufacturing systems, in contrast to its competitors' practices. Whereas American firms are still pre-occupied with the painful and costly task of adjusting labor-management relations, the Japanese are able to concentrate their energies on adjusting work rules and broadening the range of jobs the factory worker can undertake, in order to increase the flexibility of response of their labor force and the overall efficiency of their manufacturing operations. With much more stable and mutually reinforcing labor-management relationships, the Japanese are able to concentrate on improved just-in-time production and inventory management, which have become essential to CAM operations. By way of contrast, American firms are relying to a much more intensive degree upon the development of software embodying information data and expert systems to raise the levels of manufacturing performance. With the people and organization ingredients already in place and functioning at relatively high levels of performance, the Japanese are able to concentrate their efforts upon improved FMS and robotics. European firms are still heavily encumbered by the people-management problem, due to entrenched cultural and political factors that undermine production rationalization efforts.

If you were to compare the prevailing western enterprises approach with the prevailing practices of their more aggressive Japanese competitors regarding the design, production and marketing of a new product, you would find the following contracting differences:

1. Sequential versus Tandem Approach. The Japanese firm is able to complete the innovation cycle in one-third the time or less by working in tandem both within the company and with its well integrated family of component and parts suppliers. Among Japanese firms, the product manager has an integrative role in combining the design, production and marketing functions into an integrated whole. Western firms work in sequence; product designers do not take manufacturability into adequate account and there is often insufficient regard for the details of customer usage in terms of performance and servicing characteristics.

2. Cross-functional Training. The Japanese are willing to invest in the cross-functional training and work assignments of their employees so that the subcultures of design, production and marketing can more effectively harmonize design features. This applies both to changes in consumer preferences and to flexibility in manufacturing. Among Western firms, manufacturing problems often emerge at a later critical stage because of inadequate involvement of manufacturing engineers at the product design phase.

3. Forward and Backward Linkages. Forward linkages to customers and backward linkages to suppliers are taken much more seriously by the Japanese manufacturers than by their Western counterparts. Their linkages are regarded by Japanese firms as indispensable relationships in the conception and introduction of products into the marketplace. Whereas most Western firms plan tooling only after the product design has been frozen, Japanese firms typically release tentative designs to tool suppliers. Most American firms in particular have a low regard for the discernment and judgment of consumers. They also treat parts suppliers on an adversarial basis, rather than cultivating loyalty as an indispensable element of high-performance results. The exceptions have been firms such as Xerox that have drastically cut back the number of suppliers down to a tight-knit family of dedicated companies.

4. Team Spirit versus Adversarial Cultures. There is an underlying difference in "corporate cultures" values, attitudes, and social relationships which ultimately contribute to the Japanese ability to repeatedly beat American and European competitors to the marketplace. Among Western enterprises, there is perpetual rivalry and juxtapositioning among marketing, manufacturing and design people. For example, marketing people will resist design changes that imply re-educating the customer to a new or different mode of product utilization. There also is a fundamental lack of trust and rapport among the subcultures of marketing, production and design. What is needed is a harmonization of the subcultures, which may be achieved through cross-functional experience. In Japanese culture, there are strong pressures for individualism to give

way to the collective interest. Among Western societies, it is only in certain team sports or "good" wars that the collective will to win and survive is brought to bear.

5. Incremental versus Big-Leap Changes. Japanese companies rely upon continuing small incremental changes in response to shifts in consumer demands. The small increment approach also applies to emerging manufacturing technology opportunities related to materials, tooling, and process technology.

Needless to say there are exceptions to the above generalizations on both sides. But the fact remains that the widespread and prevailing tendencies in Japan does give their manufacturers a tactical advantage over the vast majority of Western firms in acquisition and implementation of the automated manufacturing technologies.

## 3.2 East-West Comparisons

In the Soviet Union as in the Western economies, human and organizational factors are overriding determinants of the rate of introduction of the new automated manufacturing technologies, and, more importantly, in the results achieved in terms of increased productivity, quality and reliability of output. In the USSR, as in the U.S., the basic inhibitors to the rapid and effective introduction of automation are: a) risk aversion and conservatism on the part of the industrial management, b) weak linkages between automated equipment suppliers and users and between component suppliers and equipment producers, and of reluctance on the part of factory workers to accept automation (for different reasons in the U.S. and the U.S.S.R.). Other characteristics of the Soviet "command economy" that have retarded the rate of diffusion of automation technology in the U.S.S.R. are:

a) priority allocation of production resources to military, over civilian needs,
b) over-ambitious production goals and "taut" economic planning,
c) emphasis of quantitative output, rather than improved productivity and diffusion of innovation,
d) incentives based on fulfilling production targets, rather than reducing costs, or improving product quality,
e) in the absence of pricing mechanisms and consumer sovereignty, failure to raise production efficiency and promote improvements in the quality and utility of consumer products and intermediary industrial products. [3]

In the absence of consumer sovereignty and the competitive forces of a buyers market, the principal attraction of automated manufacturing technologies (and forces to drive their introduction) is lost in the "seller's market" that prevails in the U.S.S.R. A major advantage inherent in the new generations of computer-aided design and manufacturing (CAD/CAM) is flexibility of response to changes in consumer demands and to the competition of cheaper, better products entering the marketplace.

The resistance of Soviet factory managers to the introduction of automated manufacturing systems is traceable in large part to the tautness of Soviet central planning, which in effect penalizes failure to meet production targets, inadequately rewards improved performance, and does not compensate for the added risks involved in innovation. But many of the technical difficulties that Soviet factory managers are encountering with robotic equipment are mirrored in American enterprises. In the U.S.S.R., Soviet factory managers have resisted the introduction of robotics into their factory operations because of the dislocating effects of restructuring production to fit around the robotic equipment and coping with shortages in required ancillary equipment or "connecting systems". Frequent breakdown of robots (coupled with the dearth of maintenance personnel and replacement parts) have compounded the difficulties. The downtime connected with these accommodations seriously jeopardizes meeting production quotas. More fundamentally Soviet managers have found that the introduction of robotics and related automated manufacturing equipment is difficult to do piecemeal and not only requires a restructuring of whole segments of the production system, but may even require redesign of the product to accommodate the new equipment - something especially difficult to achieve in a taut, centrally planned economy.

In its opening efforts to introduce robotic equipment at the factory level, Soviet ministries are better at agitating than in servicing clients. Recurrent cycles of enthusiastic campaigns generated by the planning authorities are followed by the hard crunch of trying to live with recurrent shortages of materials, components, ancillary equipment and critical support services. Often cited are deficiencies in experienced operators for automated machinery and maintenance skills and related technical support services for computer integrated equipment. Also cited are shortages of components such as electric drive mechanisms, sensors, control devices, and computer software for robotic equipment.

The shortages characteristic of the civilian side of the Soviet economy are reinforced by the prevailing "seller's market", as distinct from the economic forces at play in the market-driven, western economies (in significantly varying degrees: highly driven in Japan, less so in the United States, and much less so in the United Kingdom, for example [4]. Market forces compel enterprises in western economies to take the added risks of introducing automation in order to survive. In the absence of these market mechanisms, there is no compelling force to overcome Soviet managers' risk aversion toward innovation within the Soviet system. The Soviets are by no means unique in this regard. Different varieties and degrees of risk aversion on the part of industrial management are found in Western economies, where managers also respond to their respective economic environment. [5]

The conservatism on the part of Soviet factory managers is of a special variety and is traceable to structures and conditions described earlier. First and foremost, enterprise autonomy is severly constrained under the central planning system. On the supply side, Soviet factory managers manufacturing for the civilian sector must take what is supplied to them, whether it be equipment, components or materials, and live with the deficiencies in materials and manpower available to them. On the demand side, they are not compelled to meet sovereign consumer demands and face competing producers, as they would be under competitive conditions in a market-driven economy, to decrease production costs and continuously improve product designs. For the Soviet manager, the prospect of automation is attractive only to the extent that it will help him increase his quantitative output, <u>without</u> incurring the concomitant risk, pain and penalty for failure. In a word there is no "invisible foot" that compels the Soviet enterprise manager to incur the added risk and pain of innovation in order to survive.

There are also dramatic differences in the risk and rewards to factory management related to increased productivity and improved quality of production. Profit drives the American enterprise; in the USSR the incentives to excel are moderate as compared to the penalties for failure to meet (quantitative) production targets. The foregoing instills widespread conservatism toward the high-risk that is associated with even modest changes in manufacturing methods.

The deep-seated contrasts between the planned Soviet and market-driven American economies have profound implications in the demand-pull for automated manufacturing equipment and systems. These systems require close linkages between design, engineering and production, functions, and close management control over material and parts suppliers, if they are to achieve acceptable levels of proficiency. The two very different enterprise environments in the USSR and in the US engender fundamentally different evaluations by industrial managers of cost-benefit ratios and risk factors related to the introduction of automated technologies.

Another fundamental problem in the Soviet system - not entirely unique to the Soviets - is the weak linkage between research and design institutes and the production operations levels. Among the cited deficiencies are the following: designs that are not well coordinated, equipment that has not been pre-tested for factory operation, and ancillary equipment that is not in place. At international meetings, Soviet scientists engaged in research associated with automation and related fields such as artificial intelligence (used in programming automated equipment) are on a par with their Western counterparts. It is in the area of application and utilization, including the design of prototypes that fit effectively into factory operations, where the Soviets have experienced considerable difficulties.

The Soviet approach to design engineering of military equipment responds in part to the shortages and deficiencies experienced in a command economy. This is achieved by designing down to the level of manufacturability in the industrial sector and to the operability and maintainability of products in both the military and civilian sectors. In the United States, a good portion of the high cost of defense procurement (and related national budgetary deficits) is attributable to an industrial philosophy that anything the Department of Defense envisages it needs (including the Strategic Defense Initiative systems) can be designed, and anything that the engineers design can be manufactured. The Soviet approach reverses the process and tries to tailor the design of products to meet the new customer requirements and emerging productive capabilities, both in terms of resource costs and manageability of industrial operations. The key words in Soviet military design are "operability, maintainability, and manufacturability".

The paradox of high performance in the military procurement area, contrasted with low performance in the civilian sector, can be explained in terms of the priority placed upon defense-related production over industrial output for civilian production. The seller's market that prevails in the civilian sector is completely reversed to a buyer's market, where defense procurement is involved. In the procurement of military equipment, the Soviet Defense Ministry is able to demand high performing products, insist upon quality standards and cost effectiveness, and get whatever product configurations are required. Equally important, the Defense Ministry is able to allocate essential materials, components and industrial equipment to special industrial facilities manned by the top engineering and technical skills available in the U.S.S.R.. In the Soviet economy, "residual" human and physical resources are allocated to the civilian sector. In short, in the defense procurement area, there is an effective demand for the features that automated production technology can deliver - flexible response to changing demands and supplying high-performance products based upon quality and reliability built into the production process.

## 4. CONCLUSION

The rate of introduction of factory automation, and the ultimate contribution of automated manufacturing to the productivity and competitiveness of industrial sectors, will depend to varying degrees, on the economic environment in which the industrial facilities operate. This is because investments in factory automation involve considerable risks, and therefore government, financial structures, and government relations play an important role in the financial risks business firms are willing to take. The Soviet experience clearly indicates that the economic environment is an overriding determinant. In Japan, it is the combination of the national economic environment, along with a broad-based proficiency in the management of industrial enterprises, that has given Japanese firms a competitive edge in world markets.

In the United States and in Western Europe, the proficiency of enterprise management is the principal determinant of a rapid and effective introduction of automated manufacturing technology, but certain elements in the economic environment act as deterrents to enterprise willingness to introduce factory innovation and implement it effectively. In some respects, the environmental conditions prevailing in the United States and most of the Western European countries are the exact opposite of what characterizes the Japanese business environment, where "vision and consensus" bring together the business, government, labor and finance communities involved in or impacting upon, the growth and expansion of factory automation. It is highly probable that the absence of vision and consensus in the United States has contributed to a reluctance on the part of American manufacturers to take the financial risks associated with introducing factory automation and has necessitated a more piecemeal approach to automation. For an extended period beginning in the late 1960's, American firms in the consumer electronic and automative parts industry chose to move to offshore manufacturer and procurement in low-wage countries, as an alternative to investments in upgrading factory automation in order to meet import competition.

A major insight that emerges from the international comparisons of factory automation efforts is that the Japanese are in the forefront of successful application on the new generation of manufacturing technologies. The ability of Japan to manage technological change in a dynamic world economy has been an outstanding feature of Japanese society in the post-war period. Contributing to this success are their philosophy and practice of industrial management and the national economic environment in which Japanese firms operate. The major elements underlying their industrial management achievements are:

1) a strong reliance on long-range planning to think through and manage technological and marketing adjustments to economic change;

2) in-depth capabilities in process engineering applied to the progressive rationalization of factory automation in manageable increments;

3) a core emphasis upon the development and management of human resources as a key to successful operations; and

4) carefully structured forward linkages to customers and backward linkages to component and materials suppliers, both of which are considered essential to cost-effective production and responsiveness to customers needs and preferences. These philosophies and practices are applied both to factories in Japan and to industrial facilities located in North America and Western Europe.

Japanese firms also are in the forefront of forging transnational strategic alliances with foreign enterprise partners. These strategic alliances add to the effectiveness of Japanese firms in penetrating overseas markets through the marketing, production and technology complimentarities provided by foreign partners. They also provide an added competitive edge, by shortening the time frame for the run-in of manufacturing and marketing operations. (The Toyota-General Motors joint venture in California is a classical case in point). Business operations in Japan are further enhanced by distinct advantages in the Japanese national environment, as compared to prevailing government policies and economic structures in the U.S. and most Western European economies. The two most important characteristics in the political economy of Japanese society are "vision" and "consensus" - vision to anticipate and plan for change and an intricate political and economic structure and consensus among business, government, financial and labor communities. This combination of vision and consensus give Japanese enterprise a strong competitive edge in the continuous technological adjustments to economic change.

The combination of vision and consensus networks also are supportive of the high risks associated with investments in factory automation. The higher risk propensity in Japan is reinforced by the longer-term view of returns on investments and the reinforcement provided by financial institutions and tax structures that encourage such investments. Tax structures and consumption patterns in Japan are conducive to the high levels of personal savings, which in turn are channeled through the banking system to productive investments that include industrial rationalization and modernization. The educational system in Japan also contributes to factory automation efforts by producing the highly literate and skilled labor force that is required to design, engineer, manage, operate and maintain the new technologies. Beginning at the grade-school level, future entrants into industrial labor force are instilled with values and attitudes fundamental to the effective implementation of total quality control and just-in-time systems associated with the factory automation. Included here are pride in workmanship and individual responsibility for quality standards.

The Japanese experience particularly demonstrates the importance of education levels in factory automation systems. The substantial increase in the quantum and complexity of production management that is inherent in factory automation requires highly skilled cadres of engineers and technicians to design, engineer, manage and maintain factory automation system. It also requires a high degree of interdependence among trained technicians and operators that can handle computerized information interchange among design engineering, production and marketing functions. A broader spectrum of the labor force level of basic literacy in order to man the more complex and highly integrated systems associated with factory automation.

The intensified pace of technological change and the telescoping of the design-engineering production cycles imply deep-seated adjustments from traditional pre-employment education to continuing educational systems that can respond to ongoing adjustments to change. Industrial enterprises may have to take on a larger share of the continuing educational function. It is significant to note in this regard that most Japanese firms assume that new employees, on average, bring only 20 percent of what they need to know to function within the industrial enterprise [6]. In the United States, the impression is that most American firms expect that all new employees will have at least 80 percent of the training and skills needed to perform their jobs. This accounts for corporate attitudes leading to low investments in human resources development and a general attitude that all employees are readily replaceable. This viewpoint is generally inimical to the inherent characteristic of the new factory automation systems that rely heavily upon individual responsibility for total quality control and just-in-time systems [7].

**REFERENCES**

[1]  FERDOWS K., J.G. MILLER, J.NAKANE and T.E. VOLLMAN, "Evolving Manufacturing Strategies in Europe, Japan, and North America" Research Report Series, Manufacturing Roundtable, Boston University, School of Management, 1985.

[2]  BARANSON J., "Robotics in Manufacturing: Key to International Competitiveness" Mt. Airy, Maryland: Lomond Publications, 1983, 17-24.

[3]  BIALER S.."The Soviet Paradox: External Expansion, Internal Decline" New York: Alfred A. Knopf, 1985, 6-7.

[4]  BARANSON J."Soviet Automation: Perspectives and Prospects" Mt. Airy, Maryland: Lomond Publications, 1987, 11-17.

[5]  Ibid. pp. 54-57, 102-105.

[6]  OHAMAE, Kenichi. "Beyond National Borders - Reflections on Japan and the World", Homewood, Illinois: Dow Jones-Irwin, 1987.

[7]  "Exacting Employer-Toyota Takes Pains and Time, in Filling Jobs and Its Kentucky Plant", Wall Street Journal, 1 December 1987.

# CONTRIBUTORS

Akio Amano

Jeffrey S. Arpan

Jack Baranson

Roberto B. Bequillard

Kim B. Clark

Morris A. Cohen

Edward W. Davis

Arnoud De Meyer

Frank L. Dubois

Marshall Fisher

Therese Flaherty

Takahiro Fujimoto

Donald Gerwin

Joel D. Goldhar

Ramchandran Jaikumar

Marvin Lieberman

Michael E. McGrath

Jeffrey G. Miller

Jinichiro Nakane

Michael D. Oliff

Aleda Roth

Jean-Claude Tarondeau

**Kasra Ferdows** is Associate Professor of Production and Operations Management at the European Institute of Business Administration (INSEAD) in Fontainebleau, France.